BRITISH LITERATURE UNLOCKED

Vol V: The Victorian Age

A Complete Guide for UGC NET

ANKIT SHARMA

TO THE POINT NOTES BASED ON PREVIOUS YEARS QUESTION PAPERS

Table of Contents

<u>Foreword</u>

The journey through British Literature is one marked by profound ideas, artistic transformations, and socio-political upheavals, all of which have shaped the literary canon as we know it. In "British Literature Unlocked: A Complete Guide for UGC NET," this literary heritage is meticulously unpacked, volume by volume, to serve as an essential resource for UGC NET English aspirants. Spanning six volumes, this series guides readers from the ancient foundations of the Greco-Roman period all the way to the nuanced expressions of the Modern and Postmodern ages. With each era, readers will find to-the-point notes, questions from the last decade of UGC NET exams, mnemonic codes, and strategic insights designed to simplify and streamline the study process, making preparation not only thorough but also deeply engaging.

Volume by Volume Breakdown

Volume I: Greco-Roman to Chaucer

Dive into the roots of Western literary thought, tracing the influences of classical antiquity up through the Middle Ages and Chaucer's groundbreaking contributions. This volume introduces foundational concepts and sets the stage for the evolution of British literature.

Volume II: Elizabethan to Jacobean

Enter the vibrant Renaissance period, where the works of Shakespeare, Marlowe, and their contemporaries reflect the artistic flourishing and complex socio-political shifts of the time. Each page delves into the drama, poetry, and prose that defined these eras.

Volume III: The Age of Milton, Restoration, and The Augustan Age.

Explore an age marked by poetic grandeur, the restoration of the monarchy, and the Augustan pursuit of clarity and wit. This volume captures the transformations in language, form, and ideology as literature moved into a reflective phase of transition.

Volume IV: The Age of Transition and The Age of Romanticism

Witness the emotional and imaginative power of the Romantic movement, a response to the rigid rationality of the previous era. This volume celebrates the Romantic poets and novelists who embraced nature, individualism, and emotion in revolutionary ways.

Volume V: The Victorian Age

This volume covers the prolific Victorian era, an age of dramatic change and conflict that grappled with industrialization, social reform, and expanding empire. Here, readers can explore the complex morality, realism, and unique characters of Victorian prose and poetry.

Volume VI: Modern and Postmodern Literature

The journey concludes with an in-depth look at Modern and Postmodern literature, where literary form, narrative structure, and thematic depth are pushed to their limits. From the experimental techniques of Modernism to the playful and questioning nature of Postmodernism, this volume brings British literature into the contemporary era.

Why This Book is Essential?

Designed for aspiring NET scholars, "British Literature Unlocked" offers a unique blend of academic precision and strategic insight. With mnemonics that transform complex historical timelines and literary movements into memorable codes, this guide ensures that vital information is readily accessible. Each volume is filled with analysed questions from the last ten years of UGC NET exams, helping you understand not only what to study but also how to approach the exam strategically. This guide offers a structured pathway through the vast landscape of British literature, reducing overwhelm and empowering students to confidently tackle their preparation.

An effective study companion, "British Literature Unlocked" is the result of years of dedicated analysis, scholarly research, and an in-depth understanding of the UGC NET requirements. The goal is to provide readers with more than just a study guide—it is to offer them a roadmap that navigates through the richness of British literary history with ease and engagement. As you turn these pages, may you not only prepare but also find joy in the timeless world of British literature, its stories, and its legacy.

This series invites you on an enlightening journey, guiding you through the ages and unlocking the potential for both academic success and a deeper appreciation of the literary arts. Welcome to "British Literature Unlocked: A Complete Guide for UGC NET."

CHAPTER 1

VICTORIAN POETRY (1830- 1901)

Victorian Era (1837-1901)

- **Victorian era:** Reign of **Queen Victoria (1837–1901)**, marked by major change.
- Followed the **Georgian** and preceded the **Edwardian** periods.
- Era aligned partly with **Belle Époque** in Europe.
- **Religious drive** promoted higher **moral standards** by churches.
- Shifted away from **rationalism**; embraced **romanticism** and **mysticism**.
- Technological innovations fueled **Britain's power and prosperity**.
- Medicine progressed with **germ theory** and **epidemiology**.
- British foreign relations were shaped by **antagonism with Russia**.
- **Pax Britannica:** Britain dominated peaceful global **trade**.
- British Empire expanded into **Asia** and **Africa**.
- **Colonial autonomy** granted to **Australia, Canada, and New Zealand**.
- Apart from **Crimean War**, Britain avoided significant wars.
- **Political parties:** Whigs/Liberals and Conservatives; **Labour Party** emerged.
- Prominent politicians: **Melbourne, Peel, Disraeli, and Gladstone**.
- **Victorian literature** spans Queen Victoria's reign, **1837–1901**.
- The 19th century is considered a **Golden Age** for **English novels**.
- Novels became the leading genre, reflecting **society's transformations**.
- **Notable novelists: Dickens, Thackeray, Brontë sisters**, and **Hardy**.
- Victorian writers focused on **real-world issues** over abstract themes.
- Writers addressed **factory dangers, poverty, and women's treatment**.
- **Elizabeth Barrett Browning** wrote on **child labor**.
- **Dickens** used **humor** to critique **social issues**.
- **Hardy** questioned religion and **social norms** in his novels.
- **Poetry and theatre** also flourished in the Victorian period.
- **Robert Browning** and **Alfred Tennyson** were famous poets.

- ➤ Theatre became prominent in the **late 19th century**.
- ➤ Playwrights included **Gilbert and Sullivan**, **Shaw**, and **Wilde**.
- ➤ Victorian literature reflects **scientific and economic changes**.
- ➤ Era explores class structures, **social reform**, and **morality**.

Alfred Tennyson (1809-1892)

- ➤ **Alfred Tennyson** was born in Somersby, **Lincolnshire**, son of a clergyman.
- ➤ He attended Louth School and later Cambridge (1828).
- ➤ At Cambridge, he won the **Chancellor's Prize** for "Timbuctoo."
- ➤ He left **Cambridge** without a degree, publishing **mediocre verse**.
- ➤ For twenty years, he lived peacefully, writing **poetry**.
- ➤ Pleasant trips to **Lake District** and **Stratford** brightened his life.
- ➤ In 1844, lost funds in speculation; **pension** saved him (1845).
- ➤ Appointed Poet Laureate (1850) after Wordsworth's passing.
- ➤ Alfred Austin DL (30 May 1835 – 2 June 1913) appointed Poet Laureate in 1896, after an interval following the death of Tennyson
- ➤ Moved to **Freshwater, Isle of Wight**, after his marriage.
- ➤ Became widely celebrated and **regarded as greatest poet**.
- ➤ Created baron in 1884 and joined House of Lords.
- ➤ Died in **Surrey** and was buried in **Westminster Abbey**.

His Poetry:

- ➤ ***Poems by Two Brothers (1826):*** Collaborated with his elder brother Charles.
- ➤ ***Timbuctoo (1829):*** Won the Chancellor's Prize
- ➤ **Chiefly Lyrical (1830):** Published while he was an undergraduate
  - ○ *Isabel*
  - ○ The Kraken *is a sonnet*
  - ○ *Madeleine*
- ➤ Poems (1832):
  - ○ Mariana in the South
    - ■ The premise of "Mariana" originates in **William Shakespeare's** *Measure for Measure*
  - ○ The Palace of Art
  - ○ **"The Lady of Shalott"**
    - ■ It is a lyrical ballad

- Inspired by the 13th-century short prose text Donna di Scalotta,
- Tells the tragic story of Elaine of Astolat, a young noblewoman.
- Stranded in a tower up the river from Camelot.

➢ Poems (1833):
- *Œnone*
- *The Lotos-Eaters*
  - Based on an episode in Book 9 of Homer's **Odyssey**.
  - The inhabitants, *"the mild-eyed melancholy Lotos-eaters,"*
  - Odysseus tells his mariners to have courage,
  - Assuring them that they will soon reach the shore of their home.
  - They reach a land *"in which it always seemed afternoon"*
  - The mariners sight this *"land of streams"*
  - Mariners meet the **"mild-eyed melancholy Lotos-eaters."**
  - The **Lotos-eaters offer flower and fruit** to the mariners.
  - **Eating the lotos** causes a deep, dreamy slumber.
  - Mariners barely hear one another, lost in dreams.
  - They feel weary of **wandering** and yearn to stay.
  - Mariners resolve to remain with the **Lotos-eaters.**
  - Mariners sing of the land's **sweet music.**
  - They question why **humans must toil**, unlike nature.
  - Nature rests; **man alone endures endless sorrow.**
  - **Bloom and fade** is nature's allotted lifespan.
  - **Life's accomplishments lead nowhere; nothing is lasting.**
  - Mariners desire "long rest or death."
  - They crave **indulgent dreaming, free from toil.**
  - They imagine a life of **continuous relaxation.**
  - In peace, they remember **loved ones now buried.**
  - Mariners reason their **families have forgotten them.**
  - Homes likely decayed; **they resolve to remain.**
  - Memories of **wives and sons fade, property inherited.**
  - Returning would cause **unnecessary confusion.**
  - **Hearts worn out** from war and constellations.
  - They prefer the **"death-like existence"** of Lotos-land.

- ■ *"Than tir'd eyelids upon tir'd eyes;"*
- ➢ Poems (1842)
    - ○ *"Break, Break, Break" (1842)*
        - ■ Elegy that describes feelings of loss after Arthur Henry Hallam
    - ○ *Morte d'Arthur,*
    - ○ *Ulysses,*
        - ■ Ulysses is a blank-verse poem.
        - ■ Dramatic monologue.
        - ■ Aged title character
        - ■ **Ulysses plans to leave** his dreary Ithacan kingdom.
        - ■ The poem **reflects Tennyson's response** to Hallam's death.
        - ■ **Restless in Ithaca**, Ulysses cedes his throne.
        - ■ **Telemachus, Ulysses' son, takes the throne** dutifully.
        - ■ Ulysses **inspires his men with words** of heroism.
        - ■ **Narrative voice adds ambiguity** to Ulysses' motives.
        - ■ It's unclear if **Ulysses is noble or irresponsible**.
        - ■ The journey may prove **futile, fatal, or both**.
        - ■ Tennyson's view **draws from Homer and Dante**.
        - ■ **Ulysses feels unfulfilled as an idle king**
          "I cannot rest from travel: I will drink / Life to the lees."
        - ■ **Reflects on his past adventures and life**
            - ● *"I am become a name."*
- ➢ **Feels connected to all he has experienced**
  "Yet all experience is an arch wherethro' / Gleams that untravell'd world."
- ➢ **Yearns for continuous discovery and growth**
  "To rust unburnish'd, not to shine in use!"
- ➢ Entrusts Ithaca to his son, Telemachus
  "This is my son, mine own Telemachus."
- ➢ Acknowledges Telemachus' differing qualities
  "He works his work, I mine."
- ➢ **Rallies his old comrades for one last journey**
  "There lies the port; the vessel puffs her sail."
- ➢ **Sees opportunity for a final noble act**
  "Death closes all: but something ere the end, / Some work of noble note, may yet be done."
- ➢ **Longs to sail "beyond the sunset"**
  "It may be we shall touch the Happy Isles, / And see the great Achilles."

> **Embraces resolve despite weakened strength**
> "That which we are, we are; / One equal temper of heroic hearts."

It little profits that an idle king,
By this still hearth, among these barren crags,
Match'd with an aged wife, I mete and dole
Unequal laws unto a savage race,
That hoard, and sleep, and feed, and know not me.
I cannot rest from travel: I will drink
Life to the lees: All times I have enjoy'd
Greatly, have suffer'd greatly, both with those
That loved me, and alone, on shore, and when
Thro' scudding drifts the rainy Hyades
Vext the dim sea: I am become a name;
For always roaming with a hungry heart
Much have I seen and known; cities of men
And manners, climates, councils, governments,
Myself not least, but honour'd of them all;
And drunk delight of battle with my peers,
Far on the ringing plains of windy Troy.
I am a part of all that I have met;
Yet all experience is an arch wherethro'
Gleams that untravell'd world whose margin fades
For ever and forever when I move.
How dull it is to pause, to make an end,
To rust unburnish'd, not to shine in use!
As tho' to breathe were life! Life piled on life
Were all too little, and of one to me
Little remains: but every hour is saved
From that eternal silence, something more,
A bringer of new things; and vile it were
For some three suns to store and hoard myself,
And this gray spirit yearning in desire
To follow knowledge like a sinking star,
Beyond the utmost bound of human thought.

This is my son, mine own Telemachus,
To whom I leave the sceptre and the isle,—

Well-loved of me, discerning to fulfil
This labour, by slow prudence to make mild
A rugged people, and thro' soft degrees
Subdue them to the useful and the good.
Most blameless is he, centred in the sphere
Of common duties, decent not to fail
In offices of tenderness, and pay
Meet adoration to my household gods,
When I am gone. He works his work, I mine.

There lies the port; the vessel puffs her sail:
There gloom the dark, broad seas. My mariners,
Souls that have toil'd, and wrought, and thought with me—
That ever with a frolic welcome took
The thunder and the sunshine, and opposed
Free hearts, free foreheads—you and I are old;
Old age hath yet his honour and his toil;
Death closes all: but something ere the end,
Some work of noble note, may yet be done,
Not unbecoming men that strove with Gods.
The lights begin to twinkle from the rocks:
The long day wanes: the slow moon climbs: the deep
Moans round with many voices. Come, my friends,
'T is not too late to seek a newer world.
Push off, and sitting well in order smite
The sounding furrows; for my purpose holds
To sail beyond the sunset, and the baths
Of all the western stars, until I die.
It may be that the gulfs will wash us down:
It may be we shall touch the Happy Isles,
And see the great Achilles, whom we knew.
Tho' much is taken, much abides; and tho'
We are not now that strength which in old days
Moved earth and heaven, that which we are, we are;
One equal temper of heroic hearts,
Made weak by time and fate, but strong in will
To strive, to seek, to find, and not to yield.

> A dramatic monologue is a type of poem in which a single speaker addresses a silent listener, often revealing their thoughts, emotions, and motives in a particular situation.
>
> **Other Examples of Dramatic Monologue:**
>
> *Ulysses by Alfred, Lord Tennyson*
> *"Tithonus" by Alfred, Lord Tennyson*
> *Porphyria's Lover by Robert Browning*
> *"Medusa by Carol Ann Duffy,*
> *The Bishop Orders His Tomb at Saint Praxed's Church by Robert Browning*
> *The Love Song of J. Alfred Prufrock by T.S. Eliot*
> *Lady Lazarus by Sylvia Plath*
> *Caliban upon Setebos by Robert Browning*
> *My Last Duchess by Robert Browning*

- *Locksley Hall,*
  - Narrates the emotions of a rejected suitor upon coming to his childhood home.
  - "young life, its good side, its deficiencies, and its yearnings."
- ***The Princess (1847)***
  - **Known as "the new woman."**
  - **The Princess, a Medley, long poem**
  - **For the sake of his story Tennyson imagines a ladies'**
  - **"Tears, Idle Tears" Published as one of the "songs" in his The Princess (1847)**
- **In Memoriam (1850):**
  - **Elegy**
  - Written in four-line **ABBA stanzas of iambic tetrameter**
  - Long series of **meditations** upon the death of **Arthur Henry Hallam.**
  - Tennyson's college friend, who **died at Vienna in 1833.**
  - Called the **In Memoriam meter**—which is quite rare, is deftly managed.
  - Invocation of the "*Strong Son of God.*"
  - "*these orbs of light and shade*"
  - "*knowledge [will] grow from more to more,*"
  - "*thy [God's] creature, whom I found so fair.*"

- o *" 'Tis better to have loved and lost / Than never to have loved at all."*
- o *"so careful of the type"*
- o *"Nature, red in tooth and claw"*
- o *"And he, shall he, Man...Be blown about the desert dust, Or sealed within the iron hills?"*
- o *"dragons of the prime."*

➢ *"The Charge of the Light Brigade" (1854)*
  - o ***Narrative poem***
  - o The Battle of Balaclava during the Crimean War.
  - o He was the Poet Laureate.
  - o *"The British soldier will do his duty, even to certain death, and is not paralyzed by the feeling that he is the victim of some hideous blunder,"*

➢ *Maud and Other Poems (1855):*
  - o The chief poem is called a "monodrama"

➢ *Idylls of the King (1859)*
  - o King Arthur and the Round Table.
  - o The Idylls an allegory of the soul of man.
  - o Comprises 12 poems
  - o Four books—"Enid," "Vivien," "Elaine," and "Guinevere"

➢ *"Tithonus" (1859)*
  - o The poem is a **dramatic monologue**.
  - o Tithonus addressed his consort, Eos, the goddess of the dawn.
  - o **Tithonus speaks to Eos** "at the quiet limit of the world."
  - o Confronted by **old age**, he reflects on **mortality**.
  - o **Pride filled him** as Eos made him feel like a god.
  - o Eos granted him **immortality**, but **time aged him mercilessly**.
  - o "But thy strong Hours...beat me down and marr'd me."
  - o Tithonus begs, **"Let me go; take back thy gift."**
  - o **Eos departs** silently, leaving **tears on his cheek**.
  - o Tithonus fears, **"The Gods cannot recall their gifts."**
  - o He remembers his **youth**, revived each morning by **Eos' kiss**.
  - o **Longing for death**, he envies men who can die.
  - o His "immortal age" cannot match Eos' **"immortal youth."**
  - o Weary, he yearns for **freedom from eternal life**.

➢ *Enoch Arden (1864)*

- o *Narrative poem.*
- o **Enoch Arden** is a happily married fisherman facing **financial struggles**.
- o He becomes a **merchant seaman** to support his family.
- o **Shipwrecked**, he spends **ten years** on a desert island.
- o Returning home, he finds his **wife remarried** with a child.
- o To preserve her happiness, he **keeps his survival secret**.

- ➤ *Locksley Hall Sixty Years after (1885)*
- ➤ *Crossing the Bar (1889)*
  - o *Extended metaphor to compare death with crossing the "sandbar"*

- ➤ *The Death of Œnone (1892)*

> 📄 **Code 1:**
>
> 🖌️ **Two Brothers** penned a cracking poem **"Timbuctoo"** 🏕️ telling of **Isabel** 🕯️ and **Mad Maria** 🎭
> who reside in the **Palace of Art** 🏔️ , feasting on **Lotus** 🌸 , dreaming of **Arthur** ⚔️
> and the journey of **Ulysses** 🧭 to **Locksley Hall** 🏛️.
>
> 📄 **Code 2:**
>
> 👑 **Princess** mourns for **Maud** 🕯️ , in **Idylls** 🗡️, a **King's Arden** 🌳 .
>
> 🗂️ **Poetic Journey:**
>
> - ● **First Work:** 🖌️ **Two Brothers**
> - ● **Second Work:** 📄 **Timbuctoo**
> - ● **Middle Poems:** 📖 **Isabel, Madeleine, Mariana, The Palace of Art,**
>   **The Lotus Eater, Morte d'Arthur, Ulysses, Locksley Hall,**
>   **Princess, In Memoriam, and Maud**
> - ● **Second Last Work:** 🖼️ **Idylls of the King**
> - ● **Last Work:** ⚓ **Enoch Arden**

His Plays:

Historical plays—
  ➢ *Queen Mary (1875),*
  ➢ *Harold (1877),*
  ➢ *Becket (1884).*

Comedy Play:
  ➢ *The Falcon (1879):* Comedy based on a story from Boccaccio;
  ➢ *The Cup (1880)* is based on a story from Plutarch,
  ➢ *The Foresters (1892)*

Questions:

The poetic line "Tis better to have loved and lost than never to have loved at all" appears in :

    (1) S.T. Coleridge's "The Rime of Ancient Mariner"
    (2) Alfred Tennyson's "In Memorium A.H.H"
    (3) Shakespeare's "Let Me Not to the Marriage of True Minds"
    (4) Mathew Arnold's "Dover Beach"

Explanations:
Answer: (2) Alfred Tennyson's "In Memorium A.H.H"

The line *"'Tis better to have loved and lost than never to have loved at all"* is from Alfred Tennyson's *In Memoriam A.H.H.* This famous work is a long elegy written in memory of Tennyson's friend Arthur Henry Hallam. The line reflects Tennyson's exploration of grief, love, and loss, emphasizing the enduring value of love even in the face of bereavement.

Additional Context:

- **Option (1)** - *The Rime of the Ancient Mariner* by S.T. Coleridge does not contain this line; it focuses on themes of guilt and redemption.
- **Option (3)** - Shakespeare's *Sonnet 116*, also known as *Let Me Not to the Marriage of True Minds*, is about the steadfastness of true love, but does not include this line.
- **Option (4)** - *Dover Beach* by Matthew Arnold explores human misery and disillusionment with faith, and does not contain this line.

So, **Option (2) is correct.**

Which two poems in the following list are examples of dramatic monologue?

    A. Alfred Tennyson, "Ulysses"
    B. Philip Larkin, "Church Going"
    C. Carol Ann Duffy, "Medusa"
    D. Katherine Philips, "A Married State"

Choose the correct answer from the options given below:

1. A and D only
2. B and C only
3. C and D only
4. A and C only

Explanations:
Answer: 4. A and C only

Alfred Tennyson's poem "Ulysses" is a dramatic monologue spoken by the Greek hero Ulysses, also known as Odysseus. The poem describes Ulysses' restlessness and desire for new adventures even after his return home to Ithaca. He expresses his dissatisfaction with the mundane life of ruling his kingdom and yearns for the excitement of the sea and the unknown. The poem is often interpreted as a commentary on the human desire for exploration and the search for meaning in life.

Carol Ann Duffy's poem "Medusa" is a dramatic monologue in which the speaker is Medusa herself. Medusa is a character from Greek mythology who was once a beautiful woman but was cursed by Athena and turned into a monster with snakes for hair. In the poem, Medusa speaks about her life as a monster and her desire to turn men into stone with her gaze.

Katherine Philips' poem "A Married State" is a satirical poem that critiques the institution of marriage. Philips, who was a 17th-century poet, was known for her unconventional views on marriage and her support of same-sex relationships. In this poem, she portrays marriage as a form of enslavement for women, who are expected to submit to their husbands and bear children. The poem is a powerful statement on the unequal power dynamics between men and women in marriage.

Philip Larkin's poem "Church Going" is a meditation on the decline of religious belief and the loss of faith in modern society. The poem is narrated by a speaker who enters an empty church and reflects on the purpose and meaning of religious institutions in the modern world. The poem explores the tension between tradition and modernity and the role of religion in providing meaning and purpose in life.

Question 3

Match List I with List II

List I (First Line)	List II (Poet)
A. "Courage!" he said, and pointed toward the land...	I. G.M. Hopkins
B. I am poor brother Lippo, by your leave!	II. Alfred Tennyson
C. I caught this morning morning's minion...	III. D.G. Rossetti
D. Look in my face; my name is Might-have-been..	IV. Matthew Arnold
E. The sea is calm tonight...	V. Robert Browning

Choose the correct answer from the options given below:

1.   A-II, B-III, C-I, D-V, E-IV
2.   A-IV, B-V, C-I, D-III, E-II
3.   A-III, B-IV, C-V, D-I, E-II
4.   **A-II, B-V, C-I, D-III, E-IV**

Correct Explanations:
A. "Courage! he said and pointed toward the land" is from **"Ulysses" by Alfred, Lord** Tennyson, not "The Lotos-eaters."

B. "I am poor brother Lippo, by your leave!" - This is the opening line of the dramatic monologue **"Fra Lippo Lippi" by Robert Browning.** The poem is spoken by a Renaissance painter who defends his unconventional lifestyle and artistic methods to a group of monks.

C. "I caught this morning morning's minion..." - This is the opening line of the poem **"The Windhover" by Gerard Manley Hopkins**. The poem describes the speaker's awe and admiration for a falcon in flight and explores the beauty and complexity of the natural world.

D. Look in my face; my name is Might have been" – The Nevermore. Dante Gabriel Rossetti.

E. "The sea is calm tonight..." - This is the opening line of the poem "Dover Beach" by Matthew Arnold. The poem reflects on the loss of faith and the decline of Western culture and uses the image of the sea as a metaphor for the changing tides of history.

Question 4

Match List I with List II

List I (Author)	List II (Text)
A. Robert Browning	I. Queen Mary
B.S. T. Coleridge	II. The Second Mrs Tanqueray
C. A. W. Pinero	III. Remorse
D. Alfred Tennyson	IV. The Borderers
E. William Wordsworth	V. Strafford

Choose the correct answer from the options given below:

1. **A-V; B-III; C-II; D-I; E-IV**
2. A-II; B-IV; C-III; D-V; E-I
3. A-III; B-V; C-II; D-I; E-IV
4. A-IV; B-II; C-I; D-V; E-III

Correct Explanations:
  - ➢ *The Second Mrs. Tanqueray* **(1892) is a problem play by Arthur Wing Pinero.** It adopts the "Woman with a past" plot, popular in nineteenth century melodrama.
  - ➢ *Strafford* **is an 1837 tragedy by the British writer Robert Browning.** It portrays the downfall and execution of Lord Strafford, the advisor to Charles I shortly before the English Civil War.
  - ➢ *Osorio* **is a tragedy in blank verse by Samuel Taylor Coleridg**e. It was written in 1797 but was unperformed following its rejection by Drury Lane Theatre. Coleridge revised and recast the play sixteen years later, giving it the new title of *Remorse*.
  - ➢ *Queen Mary and Harol***d, by Alfred Lord Tennyson.**
  - ➢ *The Borderers***, by William Wordsworth.**

Question 5

A. L. Tennyson in the following lines:

"Yet I doubt not through the ages one increasing purpose runs. And the thoughts of men are widen'd with the process of the suns"

1. Reflects upon secularism
2. Reflects upon materialism
3. Reflects upon utilitarianism
4. **Reflects upon evolutionary faith**

Explanations:

The lines *"Yet I doubt not through the ages one increasing purpose runs. And the thoughts of men are widen'd with the process of the suns"* were written by Alfred, Lord Tennyson in his poem "Locksley Hall."

In *Locksley Hall*, Tennyson reflects on progress, human development, and the optimistic idea that humanity's purpose and understanding expand over time, symbolized by the movement of the suns. This sentiment captures the Victorian era's faith in progress and the advancement of knowledge.

The phrase *"one increasing purpose runs"* and *"the thoughts of men are widen'd with the process of the suns"* suggests a belief in human progress and the idea that humanity evolves intellectually and morally over time. This aligns with the concept of evolutionary faith, an optimistic Victorian view that human understanding and purpose continually expand through the ages.

Question 6

"The Princess: A Medley" by Tennyson is

1. a lyric
2. an elegy
3. **a narrative poem**
4. a dramatic monologue

Explanations:

"The Princess: A Medley" is a narrative poem written by Alfred Lord Tennyson and published in 1847. The poem tells the story of a princess who starts a women's college to prove that women can be just as intelligent and capable as men. The poem is divided into seven parts, or "cantos," and it uses a variety of poetic forms, including blank verse, rhymed couplets, and songs. "The Princess" was one of Tennyson's most popular and influential works, and it helped to establish him as one of the leading poets of the Victorian era.

Robert Browning (1812-1889)

- **Browning** was born in **Camberwell**; his father worked at the **Bank of England**.
- He was **educated semi-privately** and studied unusual subjects freely.
- Browning showed **precocious talent**, writing poetry by age twelve.
- **Shelley** notably influenced Browning's early, turbulent mind.
- After a short time at **London University**, he traveled to **Russia** in 1833.
- Lived in **London** and met leading literary, theatrical figures.
- In **1834**, he visited **Italy**, which later became a home.
- **1845**: Met poet **Elizabeth Barrett**, who fascinated him deeply.
- **Elizabeth and Browning** privately married and eloped soon after.
- Spent life traveling between **England, France, and Italy**.
- **Elizabeth Barrett Browning** died in **Florence** in 1861.
- Browning returned to **England** after her death but revisited Italy.
- In **1867**, **Oxford** awarded him an honorary **D.C.L.** degree.
- He returned to **Italy** briefly in **1878**.
- **Browning died in Italy** and was buried at **Westminster Abbey**.

Major Works:
- *Pauline: A Fragment of a Confession (1833)*
  - The First Work.
  - The poem is a wild **imitation** of the more extravagant outbursts of **Shelley**.
  - The **confession** of an **unnamed poet** to his lover, the **eponymous woman**.
  - The poem as a **"sort of spiritual biography"**
- *Paracelsus (1835)*
  - **Monologues** of the medieval charlatan whose name forms the title.
  - The work gave the public its first taste of Browning's famous **"obscurity."**
  - The poem is split into **five parts** called
    - "Paracelsus Aspires,"
    - "Paracelsus Attains,"
    - "Paracelsus,"
    - "Paracelsus Aspires,"

- "Paracelsus Attains."
- ➢ *Strafford (play) (1837)*
- ➢ *Sordello (1840)*
  - o Tells the life-story of a Mantuan troubadour.
  - o Narrative poem.
- ➢ *Bells and Pomegranates (No. I-VIII) (1841–46)*
  - o ***No. I: Pippa Passes (play) (1841)***
    - A verse drama in four parts.
    - The poem's sections—**Morning, Noon, Evening, and Night.**
    - On New Year's morning, her only holiday for the entire year,
    - Pippa, an impoverished young silk-winder, sings as she wanders.
    - **People at critical life points hear Pippa sing.**
    - **Her song influences them to make impactful decisions.**
  - o *No. III: Dramatic Lyrics (1842)*
  - o ***No. V: A Blot in the 'Scutcheon (play) (1843)***
    - A tragedy about a nobleman who falls in love with his sister-in-law.
  - o ***Porphyria's Lover***
    - Browning's first-ever short dramatic monologue.
    - In the poem, **a man strangles his lover** – Porphyria – **with her hair.**
    - *"and all her hair / In one long yellow string I wound / Three times her little throat around, / And strangled her."*
  - o *Soliloquy of the Spanish Cloister*
  - o ***My Last Duchess***
    - A **dramatic monologue.**
    - There are **28 iambic pentameter** couplets in the poem.
    - The poem was titled "Italy" in the first edition of Dramatic Lyrics.
    - The poem begins with the epigraph **"Ferrara:"**
    - **Based on Duke of Ferrara's** 16th-century life events.
    - **Duke entertains an emissary** negotiating a new marriage.
    - Visitor pauses before **a portrait of the Duchess.**

- - **Duke reminisces about the Duchess's** life and behavior.
    - Duke criticizes her **"disgraceful" flirtations with everyone.**
    - Duchess did not value his **"nine-hundred-year-old name."**
    - Duke hints he **caused the Duchess's death** with commands.
    - All her **"smiles stopped together,"** implying her end.
    - **Duke resumes discussing** his next potential marriage.
    - They leave the painting, observing **more artworks together.**
  - *The Pied Piper of Hamelin*
    - The Pied Piper of Hamelin, a Child's Story,
    - A narrative poem of 303 lines.
    - The classic legend of **Hamelin** tells of its **burghers.**
    - They hire the **Pied Piper** to remove **rats.**
    - The **Piper** leads the rats to their death **in the river.**
    - **Townspeople refuse payment** for the Piper's services.
    - He then lures their **children away** by the same means.
    - **130 children** followed him out of town and into a cave,
    - **Three children remained behind:**
      - Lame and could not follow quickly enough.
      - Deaf and therefore could not hear the music.
      - Blind and unable to see where he was going.
  - *Count Gismond*
  - *Johannes Agricola in Meditation*
- *The Lost Leader*
- *Home Thoughts from Abroad*
- *Meeting at Night*
- ***Men and Women (1855):***
  - **A collection of fifty-one poems in two volumes**
  - **All of which are monologues spoken by different narrators**
    - *Evelyn Hope*
    - *Love Among the Ruins*
    - *A Toccata of Galuppi's*
    - *Childe Roland to the Dark Tower Came*
    - ***Fra Lippo Lippi***
      - **Dramatic monologue**

- Depicts a **15th-century real-life painter, Filippo Lippi**.
- Written in **blank verse**, non-rhyming iambic pentameter.
  - *Andrea Del Sarto*
    - Also called "**The Faultless Painter**"
    - **Dramatic monologue**
    - "Paint the soul, never mind the legs and arms!"
    - About the Italian painter Andrea del Sarto.
  - *The Patriot*
  - *The Last Ride Together(1855)*
  - *Love Among the Ruins*
  - *"Bishop Blougram's Apology"*
    - *"Our interest's on the dangerous edge of things.*
      The honest thief, the tender murderer,
      The superstitious atheist..."

- *Dramatis Personae (1864)*
  - *Caliban upon Setebos*
    - **The titular Setebos refers to The brutal god in whom Caliban believes.**
    - It explores **Caliban's reflections on his god Setebos.**
    - Caliban believes in **Setebos, a brutal god.**
    - Some scholars argue **God is in the eye.**
    - A **barbaric character believes in a barbaric god.**
    - "Thou thoughtest that I was altogether such a one as thyself."
  - **Rabbi Ben Ezra**
    - About Abraham ibn Ezra (1092–1167),
    - One of the great poets and scholars of the 12th century.
    - He wrote on grammar, astronomy, the astrolabe, etc.
    - The poem begins:
      Grow old along with me!
      - *The best is yet to be — Stanza I, lines 1-2*
      - *For thence,—a paradox*
      - *Which comforts while it mocks,—*
      - *Shall life succeed in that it seems to fail:*

- - *What I aspired to be,*
      And was not, comforts me:
  - *A brute I might have been, but would not sink i'*
    the scale. — Stanza VII
  - *Abt Vogler*
    - *"art in obedience to laws,"*
    - *Abt Vogler* by **Robert Browning** explores artistic expression's depth.
    - Inspired by **musician Georg Vogler**, famous for improvisation.
    - Themes reflect **music, divine creation, and impermanence**.
    - Vogler uses **music metaphors** to reach spiritual heights.
    - Faith brings meaning to beauty's **ephemeral nature**.
  - "A Death in the Desert"

- ➢ ***The Ring and the Book (1868–69)***
  - A literary "stunt."
  - A long dramatic narrative poem.
  - A verse novel of 21,000 lines.
  - Published in four volumes from 1868 to 1869
  - Story of the murder of a young wife, **Pompilia**, by her worthless husband, in the year 1698.
  - The same story is told by **nine different people**, and continues for **twelve books**.
  - The book recounts a **1698 murder trial in Rome**.
  - **Count Guido Franceschini** is found guilty of **murdering** his wife.
  - Guido suspects his wife had an affair with **Giuseppe Caponsacchi**.
  - He appeals to **Pope Innocent XII** but is denied.
  - The poem contains **twelve books**, primarily **dramatic monologues**.
  - **Ten monologues** depict different characters' versions of events.
  - **Two books** (first and last) are by the author.

Elizabeth Barrett Browning (1806-1861)

- ➢ Born in **Durham** to a West India planter.

- ➤ She began writing poetry at age eight.
- ➤ Her first noteworthy work, *An Essay on Mind* **(1826),** is minor.
- ➤ At thirty, her **delicate health** made her nearly an invalid.
- ➤ In 1846, she married **Robert Browning** and moved to Italy.
- ➤ She supported various causes, including **Italian independence**.
- ➤ After **Wordsworth's** death, she was considered for Laureateship.
- ➤ Her main works include *Prometheus Bound* **(1835) and *The Seraphim* (1838)**.
- ➤ *Sonnet from the Portuguese* **(1846)** was published the year she married.
- ➤ *Casa Guidi Windows* **(1851) and *Aurora Leigh* (1857)** followed.
- ➤ Her final works were *Last Poems* (1861) before her death.
- ➤ *The Cry of the Children* **(1841)** appeared in **Blackwood's Magazine**.
- ➤ *The Great God Pan* **(1860)** appeared in **The Cornhill Magazine**.
- ➤ Her narrative poems often seemed **discursive and confused**.
- ➤ Her style was **sweet, clear, and passionate** yet flawed.
- ➤ She sometimes lapsed into **"falsetto masculinity,"** as **Rossetti** said.

Sonnets from the Portuguese (1850)

- ➤ A collection of **44 love sonnets**.
- ➤ **Barrett Browning** hesitated to publish, feeling the poems **too personal**.
- ➤ **Robert Browning** insisted they were the **best sonnets since Shakespeare**.
- ➤ To maintain privacy, she **published as foreign translations**.
- ➤ She first planned to title them **"Sonnets translated from the Bosnian."**
- ➤ Browning suggested claiming **Portuguese origins** instead.
- ➤ **Portuguese** referenced her admiration for **Camões** and Robert's nickname.
- ➤ The title also references **Les Lettres Portugaises** (1669).
- ➤ **"How Do I Love Thee?" (Sonnet 43, 1845)**

> *How do I love thee? Let me count the ways.*
> *I love thee to the depth and breadth and height*
> *My soul can reach, when feeling out of sight*
> *For the ends of Being and Ideal Grace.*
> *I love thee to the level of everyday's*
> *Most quiet need, by sun and candlelight.*
> *I love thee freely, as men strive for Right;*

> *I love thee purely, as they turn from Praise;*
> *I love thee with the passion put to use*
> *In my old griefs, and with my childhood's faith;*
> *I love thee with a love I seemed to lose*
> *With my lost saints,—I love thee with the breath,*
> *Smiles, tears, of all my life!—and, if God choose,*
> *I shall but love thee better after death.*

Aurora Leigh (1856)

- ➤ A novel in **blank verse.**
- ➤ The **first-person narrative** spans approximately **11,000 lines.**
- ➤ It details the heroine's **childhood and youth** in **Italy and England.**
- ➤ Aurora **self-educates** in her **father's hidden library.**
- ➤ She pursues and achieves **success in a literary career.**
- ➤ **Initially rejecting** philanthropist **Romney Leigh's marriage proposal.**
- ➤ Aurora later **marries Romney** after life tempers their ideals.
- ➤ The plot explores **poetry, social duty, and women's victimization.**
- ➤ **Book 1**: Aurora recalls her childhood, education, and self-discovery.
- ➤ **Book 2**: Romney proposes; Aurora rejects, seeking poetic independence.
- ➤ **Book 3**: Aurora gains fame but struggles with creative fulfillment.
- ➤ **Book 4**: Marian rejects Romney at wedding; both are heartbroken.
- ➤ **Book 5**: Aurora reflects on writing; plans move to Italy.
- ➤ **Book 6**: Aurora finds Marian in Paris, learns her tragic story.
- ➤ **Book 7**: Marian embraces motherhood; Aurora supports her move to Italy.
- ➤ **Book 8**: Romney arrives in Florence; they discuss past mistakes.
- ➤ **Book 9**: Marian refuses Romney; Aurora confesses her love for him.

Questions:

Which two of the following poems are by Robert Browning?

A. "Locksley Hall"
B. "The Pied Piper of Hamelin"
C. "The Lady of Shalott"
D. "Two in the Campagna"

Choose the correct answer from the options given below:

1. A and D only
2. B and C only
3. A and C only
4. B and D only

Explanations:
Answer: 4. B and D only

"The Pied Piper of Hamelin" is a poem written by Robert Browning in 1842. It tells the story of a town in Germany that is plagued by rats and a mysterious piper who is able to lure them away with his music. When the townspeople refuse to pay him, he exacts his revenge by leading their children away as well.

"Two in the Campagna" is a poem written by Robert Browning in 1855. It describes a moment of intimacy between two lovers in the countryside outside of Rome. The speaker muses on the transience of love and the beauty of the natural world, creating a sense of melancholy and longing.

Extra Perk:

"The Lady of Shalott" is a narrative poem written by Alfred Lord Tennyson in 1832. It tells the story of a young woman who is cursed to live alone in a tower, weaving a tapestry and never looking outside. When she sees Sir Lancelot riding by, she is overcome with desire and leaves her tower to follow him, ultimately leading to her tragic death.

"Locksley Hall" is a dramatic monologue written by Alfred Lord Tennyson in 1835. The poem is narrated by a man who is disillusioned with his life and society and longs for his childhood love. It reflects the changing social and political climate of the time and the anxieties and uncertainties of the speaker.

Question 8

What does the titular Setebos in Robert Browning's "'Caliban upon Setebos" refer to?

1. The Original name of Syoorax Caliban's mother
2. The brutal god in whom Caliban believes
3. The name of the island in which Caliban lives
4. The monster whom Caliban is afraid of

Explanations:
Answer: 2. The brutal god in whom Caliban believes

Setebos in Robert Browning's poem "Caliban upon Setebos" refers to the brutal god in whom Caliban believes. Setebos is depicted as a deity with tyrannical and vengeful qualities, representing Caliban's understanding of divinity and his fears. The poem explores Caliban's contemplation of his beliefs and his questioning of the nature of God.

Question 9

Which of the following poems by Robert Browning contains the lines, *"Our interest's on the dangerous edge of things. / The honest thief, the tender murderer, / The superstitious atheist. . ."?*

1. "A Death in the Desert"
2. "Count Gismond"
3. **"Bishop Blougram's Apology"**
4. "Love Among the Ruins"

Correct Explanations:
These lines are spoken by the character Bishop Blougram in Robert Browning's poem "Bishop Blougram's Apology." The bishop is defending his faith and arguing that those who do not believe in God are not necessarily immoral, but may in fact be more honest and straightforward than those who profess belief for personal gain. The lines suggest that the bishop's interest lies in exploring the gray areas of morality and human behaviour, where people may be forced to make difficult choices and act against the norm in order to survive or achieve their goals.

Other Explanations:
"A Death in the Desert" is a dramatic monologue by Robert Browning in which an elderly Saint John gives a final testament of his faith to a group of young followers. John's reflections are focused on Christ's life and teachings, his own apostolic career, and the mysterious doctrine of the Trinity, all of which challenge his listeners' comprehension of faith and belief.

"Count Gismond" is a dramatic monologue by Robert Browning that tells the story of a woman who has been forced to marry a brutal and abusive nobleman. The speaker is the woman's lover who helps her escape her husband's wrath. He recounts the story of her escape and the subsequent duel with the Count in which he kills Gismond, allowing the couple to be together.

"Bishop Blougram's Apology" is a dramatic monologue by Robert Browning that explores the relationship between faith and doubt. The poem takes the form of a conversation between the sceptical editor of a literary magazine and a bishop who admits that he is not as devout as he may appear to be. The bishop argues that faith can coexist with doubt and that his position of power in the church does not necessarily imply unwavering belief.

"Love Among the Ruins" is a poem by Robert Browning that explores the theme of love enduring in a decaying world. The speaker imagines a future where society has crumbled, but the two lovers can still find joy and meaning in their relationship despite the ruins of civilization around them. The poem is a testament to the power of love to transcend even the direst circumstances.

Question 10

In his recasting of the canon of English poetry in New Bearings in English Poetry which of the following pairs was downgraded by F.R.Leavis ?

1. **Browning and Arnold**
2. Tennyson and Swinburne
3. Pound and Hopkins
4. Milton and Shelley

Correct Explanations:

This statement is not entirely accurate. In his book "New Bearings in English Poetry," F.R. Leavis did criticize Robert Browning's work, arguing that it lacked moral seriousness, but he did not specifically downgrade the pairing of Browning and Arnold. In fact, Leavis praised Arnold's work in the book, particularly his poem "Dover Beach." Leavis did, however, argue for the inclusion of other poets, such as T.S. Eliot and Ezra Pound, in the canon of English poetry.

Question 11

Match List I with List II

List I (Author)	List II (Text)
A. Robert Browning	I. Queen Mary
B.S. T. Coleridge	II.The Second Mrs Tanqueray
C. A. W. Pinero	III. Remorse
D. Alfred Tennyson	IV. The Borderers
E. William Wordsworth	V. Strafford

Choose the correct answer from the options given below:

1. **A-V; B-III; C-II; D-I; E-IV**
2. A-II; B-IV; C-III; D-V; E-I
3. A-III; B-V; C-II; D-I; E-IV
4. A-IV; B-II; C-I; D-V; E-III

Correct Explanations:
> *The Second Mrs. Tanqueray* **(1892) is a problem play by Arthur Wing Pinero.** It adopts the "Woman with a past" plot, popular in nineteenth century melodrama.
> *Strafford* **is an 1837 tragedy by the British writer Robert Browning.** It portrays the downfall and execution of Lord Strafford, the advisor to Charles I shortly before the English Civil War.
> *Osorio* **is a tragedy in blank verse by Samuel Taylor Coleridg**e. It was written in 1797 but was unperformed following its rejection by Drury Lane Theatre. Coleridge revised and recast the play sixteen years later, giving it the new title of *Remorse*.
> *Queen Mary and Harol***d, by Alfred Lord Tennyson.**
> *The Borderers***, by William Wordsworth.**

Question 12

Abt Vogler is authored by

1. Matthew Arnold
2. **Robert Browning**
3. A. L. Tennyson
4. None of the above

Correct Explanations:

After Browning's amazing, though not particularly popular Men & Women in 1855, Browning married Elizabeth Barrett and took a lengthy hiatus. It was not until after his wife's death, that Browning published again, but when he did so, it was with a volume that didn't pale compared to his earlier works in the least. The 1864 publication of Dramatic Lyrics was, to that point, Browning's most popular book, requiring a second printing, a first for the ridiculously overlooked poet. **Not least among the poems in Dramatics Lyrics, though not most either, is Abt Vogler, a meditation on coming to terms with loss and diminishment, not that Browning himself needed to worry about any such thing just yet.**

Abt Vogler is written in the voice of an actual historic personage, as are many of Browning's dramatic monologues.

Question 13

The predominant emotion running through the poem "Cristina" by Rebert Browning is that of

1. Sadness
2. Aggression
3. Love
4. None of the above
5. **DROP**

Correct Explanations:
In the Answer Key UGC NET has marked Love as a correct Answer.

The predominant emotion running through the poem "Cristina" by Robert Browning is not love, **but rather grief and mourning.** The poem is a poignant elegy that Browning wrote in memory of his wife, Elizabeth Barrett Browning's sister, who had died young. The poem is filled with expressions of sorrow and loss, as Browning laments the passing of this young and promising life. While the poem does make reference to love and the bond between the speaker and Cristina, it is primarily focused on the theme of grief and the difficulty of coming to terms with death.

Question 14

Identify the correct ones among the following:

A. The dramatic monologue ensures the reciprocal dialogue of the narrator.
B. The nineteenth century poets fully exploited the poetic form of dramatic monologue.
C. The Poetry of Experience by Robert Langbaum outlines a discussion on a dramatic monologue,
D. The linguistic pragmatics make the narcissistic speaker of dramatic monologue speak exclusively.
E. The speaker and the listener in the dramatic: monologues of Robert Browning share the same pedestal of communication.

Choose the correct answer from the options given below:

1. A, B and C only
2. **B, C and D only**
3. C, D and E only
4. B, D and E only

Correct Expalanations:
One of the most important influences on the development of the dramatic monologue is romantic poetry. Dramatic monologue is a type of poetry written as a speech of an individual character. M.H. Abrams notes the following three features of the dramatic monologue as it applies to poetry:

➢ The single person, who is patently not the poet, utters the speech that makes up the whole of the poem, in a specific situation at a critical moment [...].
➢ This person addresses and interacts with one or more other people; but we know of the auditors' presence, and what they say and do, only from clues in the discourse of the single speaker.
➢ The main principle controlling the poet's choice and formulation of what the lyric speaker says is to reveal to the reader, in a way that enhances its interest, the speaker's temperament and character.

Langbaum's first book, The Poetry of Experience: The Dramatic Monologue in Modern Literary Tradition (1957), takes issue with T. S. Eliot whom he admires as poet and critic. He objects, however, to Eliot's redrawing of the literary tradition as beginning with the early seventeenth-century witty poets and the witty side of Shakespeare.

"The Pragmatics of Silence, and the Figuration of the Reader in Browning's Dramatic Monologues," by Jennifer A. Wagner

In this essay, Wagner elaborates on the listener's, the reader's, and the speaker's role and function in Robert Browning's dramatic monologues. Unlike other critics, who have particularly focused on the figure of the speaker, Wagner turns the critical spotlight on the role and the function of the silent listener and the reader.

Question 15

Which of the following works of Browning are pure dramas?

- A. Strafford
- B. The Last Ride Together
- C. A Blot in the 'Scutcheon
- D. Pippa Passes
- E. Porphyria's Lover

Choose the correct answer from the options given below:

1. A and C
2. B and E
3. C and D
4. B and C

Explanations:
Ans: A and C

"Strafford" and "Pippa Passes" are both plays written by Robert Browning, but they are not generally considered pure dramas. Browning is more famous for his dramatic monologues, which are often written in verse and explore the inner thoughts and motivations of a single speaker. Examples of Browning's famous dramatic monologues include **"My Last Duchess," "The Bishop Orders His Tomb at Saint Praxed's Church," and "Porphyria's Lover."**

"Strafford" is a historical play based on the life of Thomas Wentworth, the Earl of Strafford, while **"A Blot in the 'Scutcheon" is a tragedy about a**

nobleman who falls in love with his sister-in-law. "Pippa Passes" is a four-act play about a young factory worker named Pippa who spends a day off work exploring a city and interacting with various characters. **"The Last Ride Together" is a dramatic monologue in which a man confesses his love to a woman who is about to marry another man. "Porphyria's Lover" is a dramatic monologue in which a man strangles his lover, Porphyria, with her own hair.**

Question 16

Arrange the following poets in accordance with their years of birth.

    A.   Rudyard Kipling
    B.   Robert Browning
    C.   John Masefield
    D.   A.E. Housman
    E.   John Donne

Choose the correct answer from the options given below:

    1.   E, A, B, D, C
    2.   E, B, A, C, D
    3.   E, B, A, D, C
    4.   A, D, B, C, E

Explanations:
Ans: E, B, A, D, C

Here are the poets in order of their years of birth, along with their life spans:

    ➢   John Donne (1572-1631)
    ➢   Robert Browning (1812-1889)
    ➢   Rudyard Kipling (1865-1936)
    ➢   A.E. Housman (1859-1936)
    ➢   John Masefield (1878-1967)

John Donne was born in 1572 and lived until 1631. He is considered a leading figure of the Metaphysical poets, known for their use of extended metaphors, paradoxes, and intellectual wit.

Robert Browning was born in 1812 and lived until 1889. He is known for his dramatic monologues, which give voice to a range of characters and perspectives.

Rudyard Kipling was born in 1865 and lived until 1936. He was a prolific writer of poetry and prose, and his work often celebrated British imperialism and the values of the British Empire.

A.E. Housman was born in 1859 and lived until 1936. He is known for his elegiac poems about unrequited love and the transience of life.

John Masefield was born in 1878 and lived until 1967. He was appointed Poet Laureate of the United Kingdom in 1930 and is known for his lyrical, narrative poetry.

Question 17

Find the chronological order of publication of the given works:

- A. Darwin's Origin of Species
- B. Macaulay's "Essay on Milton"
- C. Stevenson's Treasure Island
- D. Browning's "Pauline"
- E. Arnold Bennet's Old Wives Tale

Choose the correct answer from the options given below:

1. ABCDE
2. **BDACE**
3. CDABE
4. DEACB

Explanations:
- ➤ Browning's "Pauline" (1833)
- ➤ Darwin's Origin of Species (1859)
- ➤ Macaulay's "Essay on Milton" (1859)
- ➤ Stevenson's Treasure Island (1883)
- ➤ Arnold Bennet's Old Wives Tale (1908)

Which of the following two poems are linked with each other in terms of form?

A.   "The Last Ride Together"
B.   "Ulysses"
C.   "Upon Appleton House: To My Lord Fairfax"
D.   "To Penshurst"
E.   "The Waste Land"

Choose the correct answer from the options given below:

1.   A and E only.
2.   A and B only.
3.   A and D only.
4.   **C and D only.**

Explanations:
"Upon Appleton House: To My Lord Fairfax" and "To Penshurst" are linked with each other in terms of form. Both poems are examples of **country-house poems, which were popular in the seventeenth century.** These poems describe the beauty and tranquility of country estates and the noble families who lived there. They often use a descriptive and contemplative style, praising the virtues of country life and rural landscapes. Additionally, both poems were written by poets associated with the metaphysical school of poetry: Andrew Marvell wrote "Upon Appleton House," and Ben Jonson wrote "To Penshurst."

Other Explanations:
"The Last Ride Together" is a poem by Robert Browning that explores the theme of unrequited love. The speaker is addressing his beloved, who is about to marry someone else. He asks for one last ride together before he lets her go. The poem is structured as a dramatic monologue, with the speaker trying to persuade his beloved to spend one last moment with him. The poem is notable for its use of dramatic irony, as the reader knows that the beloved will not accept the speaker's offer.

"Ulysses" is a poem by Alfred, Lord Tennyson that explores the theme of the search for meaning and purpose in life. The poem is written in the voice of the legendary hero Ulysses, who is now an old man, looking back on his life. He expresses his desire to set out on one final adventure, to seek new experiences and regain his former glory. The poem is notable for its use of blank verse and its complex syntax, which reflects Ulysses' restless, searching spirit.

"Upon Appleton House: To My Lord Fairfax" is a poem by Andrew Marvell that celebrates the beauty and harmony of nature. The poem is written in the voice of the speaker, who is visiting his friend's country estate. The poem is structured as a series of descriptions of the landscape, the animals, and the people who inhabit the estate. The poem is notable for its use of vivid imagery and its celebration of the natural world.

"To Penshurst" is a poem by Ben Jonson that celebrates the beauty and harmony of country life. The poem is written in the voice of the speaker, who is visiting the country estate of his patron. The poem is structured as a series of descriptions of the landscape, the animals, and the people who inhabit the estate. The poem is notable for its use of vivid imagery and its celebration of the natural world.

"The Waste Land" is a poem by T.S. Eliot that is widely regarded as one of the most important works of modernist poetry. The poem is structured as a series of fragmented scenes and voices, which reflect the dislocation and fragmentation of modern life. The poem is notable for its use of allusions and quotations from a wide range of literary and cultural sources, including Shakespeare, Dante, and Hindu mythology.

Matthew Arnold (1822-1888):

- ➤ **Most significant poet and critic** of the 19th century.
- ➤ Mathew Arnold addressed **social, religious, and cultural issues**.
- ➤ **Born into a distinguished English family**; father was headmaster.
- ➤ Graduated from **Balliol College, Oxford** with distinction.
- ➤ Worked as a **school inspector, traveling across England**.
- ➤ First **Oxford poetry professor to lecture in English** (1857).
- ➤ **Walt Whitman called him** a "literary dude."
- ➤ **Arnold's poetry strongly influenced later writers**.
- ➤ Recognized as **one of the earliest Modern poets**.

> *Matthew Arnold, after reading Villette, wrote that her mind "contained nothing but hunger, rebellion, and rage":*

Notable Works:
- *"Culture and Anarchy"*
- *"Dover Beach"*
- *"Empedocles on Etna"*
- *"Essays in Criticism"*
- *"God and the Bible"*
- *"On Translating Homer"*
- *"On the Study of Celtic Literature"*
- *"Sohrab and Rustum"*
- *"The Forsaken Merman"*
- *"The Scholar Gipsy"*
- *"The Strayed Reveller, and Other Poems"*
- *"The Study of Poetry"*
- *"Thyrsis"*

The Scholar Gipsy (1853)

- **A lyric poem** by Matthew Arnold, was published in Poems (1853).
- **10-line stanza** that John Keats used in many of his odes.
- The poem's subject is an **Oxford scholar** turned wanderer.
- He abandons academia to join **a band of gypsies**.
- The poem describes the **countryside around Oxford** vividly.
- Arnold includes an extract from **Glanvill's story** as a preface.
- The student learns **gypsies' secrets** and their imaginative powers.
- He vows to reveal their wisdom to **the world** someday.
- Arnold begins the poem in **pastoral mode** with Oxford in view.
- He retells **Glanvill's tale**, extending with rumors of sightings.
- The scholar gypsy appears as a **shadowy, elusive figure**.
- Arnold himself claims to have seen him in **the countryside**.
- The gypsy is imagined "waiting for the **spark from Heaven**."
- Arnold doubts but quickly dismisses **thoughts of his death**.
- He believes the scholar gypsy **remains immortal** over time.
- The gypsy figure endures as **a timeless spirit of learning**.

Sohrab and Rustum (1853)

- **Sohrab and Rustum: An Episode** by Matthew Arnold, **published in 1853**.
- Poem retells **Rustum unknowingly killing son Sohrab** in battle.
- Arnold relied on **summaries in Malcolm's History of Persia**.
- Arnold aimed to **imitate Homer's "grandeur and rapidity"** style.
- Poem has **892 lines of blank verse**.

Thyrsis (1866):

- **"Thyrsis,"** an elegiac poem by **Matthew Arnold**, published **1866**.
- Included in Arnold's **New Poems** collection in **1867**.
- **One of Arnold's finest poems**, using a **10-line stanza**.
- Composed of **24 stanzas** eulogizing his friend, **Clough**.
- **Clough** is portrayed as **Thyrsis**, a **shepherd-poet**.
- Uses **pastoral imagery** to remember **Oxford countryside**.
- Arnold recalls **student days** with Clough in the **1840s**.
- Reflects on **youthful ideals** and their fate post-**university**.

Dover Beach (1867)

- A lyric poem.
- First published in 1867 in a collection called New Poems.
- The poem's **title, location**, and **subject** are the **Strait of Dover**.
- **Arnold** spent his honeymoon there in **1851**.
- He describes the sea's **"grating roar"** on stony beaches.
- The **beaches** are made of **stones and pebbles**, not sand.
- **Tinker and Lowry** note the poem's **early draft**.
- First **twenty-eight lines** written on a **folded sheet**.
- **Draft included notes** on the career of **Empedocles**.
- **Allott** estimates **notes** from **1849s or 1850s**.
- "Empedocles on Etna" likely **written in 1849–52**.
- **Notes on Empedocles** probably from the **same time**.

> ***The sea is calm tonight.***
> *The tide is full, the moon lies fair*
> *Upon the straits; on the French coast the light*
> *Gleams and is gone; the cliffs of England stand,*
> *Glimmering and vast, out in the tranquil bay.*
> *Come to the window, sweet is the night-air!*

Only, from the long line of spray
Where the sea meets the moon-blanched land,
Listen! you hear the grating roar
Of pebbles which the waves draw back, and fling,
At their return, up the high strand,
Begin, and cease, and then again begin,
With tremulous cadence slow, and bring
The eternal note of sadness in.

Sophocles long ago
Heard it on the Ægean, and it brought
Into his mind the turbid ebb and flow
Of human misery; we
Find also in the sound a thought,
Hearing it by this distant northern sea.

The Sea of Faith
Was once, too, at the full, and round earth's shore
Lay like the folds of a bright girdle furled.
But now I only hear
Its melancholy, long, withdrawing roar,
Retreating, to the breath
Of the night-wind, down the vast edges drear
And naked shingles of the world.

Ah, love, let us be true
To one another! for the world, which seems
To lie before us like a land of dreams,
So various, so beautiful, so new,
Hath really neither joy, nor love, nor light,
Nor certitude, nor peace, nor help for pain;
And we are here as on a darkling plain
Swept with confused alarms of struggle and flight,
Where ignorant armies clash by night.

The Study of Poetry (1880)

- ➤ Arnold explores poetry's **"high destiny"**.
- ➤ He acknowledges that **"*mankind will discover that we have to turn to poetry to interpret life for us, to console us, to sustain us*"**.

- He describes that science and philosophy will **ultimately prove flimsy and unstable**.
- The purpose of Arnold's essay is to establish a **"high standard"** and **"strict judgment"** to avoid the mistake of overvaluing **certain poems (and poets)**.
- It applies a method for distinguishing only the best and, therefore, **"classic" poets: Milton, Shakespeare, Dante, and Homer.**
- Arnold says that their poetry is timeless and moving.
- In Arnold's view, sincerity and feeling are paramount, as is the seriousness of the subject: "*The superior character of truth and* **seriousness,** *in the matter and substance of the best poetry, is inseparable from the superiority of diction and movement marking its style and manner.*"
- In Arnold's view, Geoffrey **Chaucer is an indispensable poet**.
- Chaucer does not fall under the "classic" designation because **Chaucer lacks the "high seriousness"** of classic poetry.
- Arnold considers poetry **as a criticism of life,** rebutting Plato's charge.
- There are three types of estimation - **the real estimate, the historical estimate, and the personal estimate.**
- Arnold discusses the **idea of imitation**.
- According to him, whatever one reads or knows keeps coming back to him.
- Arnold introduces the **'touchstone'** analysis method.
- This method is borrowed **from Longinus,** who said that if an example of sublimity can be pleasing to anyone regardless of habits, tastes, or age and can be pleasant at any time, this is an example of the sublime.
- Arnold discusses Thomas **Gray** after John **Dryden** and Alexander **Pope**.
- Despite writing little, **Gray's poems are highly regarded**.
- Arnold regards Thomas **Gray as a classic**.
- According to Arnold, **Robert Burns composed better poetry in Scottish than in English**.
- Burns, like **Chaucer, is not considered a classic**.
- Arnold then talks about **Byron, Shelley, and Wordsworth** without judging their poetry.
- Arnold acknowledges that his passion will influence his estimate of these poets as they are closer to his age than the classics.
- Their writings are more personal.

> ➤ Arnold concludes by discussing the **preservation of classics**.
> ➤ **Arnold argues that there are two types of fallacious evaluations of poetry: the historic estimate and the personal estimate.**
> ➤ *"Yes; constantly in reading poetry, a sense for the best, the really excellent, and of the strength and joy to be drawn from it, should be present in our minds and should govern our estimate of what we read. But this real estimate, the only true one, is liable to be superseded, if we are not watchful,* **by two other kinds of estimate, the historic estimate and the personal estimate,** *both of which are fallacious. A poet or a poem may count to us historically, they may count to us on grounds personal to ourselves, and they may count to us really. They may count to us historically."*

Touchstone Method:

> ➤ **Arnold compares** classic poems to assess high standards.
> ➤ Poems **need not resemble** the touchstones exactly.
> ➤ With **touchstones in mind**, critics detect poetic quality.
> ➤ **Arnold cites Homer, Dante, Shakespeare,** and Milton.
> ➤ These poets represent **high poetic quality**.
> ➤ Examples of **top-quality poetry clarify poetry's importance**.
> ➤ High poetry quality depends on **matter and manner**.
> ➤ Following **Aristotle**, he values **truthfulness and seriousness**.
> ➤ **Arnold stresses** that this method's strength is its **application**.
> ➤ He believes critics should **apply the touchstone method**.

The Function of Criticism (1865):

> ➤ Arnold focuses on his interpretation of criticism and criticism of writers who write politically or religiously biased literature.
> ➤ Arnold **begins** *"Of the literature of France and Germany, as of the intellect of Europe."*
> ➤ Here Arnold explains **the primary task of any critic**.
> ➤ Critics must see any **object (work) as it is without considering other factors**.
> ➤ Critics should always **interpret the text as a whole** and never look to other texts.
> ➤ According to Arnold, **the creator of a text is more significant** than its critic since *"creative activity is the true function of man"*.
> ➤ A critic is responsible for determining the true meaning of a particular work of literature.

- A great literary work is produced by *"the power of man"* and *"the power of moment"*.
- The absence of any of them will prevent the creation of a great work of literature.
- In his essay, Arnold provides the example of two poets, **Goethe and Byron**.
- Goethe and Byron **both possessed a great deal of productive power**.
- However, the works of Goethe are more valuable than those of Byron due to the former's rich cultural background.
- According to Arnold, **Shakespeare did not have a deep reading habit**.
- His fame and glory are primarily due to the **climate of great ideas during his time**.
- He argues that the French Revolution, with its writers such as Rousseau and Voltaire, was more powerful than the English Revolution under Charles (of great ideas of Renaissance).
- French Revolution was followed by **the "Epoch of Concentration"** (period of single-mindedness) followed by **the "Epoch of Expansion"** (period of creative ideas).

Use of Disinterestedness:

- Arnold's argument shifts to the **nature of criticism,** his thinking, and his work.
- He argues that a critic must maintain *"disinterestedness,"* i.e. keeping aloof from *"the practical view of things "*in order to *"know the best that is known and thought in the world, and in its turn making this known, to create a current of true and fresh ideas."*
- In these lines, he provides a threefold explanation of the responsibility of a critic:
  - A **critic must know about life** and the world before writing anything and see things as they are.
  - A **critic should convey his ideas** to others and strive to ensure that the best ideas prevail in society.
  - A **critic must create an atmosphere** for developing noble, honest, and true ideas to create the future's genius.

Culture and Anarchy (1869):

- ➤ ***Culture and Anarchy: An Essay in Political and Social Criticism*** was first published in Cornhill Magazine.
- ➤ The **preface was added in 1869.**
- ➤ He says, *"Culture [...] is a study of perfection"*.
- ➤ He further wrote: *"[Culture] seeks to do away with classes; to make the best that has been thought and known in the world current everywhere; to make all men live in an atmosphere of sweetness and light [...]"*.
- ➤ His often-quoted phrase ***"[culture is] the best which has been thought and said"*** comes from the Preface to *Culture and Anarchy*:
- ➤ This essay is primarily concerned with recommending culture as an excellent tool for overcoming our current challenges.
- ➤ Getting to know the best that has been said and thought in the world is what represents the pursuit of our total perfection through culture.
- ➤ The book contains most of the terms:
    - ○ **Culture,**
    - ○ **Sweetness and light,**
    - ○ **Barbarian,**
    - ○ **Philistine,**
    - ○ **Hebraism**
- ➤ **Matthew Arnold used the term "Hebraism" to refer to the moral and ethical values of the Hebrew people.**

Questions

Question 19

Match List - I with List - II.

List - I (Poem)	List - II (Poet)
A. To His Coy Mistress	I. Rudyard Kipling
B. The Scholar Gypsy	II. Andrew Marvel
C. Still I Rise	III. Matthew Arnold
D. If	IV. Maya Angelou

Choose the correct answer from the options given below :

(1) A-II, B-III, C-IV, D-I

(2) A-I, B-II, C-IV, D-III

(3) A-III, B-II, C-IV, D-I
(4) A-IV, B-III, C-I, D-II

Explanations:
Answer: (1) A-II, B-III, C-IV, D-I

A. To His Coy Mistress – II. Andrew Marvell
B. The Scholar Gypsy – III. Matthew Arnold
C. Still I Rise – IV. Maya Angelou
D. If – I. Rudyard Kipling

Question 20

The line - "He who works for sweetness and light united, works to make reason and the will of God prevail", occurs in:

1. Raymond Williams' *Culture and Society*
2. Julia Kristeva's *Revolution in Poetic Language*
3. Matthew Arnold's *Culture and Anarchy*
4. Sigmund Freud's *Civilization and Its Discontents*

Explanations:
Answer: 3. Matthew Arnold's *Culture and Anarchy*

The quote:

> "He who works for sweetness and light united, works to make reason and the will of God prevail."

was written by **Matthew Arnold** in his work, **"Culture and Anarchy."**

In *Culture and Anarchy*, Arnold emphasizes the importance of cultivating both intellectual and moral values, which he calls "sweetness and light." By working towards a union of beauty (sweetness) and intelligence or enlightenment (light), Arnold believes we align with reason and divine will, ultimately contributing to a harmonious and moral society.

Other Explanations:

Raymond Williams' *Culture and Society* (1958)

This foundational text examines how the concept of "culture" evolved from the late 18th century to the 20th century, especially through the works of writers like Coleridge, Arnold, and Marx. Williams argues that culture is central to social and political life, and he analyzes its influence in shaping societal values.

Julia Kristeva's *Revolution in Poetic Language* (1974)

In this influential work, Kristeva introduces the idea of the *semiotic* as a pre-linguistic dimension of language that interacts with the symbolic (structured language) to create meaning. She explores how poetic language challenges conventional linguistic norms and pushes boundaries in the expression of identity and social norms.

Matthew Arnold's *Culture and Anarchy* (1869)

Arnold critiques the materialism and individualism of his time, advocating for "culture" as the pursuit of human perfection through knowledge and appreciation of "sweetness and light." He sees culture as a guiding force for moral and social reform, opposed to the chaos he associates with "anarchy."

Sigmund Freud's *Civilization and Its Discontents* (1930)

Freud examines the tension between individual desires and societal expectations. He argues that civilization is built upon the suppression of primal urges, leading to a collective sense of dissatisfaction. Freud explores the cost of societal order and the inevitability of inner conflict in the civilized individual.

Question 21

Arrange the following critical works in their chronological order of publication:

> A. "Preface to Lyrical Ballads"
> B. "A Defence of Rhyme"
> C. "Life of Cowley"
> D. "The Frontiers of Criticism"

Choose the correct answer from the options given below:

1. A, C, B and D
2. B, A, C and D
3. B, C, A and D
4. C, A, D and B

Explanations:
Answer: 3. B, C, A and D

Samuel Daniel (1562–1619) was an English poet, playwright and historian in the late-Elizabethan and early-Jacobean eras. He was an innovator in a wide range of literary genres. His best-known works are the sonnet cycle Delia, the epic poem The Civil Wars Between the Houses of Lancaster and York, the dialogue in verse Musophilus, and the essay on English poetry *A Defence of Rhyme (1603)*.

"Life of Cowley": This is a biography of the English poet Abraham Cowley, written by Samuel Johnson and first published in 1779. The biography was part of a larger project by Johnson to write biographies of English poets from the time of William Shakespeare to his own time. The "Life of Cowley" is notable for its detailed analysis of Cowley's poetry and its place in English literary history.

"Preface to Lyrical Ballads": This is a critical essay written by William Wordsworth and originally published in 1800 as the preface to the first edition of "Lyrical Ballads," a collection of poems co-authored by Wordsworth and Samuel Taylor Coleridge. The preface is considered a landmark in the development of English Romanticism and contains Wordsworth's famous declaration that "poetry is the spontaneous overflow of powerful feelings."

"The Frontiers of Criticism" is a lecture given by T. S. Eliot at the University of Minnesota in 1956. It was reprinted in On Poetry and Poets, a collection of Eliot's critical essays, in 1957.

Question 22

Name the British poet who wrote Sohrab and Rustum :

(1) Mary Shelley
(2) Edward Fitzgerald
(3) Matthew Arnold
(4) Alfred Tennyson

Explanations:
Answer: (3) Matthew Arnold

Sohrab and Rustum (1853)

- ➢ **Sohrab and Rustum: An Episode** by Matthew Arnold, **published in 1853**.
- ➢ Poem retells **Rustum unknowingly killing son Sohrab** in battle.
- ➢ Arnold relied on **summaries in Malcolm's History of Persia**.
- ➢ Arnold aimed to **imitate Homer's "grandeur and rapidity"** style.
- ➢ Poem has **892 lines of blank verse**.

Question 23

Match the following

List I (Critics)	List II (Essays)
a. L.C. Knights	(i) "The Study of Poetry"
b. Lionel Trilling	(ii) "Restoration Comedy: The Reality and the Myth"
c. Matthew Arnold	(iii) "Poetry for Poetry's Sake
d. A.C. Bradley	(iv) "The Sense of the Past"

Choose the correct answer from the options given below:

1. (a)-(iii), (b)-(iv), (c)-(i), (d)-(ii)
2. (a)- (iv). (b) -(i). (c) -(ii), (d)-(iii)
3. (a)-(ii). (b) -(iv). (c)-(i). (d)-(iii)
4. (a)-(iv). (b)-(iii), (c)-(i), (d)-(ii)

Explanations:

Answer: 3. (a)-(ii). (b) -(iv). (c)-(i). (d)-(iii)

- ➢ L.C. Knights is known for his essay "Restoration Comedy: The Reality and the Myth."
- ➢ Lionel Trilling wrote the essay "The Sense of the Past."
- ➢ Matthew Arnold's essay is titled "The Study of Poetry."
- ➢ A.C. Bradley's essay is named "Poetry for Poetry's Sake."

Question 24

Match List I with List II

List I (First Line)	List II (Poet)
A. "Courage!" he said, and pointed toward the land...	I. G.M. Hopkins
B. I am poor brother Lippo, by your leave!	II. Alfred Tennyson

C. I caught this morning morning's minion...	III. D.G. Rossetti
D. Look in my face; my name is Might-have-been..	IV. Matthew Arnold
E. The sea is calm tonight...	V. Robert Browning

Choose the correct answer from the options given below:

1. A-II, B-III, C-I, D-V, E-IV
2. A-IV, B-V, C-I, D-III, E-II
3. A-III, B-IV, C-V, D-I, E-II
4. **A-II, B-V, C-I, D-III, E-IV**

Correct Explanations:

A. "Courage! he said and pointed toward the land" is from **"Ulysses" by Alfred, Lord** Tennyson, not "The Lotos-eaters."

B. "I am poor brother Lippo, by your leave!" - This is the opening line of the dramatic monologue **"Fra Lippo Lippi" by Robert Browning.** The poem is spoken by a Renaissance painter who defends his unconventional lifestyle and artistic methods to a group of monks.

C. "I caught this morning morning's minion..." - This is the opening line of the poem **"The Windhover" by Gerard Manley Hopkins**. The poem describes the speaker's awe and admiration for a falcon in flight and explores the beauty and complexity of the natural world.

D. Look in my face; my name is Might have been" – The Nevermore. Dante Gabriel Rossetti.

E. "The sea is calm tonight..." - This is the opening line of the poem "Dover Beach" by Matthew Arnold. The poem reflects on the loss of faith and the decline of Western culture and uses the image of the sea as a metaphor for the changing tides of history.

Question 25

In *The Function of Criticism at the Present Time*, what is proposed by Matthew Arnold as the essence of criticism?

1. Affirmation
2. Judiciousness
3. **Disinterestedness**
4. Cohesiveness

Correct Explanations:

In *"The Function of Criticism at the Present Time,"* Matthew Arnold argued that disinterestedness is the essence of criticism, and that criticism should strive to see things as they are, rather than simply expressing personal feelings or preferences. He believed that good criticism was a way of maintaining a sense of balance and proportion in society and that it played an important role in preserving cultural values and promoting social harmony.

"It is of the last importance that English criticism should clearly discern what rule for its course, in order to avail itself of the field now opening to it, and to pro- duce fruit for the future, it ought to take. The rule may be summed up in one word, -- disinterestedness. And how is a criticism to show disinterestedness?"

In his recasting of the canon of English poetry in New Bearings in English Poetry which of the following pairs was downgraded by F.R.Leavis ?

1. **Browning and Arnold**
2. Tennyson and Swinburne
3. Pound and Hopkins
4. Milton and Shelley

Correct Explanations:

This statement is not entirely accurate. In his book "New Bearings in English Poetry," F.R. Leavis did criticize Robert Browning's work, arguing that it lacked moral seriousness, but he did not specifically downgrade the pairing of Browning and Arnold. In fact, Leavis praised Arnold's work in the book, particularly his poem "Dover Beach." Leavis did, however, argue for the inclusion of other poets, such as T.S. Eliot and Ezra Pound, in the canon of English poetry.

Question 27

According to Matthew Arnold's "The Study of Poetry", which two of the following are fallacious evaluations of poetry?

    A. contextual estimate
    B. personal estimate
    C. comparative estimate
    D. historic estimate

Choose the correct answer from the options given below:

    1. A and B only
    2. B and C only
    3. C and D only
    4. B and D only

Correct Explanations:
In "The Study of Poetry," Matthew Arnold argues that there are two types of fallacious evaluations of poetry: the historic estimate and the personal estimate.

The historic estimate, according to Arnold, is the evaluation of poetry based on its historical significance or influence. This approach judges a poem's value based on its place in the development of literary history or its influence on subsequent writers. Arnold argues that this approach is fallacious because it does not take into account the enduring qualities of the poem itself, such as its beauty, truth, and power to move the reader.

The personal estimate, on the other hand, is the evaluation of poetry based on personal taste or preference. This approach judges a poem's value based on the emotional or subjective response it elicits in the reader. Arnold argues that this approach is also fallacious because it does not take into account the objective qualities of the poem or its ability to speak to universal human experiences.

Arnold argues that the true evaluation of poetry should be based on a combination of these two approaches, along with a critical sense of judgment that can discern the enduring qualities of a poem and its ability to speak to the human condition. He believed that poetry has the power to elevate and refine the reader, and that its study is an essential part of a liberal education.

"Yes; constantly in reading poetry, a sense for the best, the really excellent, and of the strength and joy to be drawn from it, should be present in our minds and should govern our estimate of what we read. But this real estimate, the only true one, is liable to be superseded, if we are not watchful, by two other kinds of estimate, the historic estimate and the personal estimate, both of which are fallacious. A poet or a poem may count to us historically, they may count to us on grounds personal to ourselves, and they may count to us really. They may count to us historically."

Question 28

Identify the poems termed as "pastoral elegies" :

    A.   Lycidas
    B.   In Memory of W.B. Yeats
    C.   Adonais
    D.   Thyrsis
    E.   In Memoriam

Choose the most appropriate answer from the options given below :
    1.   C, D and E only
    2.   A, C and D only
    3.   B, C and E only
    4.   A, B and C only

Correct Explanations:
Lycidas, a poem by John Milton, written in 1637 for inclusion in a volume of elegies published in 1638 to commemorate the death of Edward King, Milton's contemporary at the University of Cambridge, who had drowned in a shipwreck in August 1637. The poem mourns the loss of a virtuous and promising young man about to embark upon a career as a clergyman. Milton muses on fame, the meaning of existence, and heavenly judgment, adopting **the conventions of the classical pastoral elegy** (Lycidas was a shepherd in Virgil's Eclogues).

Adonais, a pastoral elegy by Percy Bysshe Shelley, was written and published in 1821 to commemorate the death of his friend and fellow poet John Keats earlier that year. Referring to Adonis, the handsome young man of

Greek mythology who a wild boar killed, the title was probably taken from Bion's Lament for Adonis, which Shelley had translated into English. Written in 55 Spenserian stanzas, Adonais is ranked with John Milton's "Lycidas" for its purity of classical form.

Thyrsis, an elegiac poem by Matthew Arnold, was first published in Macmillan's Magazine in 1866. It was included in Arnold's New Poems in 1867. It is considered one of Arnold's finest poems. In Thyrsis, Arnold mastered an intricate 10-line stanza form. The 24-stanza poem eulogizes his friend, poet Arthur Hugh Clough, who died in 1861. Arnold portrays Clough as Thyrsis, a traditional Greek name for a shepherd-poet. **In rich pastoral imagery, Arnold recalls the Oxford countryside** the two explored as students in the 1840s and reviews the fate of their youthful ideals after they left the university.

Other Explanations:
In 'In Memory of W.B. Yeats, ' Auden taps into themes of life after death, the power of poetry, and the human condition. The powerful and wide-ranging themes are discussed within the context of Yeats' life and death. Auden uses an exacting tone and direct language to depict the events around Yeat's death. The mood is at times uplifting and others concerning and worrying. There are many dark images and many fewer hopeful ones.

In Memoriam, in full In Memoriam A.H.H., a poem by Alfred, Lord Tennyson, was written between 1833 and 1850 and published anonymously in 1850. Consisting of 131 sections, a prologue, and an epilogue, this chiefly elegiac work examines the different stages of Tennyson's mourning over the death of his close friend Arthur Henry Hallam.

Question 29

Who among the following refers to "high seriousness" as a quality of a great poet and quotes John Milton to prove the same?

    A.   T.S. Eliot
    B.   Ezra Pound
    C.   Matthew Arnold
    D.   I. A Richards:
    E.   G. M, Hopkins-

Choose the correct answer from the options given below:

1. A and B only
2. B and C only
3. D and E only
4. **C only**

Correct Explanation:

High Seriousness means the grand style or the serious treatment of the subject matter. A poet can achieve the quality of high seriousness when he treats a serious subject in a simple and intense matter.

"The Study of Poetry" is a milestone in the history of English literary criticism. In this critical essay, Matthew Arnold gives poetry a very high position. He is confident in the high of poetry. According to him, poetry attains the place of religion. It is able to make room in the heart of man. It is an application of ideas to human life. The best kind of poetry is a criticism of life. It is an interpretation of life. It has the power to console, sustain and form us. At the same time, it delights us too. Thus Arnold sets high standards for poetry. He proclaims that truth and high seriousness are two essential qualities of excellent poetry. He tries to represent them as a proper standard for the evaluation of poetry.

Arnold has a very high opinion of Chaucer. It is Chaucer who establishes romantic poetry in England. Chaucer is the father of splendid English poetry. His poetry has largeness, freedom, and kindness. Arnold thus showers high praise on Chaucer. But surprisingly he also remarks that Chaucer is not a classic. **He argues that this immortal poet lacks high seriousness. Chaucer does not have the high seriousness that Homer, Shakespeare, Milton, and many others had.**

Question 30

What did Matthew Arnold imply by the term "Hebraism" in his Culture and Anarchy?

1. Moral education
2. Intellectual autonomy
3. Rational outlook
4. Pragmatic attitude

Explanations:

Ans: Moral education.

In his book ***Culture and Anarchy,* Matthew Arnold used the term "Hebraism" to refer to the moral and ethical values of the Hebrew people**, particularly as expressed in the Old Testament of the Bible. He contrasted this with "Hellenism," which he saw as representing the aesthetic and intellectual values of ancient Greece. According to Arnold, Hebraism emphasized the importance of duty, obedience, and **moral righteousness,** while Hellenism focused on the pursuit of beauty, reason, and intellectual excellence.

Close Explanations: Matthew Arnold used the term "Hebraism" in his book *Culture and Anarchy* to refer to the moral and ethical teachings of the Hebrew prophets, which he saw as a vital part of the education of the English people. **Hebraism, for Arnold, was a system of moral education that emphasized the importance of personal responsibility, duty, and self-discipline, and it stood in contrast to Hellenism, which he saw as a more individualistic and aesthetic approach to life.**

Question 31

Match List I with List II

LIST I	LIST II
A. "Negative Capability"	I. Matthew Arnold
B. "Sweetness and light"	II. Samuel Taylor Coleridge
C. "Esemplastic"	III. T.S. Eliot
D. "Dissociation of Sensibility"	IV. John Keats

Choose the correct answer from the options given below:

1. A-II, B-IV, C-I, D-III
2. A-II, B-I, C-IV, D-III
3. A-IV, B-III, C-II, D-I
4. A-IV, B-I, C-II, D-III

Explanations:
Ans: A-IV, B-I, C-II, D-III

A. "Negative Capability" - John Keats: Negative Capability is a term coined by John Keats in a letter to his brothers in 1817, where he described it as the ability to tolerate uncertainty and the mysterious without resorting to oversimplification, explanation or absolute knowledge.

B. "Sweetness and light" - Matthew Arnold: "Sweetness and light" is a phrase used by Matthew Arnold to describe the goal of cultural criticism, which is to help people to see the world more clearly, to appreciate beauty, and to lead better lives.

C. "Esemplastic" - Samuel Taylor Coleridge: Esemplastic is a term coined by Samuel Taylor Coleridge to describe the power of imagination to unify or combine different elements into a single, integrated whole.

D. "Dissociation of Sensibility" - T.S. Eliot: "Dissociation of Sensibility" is a term coined by T.S. Eliot in his essay "The Metaphysical Poets" to describe a separation of thought and feeling in 17th century poetry. Eliot argues that the poetry of Donne and his contemporaries is marked by a dissociation of sensibility, which is the result of the fragmentation of experience caused by the rise of rationalism and the scientific method.

Question 32

Choose the correct chronological sequence in which the following texts were published:

- A. Madness and Civilization
- B. The Archaeology of Knowledge
- C. The Language of the Self: The Function of Language in Psychoanalysis
- D. The Birth of the Clinic
- E. Culture and Anarchy

Choose the correct answers from the options given below:
1. E, B, D, C, A
2. E, A, C, B, D
3. E, B, D, A, C
4. C, A, B, D, E

Explanations:
Ans: E, A, C, B, D

> ➤ *Culture and Anarchy - by Matthew Arnold (1869)*
> ➤ *The Birth of the Clinic - by Michel Foucault (1963)*
> ➤ *Madness and Civilization - by Michel Foucault (1964)*
> ➤ *The Archaeology of Knowledge - by Michel Foucault (1969)*
> ➤ *The Language of the Self: The Function of Language in Psychoanalysis - by Jacques Lacan (1975)*

Extra Perk:

Culture and Anarchy, written by Matthew Arnold in 1869, is a critique of the state of society in Victorian England. Arnold argues that the pursuit of perfection in culture, **education, and morality should be the ultimate goal of society,** rather than the pursuit of power, material wealth, or political dominance. He advocates for the establishment of a "high culture" which would emphasize critical thinking and a sense of shared values, as opposed to the "popular culture" of his time, which he viewed as superficial and debased.

Michel Foucault's The Birth of the Clinic, published in 1963, is an exploration of the emergence of the **clinical gaze in medicine.** The book examines the shift from the earlier, more holistic approach to medicine to the more specialized, technical, and scientific approach that emerged in the 18th and 19th centuries. Foucault argues that this shift was part of a broader historical transformation in which new forms of power and knowledge emerged in the modern era.

Madness and Civilization, also by Michel Foucault and published in 1964, is a study of the history of mental illness and its treatment in Europe from the Middle Ages to the 19th century. **The book argues that the treatment of the mentally ill has been closely tied to larger social, political, and cultural developments, and that the "mad" have been treated as outcasts from society.**

The Archaeology of Knowledge, published by Michel Foucault in 1969, is an exploration of the relationship between knowledge and power. Foucault argues that knowledge is not objective or neutral, but is shaped by power relations in society. He examines the ways in which knowledge is produced, classified, and organized, and how it is used to maintain and reproduce social hierarchies.

Jacques Lacan's The Language of the Self: The Function of Language in Psychoanalysis, published in 1975, is a collection of essays that explore the relationship between language and subjectivity in psychoanalytic theory. Lacan argues that language is not simply a means of communication, but is deeply implicated in the formation of the self. He proposes a radical rethinking of the relationship between language, subjectivity, and psychoanalytic practice, and his work has had a significant impact on subsequent developments in psychoanalytic theory and practice.

Question 33

Arrange the works in chronological sequence:

- A.   Matthew Arnold's Culture and Anarchy
- B.   Thomas Browne's The Anatomy of Melancholy
- C.   Thomas Hobbes' Leviathan
- D.   Walter Pater's Studies in the History of the Renaissance
- E.   PB Shelley's Defense of Poesie

Choose the correct answer from the options given below:

1.   B, C, E, A, D
2.   A, B, C, D, E
3.   C, D, E, A, B
4.   D, C, B, A, E

Explanations:
Ans: B, C, E, A, D

Thomas Browne's The Anatomy of Melancholy (1621): The Anatomy of Melancholy is a medical treatise on melancholy, now known as depression, written by Thomas Browne. It was first published in 1621.

Thomas Hobbes' Leviathan (1651): Leviathan is a political treatise written by Thomas Hobbes, published in 1651. The book concerns the structure of society and legitimate government, and is considered one of the earliest and most influential examples of social contract theory.

Matthew Arnold's Culture and Anarchy (1869): Culture and Anarchy is a series of essays by Matthew Arnold, published in 1869. It critiques the contemporary culture of Victorian England, and advocates for a "sweetness and light" approach to life and culture.

Walter Pater's Studies in the History of the Renaissance (1873): Studies in the History of the Renaissance is a collection of essays by Walter Pater, published in 1873. It discusses the art, literature, and culture of the Italian Renaissance, and is considered a key text in the development of aestheticism.

PB Shelley's Defense of Poesie (written in 1821, published in 1840): A Defence of Poetry is an essay by the English poet Percy Bysshe Shelley, written in 1821 and first published posthumously in 1840. It argues that poets are the unacknowledged legislators of the world, and that poetry has the power to inspire revolution and social change.

Question 34

Find the chronological order of the writers in terms of the period they belonged to:

A. Richard Steele
B. Charles Lamb
C. John Dryden
D. Francis Bacon
E. Matthew Arnold

Choose the correct answer from the options given below:

1. ABCDE
2. BDECA
3. CBDAE
4. **DCABE**

Explanations:
- Francis Bacon (1561-1626)
- John Dryden (1631-1700)
- Richard Steele (1672-1729)
- Charles Lamb (1775-1834)
- Matthew Arnold (1822-1888)

Question 36

Match List I with List II

List I	List II
A. Response to Stephen Gosson	I. Aristotle
B. The Individual Talent	II. Matthew Arnold
C. Catharsis	III. T.S. Eliot
D. Sweetness and Light	IV. Philip Sidney

Choose the correct answer from the options given below:

1. A- IV. B- II, C- III. D-I
2. A - IV, B - III. C - I. D -II
3. A - IV. B - III, C - II, D - I
4. A- IV. B - I, C - II, D - III

Explanations
Answer: 2. A - IV, B - III, C - I, D -II

I. Aristotle - Catharsis: In his work "Poetics," Aristotle introduced the concept of catharsis, which refers to the **emotional release or purification experienced by the audience of a tragedy**. According to Aristotle, through witnessing the suffering and downfall of tragic characters, audiences experience a cathartic purging of their own emotions. Catharsis allows for a psychological and emotional transformation, providing a sense of relief and a heightened understanding of the human condition.

II. Matthew Arnold - Sweetness and Light: Matthew Arnold, a prominent Victorian critic, advocated for the pursuit of "sweetness and light" in his essay "Culture and Anarchy." He believed that true culture, achieved through education and intellectual development, could lead to the harmonious progress of society. **"Sweetness" represents the aesthetic** and **artistic aspects of culture, while "light"** refers to rational and intellectual enlightenment. Arnold emphasised the importance of cultivating both aspects to create a balanced and enlightened society.

III. T.S. Eliot - The Individual Talent: T.S. Eliot, in his influential essay "Tradition and the Individual Talent," discusses the role of the individual poet in relation to literary tradition. Eliot argues that the poet's creative expression is shaped by the collective wisdom of the past, and true originality emerges from the assimilation and transformation of that tradition. He highlights the necessity of humility and the ability to detach oneself from personal emotions and biases, urging poets to embrace the wider cultural and historical context in their work.

IV. Philip Sidney - Response to Stephen Gosson: Philip Sidney, in his critical work "An Apology for Poetry," responds to the attacks on poetry made by Stephen Gosson. Gosson criticised poetry for its alleged moral corruption and lack of educational value. In his response, Sidney defends poetry as a noble art form that holds the power to inspire and educate through imaginative storytelling. He argues that poetry has the ability to convey moral and philosophical truths while entertaining and engaging the audience, refuting Gosson's negative portrayal and advocating for the value and significance of poetry in society.

Question 37

Some of the following are significant texts of Victorian Criticism. Identify them.

    A. Studies in the History of the Renaissance
    B. From Rituals to Romance
    C. "Hamlet and His Problems"
    D. "The Function of Criticism in the Present Time"
    E. Modern Painters

Choose the correct answer from the options given below:

    1. B, C, and D
    2. A, D, and E
    3. A, C, and D
    4. B, D, and E

Explanations
Answer: 2. A, D, and E

Walter Pater (1839-1894) was a Victorian English essayist, art and literary critic, and fiction writer, regarded as one of the great stylists. His first and most often reprinted book, *Studies in the History of the Renaissance (1873)*, revised as *The Renaissance: Studies in Art and Poetry (1877),* in which he outlined his approach to art and advocated an ideal of the intense inner life, was taken by many as a manifesto (whether stimulating or subversive) of Aestheticism.

Modern Painters **(1843–1860) is a five-volume work by the Victorian art critic, John Ruskin**, begun when he was 24 years old based on material collected in Switzerland in 1842. Ruskin argues that recent painters emerging from the tradition of the picturesque are superior in the art of landscape to the old masters. The book was primarily written as a defence of the later work of J. M. W. Turner. Ruskin used the book to argue that art should devote itself to the accurate documentation of nature.

Arnold is famous for introducing a methodology of literary criticism somewhere between the historicist approach common to many critics at the time and the personal essay; he often moved quickly and easily from literary subjects to political and social issues. His *Essays in Criticism* **(1865, 1888)**, remains a significant influence on critics to this day, and his prefatory essay to that collection, **"The Function of Criticism at the Present Time"**, is one of the most influential essays written on the role of the critic in identifying and elevating literature – even while saying, "The critical power is of lower rank than the creative."

Other Explanation
From Ritual to Romance is a 1920 book written by Jessie Weston. It is an examination of the roots of the King Arthur legends. It seeks to make connections between the early pagan elements and the later Christian influences. The book's main focus is on the Holy Grail tradition and its influence, particularly the Wasteland motif.

Hamlet and His Problems is an essay written by T.S. Eliot in 1919 that offers a critical reading of Hamlet. The essay first appeared in Eliot's The Sacred Wood: Essays on Poetry and Criticism in 1920. It was later reprinted by Faber & Faber in 1932 in Selected Essays, 1917-1932. Eliot's critique gained attention partly due to his claim that Hamlet is "most certainly an artistic failure." Eliot also popularised the concept of the objective correlative—a mechanism used to evoke emotion in an audience—in the essay. The essay is also an example of Eliot's use of what became known as new criticism.

Question 38

Who, among the following, wrote about Charlotte Bronte that her mind contained nothing but hunger, rebellion, and rage"?

1. Elizabeth Gaskell
2. Matthew Arnold
3. Charles Dickens
4. Mary Shelley

Explanations:
Answer: 2. Matthew Arnold

Jane Eyre, published within seven weeks of submission under the pseudonym Currer Bell, was an instant success. With its emphasis on the gothic and romantic, it was considered coarse by some of Charlotte's contemporaries, as was Wuthering Heights (though it has a strong moral dimension). Praised by Queen Victoria as "really a wonderful book", it is often pointed out these days that in plot it is indistinguishable from a Mills & Boon. During her lifetime, Charlotte was the best-known and most celebrated of the Brontë sisters, moving in literary circles with greats such as WM Thackeray and Elizabeth Gaskell. **Matthew Arnold and Virginia Woolf caught on the violent aspects of Brontë's work when the former complained that her mind "contained nothing but hunger, rebellion, and rage"** and the latter asserted that "All her force, and it is the more tremendous for being constricted, goes into the assertion, 'I love,' 'I hate,' 'I suffer.'"

Question 39

What is the correct chronological sequence of the following English non-fictional prose writers according to their years of birth?

A. Joseph Addison
B. Francis Bacon
C. Charles Lamb
D. Virginia Woolf

E. Matthew Arnold

Choose the correct answer from the options given below:

1. A. D. C. B. E
2. B. A. C. E. D
3. C. A. D. E. B
4. D. C. B, A, E

Explanations:
Answer: 2. B. A. C. E. D

Sir Francis Bacon (1561-1626) was an influential English philosopher and statesman who held the positions of Attorney General and Lord Chancellor of England during the reign of King James I.

Joseph Addison (1672-1719) was an English essayist, poet, and dramatist. Alongside Richard Steele, he played a leading role in the creation and direction of the periodicals The Tatler and The Spectator. Addison's remarkable writing abilities earned him significant government positions during the Whig party's tenure.

Charles Lamb (1775-1834) was an English essayist and critic, renowned for his collection of essays titled Essays of Elia (1823–33). Lamb attended Christ's Hospital, where he studied until 1789. He was a contemporary of Samuel Taylor Coleridge and Leigh Hunt during his time there.

Matthew Arnold (1822-1888) was an English Victorian poet and a prominent literary and social critic. Notably, he launched scathing attacks on the contemporary tastes and manners of different social classes such as the "Barbarians" (the aristocracy), the "Philistines" (the commercial middle class), and the "Populace." Arnold championed the concept of "culture" in works like Culture and Anarchy (1869).

Virginia Woolf (1882-1941) is best known as a novelist, particularly for her works Mrs. Dalloway (1925) and To the Lighthouse (1927). However, Woolf also made significant contributions to the field of literary criticism, writing groundbreaking essays on artistic theory, literary history, women's writing, and power dynamics.

Question 40

Match List I with List II

List I	List II
A. Egotistical sublime	I. Matthew Arnold
B. Willing suspension of disbelief	II. Joseph Addison
C. Touchstone	III. John Keats
D. Pleasures of the Imagination	IV. Samuel Taylor Coleridge

Choose the correct answer from the options given below:

1. (A)-(III), (B)-(IV), (C)-(I), (D)-(II)
2. (A)-(III), (B)-(IV), (C)-(II), (D)-(I)
3. (A)-(II), (B)-(IV), (C)-(I), (D)-(III)
4. (A)-(II), (B)-(IV), (C)-(I), (D)-(II)

Explanations:
Answer: 1. (A)-(III), (B)-(IV), (C)-(I), (D)-(II)

**Joseph Addison's philosophical essay "Pleasures of the Imagination,"
published in The Spectator (1712),** takes a wary approach to the
imagination. According to Addison, if employed properly, the imagination can
be a means for one to avoid falling into slothful or illicit ways.

**Suspension of disbelief is the avoidance—often described as willing—of
critical thinking and logic in understanding something that is unreal or
impossible in reality,** such as something in a work of speculative fiction, in
order to believe it for the sake of enjoying its narrative. **The phrase first
appeared in English poet and aesthetic philosopher Samuel Taylor
Coleridge's Biographia Literaria (1817),** where he suggested that if an
author could infuse a "human interest and a semblance of truth" into a story
with implausible elements, the reader would willingly suspend judgement
concerning the implausibility of the narrative.

**The 'egotistical sublime' is a phrase coined by John Keats to describe the
poetry of William Wordsworth in an 1818 letter to Richard Woodhouse.**
The phrase expresses the **underlying self-centred nature of Wordsworth's
poetry,** particularly his use of the narrative voice to convey his own
conception of a singular truth. The egotistical sublime contrasts with Keat's

perception of 'negative capability', which he believed to be the ideal and exemplified by the sonnets of William Shakespeare.

As a metaphor, a touchstone refers to any physical or intellectual measure by which the validity or merit of a concept can be tested. It is similar in use to an acid test, a litmus test in politics, or, from a negative perspective, a shibboleth where some consider the criterion to be out-of-date. **The word was introduced into literary criticism by Matthew Arnold in "Preface to the volume of 1853 poems" (1853)** to denote short but distinctive passages selected from the writings of the greatest poets, which he used to determine the relative value of passages or poems which are compared to them.

Question 41

Arrange the correct chronological sequence of the publication of the following texts:

    A. Essay of Dramatic Poesy
    B. A Room of One's Own
    C. Culture and Anarchy
    D. The Lives of the Poets
    E. "Preface to the Lyrical Ballads"

Choose the correct answer from the options given below:

    1. A, D, E, C, B
    2. D, A, E, B, C
    3. A, C, D, E, B
    4. E, D, C, A, B

Explanations
Answer: 1. A, D, E, C, B

A. John Dryden's *Essay of Dramatick Poesy* was likely written in 1666 during the Great Plague of London and published in 1668. In this essay, Dryden argues that poetic drama with English and Spanish influence is a justifiable art form when compared to traditional French poetry.

D. *Lives of the Most Eminent English Poets* **(1779–81)**, alternatively known as Lives of the Poets, is a work by Samuel Johnson that includes short biographies and critical appraisals of 52 poets who lived during the eighteenth century. The poets are arranged roughly by the date of death.

E. *The Preface to Lyrical Ballads* **is an essay by William Wordsworth, first published in the second edition of the poetry collection Lyrical Ballads in 1800** and later expanded in the third edition of 1802. It is considered a de facto manifesto of the Romantic movement, with four guidelines: using ordinary life as the best subject for poetry, employing everyday language, prioritising the expression of feelings over action or plot, and defining poetry as the spontaneous overflow of powerful emotions.

C. *Culture and Anarchy: An Essay in Political and Social Criticism* **is a series of periodical essays by Matthew Arnold, first published in Cornhill Magazine from 1867 to 1868** and later collected as a book in 1869. The preface was added in 1869. The essays address political and social issues and offer Arnold's views on culture and society.

B. *A Room of One's Own* **is an essay by Virginia Woolf, published in 1929,** based on two lectures she gave in 1928 at Newnham College and Girton College, the first two colleges for women at Cambridge. In the essay, Woolf discusses the status of women, particularly women artists, and argues that financial independence and a dedicated space are essential for women to pursue their creative endeavours.

Question 42

Arrange the chronological sequence in which the following works were published:

    A. Culture and Society
    B. Culture and Anarchy
    C. To Hell with Culture
    D. Studies in Dying Culture
    E. Notes towards the Definition of Culture

Choose the correct answer from the options given below:

    1. (E), (B), (A), (D),(C)

2. (C),(E),(D), (B),(A)
3. (A),(D),(E), (B), (C)
4. (B),(A),(D), (C),(E)

Explanations:
Answer: 3. (A),(D),(E), (B), (C)

Culture and Anarchy: An Essay in Political and Social Criticism (1867-1868) by Matthew Arnold

"Culture and Anarchy," a collection of essays first serialized in Cornhill Magazine during 1867-68 and later compiled into a book with a preface added in 1869, is Matthew Arnold's seminal work that introduced his High Victorian cultural agenda. In this influential piece, Arnold delves into the role of culture amidst the tumultuous social changes of his time, arguing for culture as the pursuit of perfection and a remedy to the class divisions and societal upheavals of the 19th century. His vision of culture as a harmonizing and civilizing force set the tone for cultural debates in England for decades, emphasizing the importance of intellectual and aesthetic development in contributing to societal progress and cohesion.

Notes Towards the Definition of Culture (1948) by T.S. Eliot

T.S. Eliot's "Notes Towards the Definition of Culture," published in 1948, represents a pivotal exploration into the multifaceted nature of culture and its significance within society. In this work, Eliot critically examines the complex layers of culture, including its relationship with religion, class, and regional distinctions, proposing that a true understanding of culture necessitates a comprehensive appreciation of these interwoven aspects. By situating culture within a broader social and spiritual context, Eliot contributes to the ongoing dialogue about culture's role in shaping and reflecting the values, practices, and identity of a community.

To Hell With Culture by Sir Herbert Read (1941)

"To Hell With Culture," an essay by Sir Herbert Read first published in 1941, challenges the conventional views on culture's role within society. Read, an esteemed art critic and theorist, critiques the commodification of culture and its institutionalization, arguing for an organic, intrinsic approach to cultural engagement and creation. Through his essay, Read advocates for the liberation of culture from societal constraints and the recognition of art's fundamental role in human expression and emancipation. His insights into the interplay between art, individual creativity, and society encourage a reevaluation of culture's place and purpose beyond the boundaries of traditional institutions and commercialization.

Culture and Society (1958) by Raymond Williams

In "Culture and Society," published in 1958, Raymond Williams explores the evolution of the concept of culture in Great Britain from the 18th to the 20th century, analyzing its development against the backdrop of the Industrial Revolution and subsequent social and political transformations. Williams conducts a series of studies on prominent British writers and thinkers, including Edmund Burke, William Cobbett, and William Blake, to trace how notions of culture responded to and were shaped by these historical changes. By highlighting the dialectical relationship between culture and society, Williams provides a critical framework for understanding culture as a dynamic, contested field that both influences and is influenced by the shifting landscapes of social, economic, and political life.

Further Studies in a Dying Culture by Christopher Caudwell (Publication Date Unknown)

"Further Studies in a Dying Culture" by Christopher Caudwell, while the publication date is not specified here, continues the critical examination of culture within the context of societal decay and transformation. Caudwell, known for his Marxist theoretical perspective, extends the discussion on the role of culture amidst the crises and contradictions of contemporary society. Though specific details of this work are not provided, Caudwell's contributions are recognized for their incisive analysis of cultural phenomena through a Marxist lens, offering insights into the ways in which culture both reflects and contends with the underlying forces of economic and social change.

Christina Rossetti (1830-1894)

- ➢ **Christina Rossetti** was born December 5, 1830, in London.
- ➢ She was one of four children of **Italian parents**.

- Her father, **Gabriele Rossetti**, was a poet.
- Her brother, **Dante Gabriel Rossetti**, became a poet and painter.
- Rossetti's first poems were written in **1842**.
- Published in **her grandfather's private press**.
- In **1850**, wrote under pseudonym **Ellen Alleyne**.
- Contributed seven poems to **Pre-Raphaelite journal The Germ**.
- **Known for ballads, mystic and religious lyrics.**
- Her famous work, **Goblin Market and Other Poems** (1862).
- This collection made her a significant Victorian poet.
- **The Prince's Progress and Other Poems** published in 1866.
- **Sing-Song** (1872) included verses for children.
- In 1880s, **Graves' disease limited her work.**
- Published **A Pageant and Other Poems** in 1881.
- Wrote religious prose, including **Seek and Find** (1879).
- **Called To Be Saints** published in **1881**.
- **The Face of the Deep** published in **1892**.
- Developed **cancer in 1891**, died December 29, 1894.
- William Michael edited her **collected works in 1904**.

Goblin Market (1862)

- **Goblin Market** was composed in April 1859, published 1862.
- The poem centers on sisters **Laura and Lizzie**.
- They are tempted by **goblin merchants** selling fruits.
- Rossetti claimed it wasn't intended for children.
- Illustrated by her brother **Dante Gabriel Rossetti**.
- **Laura and Lizzie** live alone, fetching water daily.
- Goblins call out, **selling strange fruits** at twilight.
- Curious, Laura lingers by the **goblin stream**.
- Goblin men appear animal-like, with **wombat faces**.
- Laura trades a **lock of her hair** for fruit.
- She indulges, returning home in a **trance**.
- Lizzie warns her, citing **Jeanie's tragic fate**.
- Laura disregards, planning to return for more.
- Laura, longing, can no longer hear **goblin cries**.
- Without fruit, Laura **weakens and withers**.
- She plants a **seed**, but nothing grows.
- **Lizzie resolves to help** her dying sister.
- Lizzie goes to **buy goblin fruit** with silver.
- Goblins attack, trying to force-feed her fruit.

- ➤ Lizzie resists, drenched with juice and pulp.
- ➤ She runs home, covered in **goblin pulp**.
- ➤ Laura tastes it, suffers a terrifying **paroxysm**.
- ➤ By morning, **Laura's health is restored**.
- ➤ **Both sisters live** to share their tale.
- ➤ They tell children of **goblin fruit's danger** and sisterly bond.

Pre-Raphaelite Brotherhood (1848)

- ➤ **Pre-Raphaelite Brotherhood** was a group of young British painters.
- ➤ Formed in **1848** in reaction against **Royal Academy's style**.
- ➤ They opposed **unimaginative, artificial historical painting**.
- ➤ **Aimed to express moral seriousness and sincerity**.
- ➤ Inspired by **14th and 15th-century Italian art**.
- ➤ Admired **direct depiction of nature** before the High Renaissance.
- ➤ Their active period lasted **under five years**.
- ➤ **Profound influence on British painting and decorative arts**.
- ➤ The Pre-Raphaelite Brotherhood was formed in 1848 by three Royal Academy students:
    - o **Dante Gabriel Rossetti**, who was a gifted poet as well as a painter,
    - o **William Holman Hunt**
    - o **John Everett Millais**, all under 25 years of age.
    - o The painter **James Collinson**
    - o The painter and critic **F.G. Stephens**,
    - o The sculptor **Thomas Woolner**,
    - o The critic **William Michael Rossetti (Dante Gabriel's brother)** joined them by invitation.
    - o The painters **William Dyce and Ford Madox Brown**, who acted in part as mentors to the younger men, came to adapt their work to the Pre-Raphaelite style.

The Fleshly School of Poetry

- ➤ **The Fleshly School** term coined by **Robert Buchanan**.
- ➤ Poets **Rossetti, Morris, Swinburne** were part of this school.
- ➤ Buchanan accused them of **immorality** in "The Fleshly School of Poetry."
- ➤ Article published in **The Contemporary Review** in **October 1871**.

- ➤ Expanded into a **pamphlet in 1872**, later withdrawn by Buchanan.
- ➤ Rossetti responded in **The Stealthy School of Criticism** (Athenaeum).
- ➤ Swinburne's reply appeared in **Under the Microscope** (1872).

Dante Gabriel Rossetti (1828-1882)

- ➤ **Dante Gabriel Rossetti** was an English poet and painter.
- ➤ **Founded the Pre-Raphaelite Brotherhood** with Hunt and Millais in 1848.
- ➤ Inspired a second generation, notably **William Morris** and **Edward Burne-Jones**.
- ➤ Influenced **European Symbolists** and was a precursor of **Aesthetic movement**.
- ➤ Rossetti's art is **sensual** with **medieval revivalism** themes.
- ➤ **John Keats** and **William Blake** influenced his early poetry.
- ➤ Later poetry, like **The House of Life**, combines thought and feeling.
- ➤ **Poetry and image are entwined** in Rossetti's work.
- ➤ His works include **The Girlhood of Mary Virgin** (1849) and **Astarte Syriaca** (1877).
- ➤ Illustrated poems like **Goblin Market** by his sister, Christina Rossetti.
- ➤ Personal life influenced his work, especially **muses like Elizabeth Siddal**.

The Blessed Damozel (1850)

- ➤ **"The Blessed Damozel"** is Rossetti's best-known poem and painting.
- ➤ Published first in **1850 in The Germ** journal.
- ➤ Rossetti revised and republished it in **1856, 1870, and 1873**.
- ➤ **Inspired by Poe's "The Raven,"** showing grief in reverse.
- ➤ Depicts a **damozel observing her lover from heaven**.
- ➤ Describes her **yearning for reunion in heaven**.
- ➤ **Four stanzas** are inscribed on the painting's frame.
- ➤ Expresses **unfulfilled longing for the lover on Earth**.

William Morris (1834-1896)

- ➤ **William Morris** was a British textile designer, poet, artist.
- ➤ Associated with the **British Arts and Crafts Movement**.
- ➤ Significant in reviving **British textile arts** and methods.

- ➤ Helped establish **modern fantasy genre** in literature.
- ➤ Promoted socialism in **fin de siècle Great Britain**.
- ➤ Rented **Kelmscott Manor** as a rural retreat in 1871.
- ➤ Influenced by **Icelandic visits with Eiríkr Magnússon**.
- ➤ Produced **translations of Icelandic Sagas** in English.
- ➤ Published **epic poems and novels** like *The Earthly Paradise*.
- ➤ Founded **Society for the Protection of Ancient Buildings**.
- ➤ Embraced **Marxism and anarchism** in the 1880s.
- ➤ Founded **Socialist League in 1884**, left SDF in 1890.
- ➤ Established **Kelmscott Press** for illuminated print books in 1891.
- ➤ Known in his time as **poet and designer**.
- ➤ William Morris Society, founded in 1955, **honors his legacy**.
- ➤ Biographies and studies of his work **have been published**.
- ➤ **Buildings associated with Morris are open** for visitors.
- ➤ His designs **remain in art galleries and museums**.

News From Nowhere (1890)

- ➤ **News from Nowhere** (1890) is by **William Morris**.
- ➤ It blends **utopian socialism** and **soft science fiction**.
- ➤ First published serially in **Commonweal journal** (1890).
- ➤ The narrator, **William Guest**, awakens in a future society.
- ➤ Society is based on **common ownership** and **democratic control**.
- ➤ There is **no private property** or **big cities**.
- ➤ **No authority, monetary system, marriage, or divorce** exists.
- ➤ There are no **courts, prisons,** or **class systems**.
- ➤ Society operates by **people's pleasure in nature**.
- ➤ People find fulfillment and pleasure in their **work**.

Questions

Question 43

Who among the following were associated with Pre-Raphaelite Brotherhood ?

1. Dante Gabriel Rossetti and John Everett Millais
2. Elizabeth Barrett Browning and Leigh Hunt
3. John Everett Millais and Elizabeth Barrett Browning
4. Dante Gabriel Rossetti and Leigh Hunt

Explanations:
Answer: 1. Dante Gabriel Rossetti and John Everett Millais

Pre-Raphaelite Brotherhood (1848)

- **Pre-Raphaelite Brotherhood** was a group of young British painters.
- Formed in **1848** in reaction against **Royal Academy's style.**
- They opposed **unimaginative, artificial historical painting.**
- **Aimed to express moral seriousness and sincerity.**
- Inspired by **14th and 15th-century Italian art.**
- Admired **direct depiction of nature** before the High Renaissance.
- Their active period lasted **under five years.**
- **Profound influence on British painting and decorative arts.**
- The Pre-Raphaelite Brotherhood was formed in 1848 by three Royal Academy students:
  - **Dante Gabriel Rossett**i, who was a gifted poet as well as a painter,
  - **William Holman Hunt**
  - **John Everett Millais**, all under 25 years of age.
  - The painter **James Collinson**
  - The painter and critic **F.G. Stephens,**
  - The sculptor **Thomas Woolner,**
  - The critic **William Michael Rossetti (Dante Gabriel's brother)** joined them by invitation.
  - The painters **William Dyce and Ford Madox Brown**, who acted in part as mentors to the younger men, came to adapt their work to the Pre-Raphaelite style.

Question 44

Who among the following in the article "Fleshly School of Poetry" attacked the Pre-Raphaelites, especially D.G. Rossetti?

1. Robert Browning
2. William Holeman Hunt
3. **Robert Buchanan**
4. Christina Rossetti

Correct Explanations:

The Fleshly School is the name Robert Buchanan gave to a realistic, sensual school of poets to which Dante Gabriel Rossetti, William Morris, and Algernon Charles Swinburne belonged. He accused them of immorality in an article entitled "The Fleshly School of Poetry" in The Contemporary Review in October 1871. This article was expanded into a pamphlet (1872), but he subsequently withdrew from the criticisms it contained. It is chiefly remembered by the replies it evoked from Rossetti in a letter to the Athenaeum (December 16, 1871), entitled The Stealthy School of Criticism, and from Swinburne in Under the Microscope (1872).

VICTORIAN PROSE (1830- 1901)

Victorian Novels:

- ➤ **Charles Dickens** is the most famous **Victorian novelist**.
- ➤ Known for **strong characterization**, Dickens became incredibly popular.
- ➤ His first novel, **The Pickwick Papers** (1836–37), was successful.
- ➤ **Comedy with satire** in his writing gained readers.
- ➤ **Pickwick Papers** serialized monthly (1836-1837) became popular.
- ➤ Serialization kept interest with **new twists or characters**.
- ➤ Dickens highlighted **social issues and the poor's plight**.
- ➤ Major works include **Oliver Twist** and **Great Expectations**.
- ➤ Dickens' later works show **darker themes**.
- ➤ **William Thackeray**, Dickens' rival, was a Victorian satirist.
- ➤ His **Vanity Fair** (1848) depicts **middle-class society**.
- ➤ The **Brontë sisters** wrote **unique Gothic fiction**.
- ➤ **Wuthering Heights** (1847) shows **women's Gothic perspective**.
- ➤ **Jane Eyre** (1847) and **Tenant of Wildfell Hall** (1848) explored **gender and realism**.
- ➤ **George Eliot's Middlemarch** (1872) followed in **realistic style**.
- ➤ **Thomas Hardy** depicted **English countryside** against urbanization.
- ➤ Hardy's works include **Tess of the d'Urbervilles**.
- ➤ **Elizabeth Gaskell** explored **working-class lives**.
- ➤ **Anthony Trollope** highlighted **British class and society**.
- ➤ **George Meredith** and **George Gissing** examined **Victorian society**.
- ➤ Victorian literature reflects **social change and urbanization**.

The New Woman

- **The New Woman** was a feminist ideal from the late 19th century.
- Irish writer **Sarah Grand** coined "new woman" in 1894.
- English writer **Ouida** used it in a follow-up article.
- **Henry James** popularized the term describing independent women.
- Independence involved changes in **activity and dress**.
- **Bicycling expanded** women's engagement in the broader world.
- **New Woman** defied limits set by male-dominated society.
- **Ibsen's plays** modeled this defiance, inspiring women.
- Early **literary explorations** included Edgeworth's *Belinda* and Barrett's *Aurora Leigh*.
- Plays like **Ibsen's *A Doll's House*** showcased new ideals.
- **Shaw's *Mrs. Warren's Profession*** also challenged societal norms.
- Max Beerbohm joked, **"The New Woman sprang from Ibsen's brain."**
- In **Stoker's *Dracula***, Mina and Lucy discuss changing roles.
- Feminist critiques of **Dracula** highlight male anxiety.
- Charles Reade's **A Woman Hater** featured the New Woman.
- New Woman authors include **Olive Schreiner, Sarah Grand**, and **Mona Caird**.
- Key works: **Cross's *Anna Lombard*** and **Wells's *Ann Veronica* (1909)**.
- **Kate Chopin's *The Awakening*** explored female independence.
- **Chopin and Flaubert** both show women's struggle for autonomy.
- The **flapper** era of the 1920s ended New Woman culture.
- New Woman movement led into **First-wave feminism**.

Benjamin Disraeli (1804-1981)

- **Benjamin Disraeli**, politician, novelist, and **bon viveur**.
- Known for fame as a **Conservative politician**.
- Served as **PM for almost seven years**.
- Promoted legislation improving **education and work lives**.
- **Educated** at small private schools.
- At **17**, he joined a **firm of solicitors**.
- Desired a **notable, sensational career**.
- **Speculated in South American mining** in 1824.
- Lost money, leaving him **in debt for years**.
- Persuaded **John Murray** to launch the **Representative**.

- ➢ The **newspaper failed; relationships soured**.
- ➢ **Vivian Grey** criticized Murray, causing public backlash.

Vivien Grey (1826)

- ➢ **Vivian Grey** is **Benjamin Disraeli's first novel**, published 1826.
- ➢ **Published anonymously** as by a "man of fashion."
- ➢ Part 1 caused **sensation in London society**.
- ➢ Reviewers identified **Disraeli as the author**.
- ➢ Disraeli released **a second volume in 1826**.
- ➢ Three additional books followed in **1827**.
- ➢ The **1853 edition was severely censored**.
- ➢ **Critic Wendy Burton** says it lost **original charm**.
- ➢ The book remains a **touchstone of Disraeli's career**.

Sybil, or The Two Nations (1845)

- ➢ **Sybil, or The Two Nations** is an 1845 novel.
- ➢ Published the same year as **Engels's** *The Condition of the Working Class*.
- ➢ **Sybil** explores the **plight of England's working classes**.
- ➢ **Disraeli** addresses **horrific conditions** for the **working class**.
- ➢ This issue was called the **"Condition of England" question**.

Question 45

The Two Nations is the subtitle of:

1. Charles Dickens' A Tale of Two Cities
2. Benjamin Disraeli's Sybil
3. Anthony Trollope's The Warden
4. Robert Louis Stevenson's Treasure Island

Explanations:

Answer: 2. Benjamin Disraeli's Sybil

Sybil, or The Two Nations is an 1845 novel by Benjamin Disraeli. Published in the same year as Friedrich Engels's The Condition of the Working Class in England in 1844, Sybil traces the plight of the working classes of England. Disraeli was interested in dealing with the horrific

conditions in which the majority of England's working classes lived — or, what is generally called the Condition of England question.

Elizabeth Gaskell (1810- 1865)

- ➤ **Elizabeth Cleghorn Gaskell** (1810-1865), also known as **Mrs. Gaskell**.
- ➤ She was an **English novelist, biographer, and short story writer**.
- ➤ Her novels depict **many strata of Victorian society**.
- ➤ Her first novel, **Mary Barton**, was published in **1848**.
- ➤ **The Life of Charlotte Brontë** (1857) was her first biography.
- ➤ Biography omits **salacious aspects of Brontë's life**.
- ➤ Best-known novels include **Cranford** (1851–53).
- ➤ **North and South** published between **1854-55**.
- ➤ **Wives and Daughters** (1865) adapted by **BBC** for television.
- ➤ **Notable Works:**
  - o *Mary Barton (1848)*
  - o *Cranford (1851–53)*
  - o *Ruth (1853)*
  - o *North and South (1854–55)*
  - o *My Lady Ludlow (1858)*
  - o *A Dark Night's Work (1863)*
  - o *Sylvia's Lovers (1863)*
  - o *Wives and Daughters: An Everyday Story (1864–66)*
  - o *The Life of Charlotte Brontë (1857)*

Mary Barton (1848)

- ➤ Mary Barton, in full *Mary Barton: A Tale of Manchester Life.*
- ➤ **Mary Barton**, Elizabeth Gaskell's first novel, published **1848**.
- ➤ Story of a **working-class family** facing desperation in **1839**.
- ➤ Describes **squalid slums** that stirred national conscience.
- ➤ **John Barton**, respected laborer, loses job in hard times.
- ➤ Becomes **union organizer** and takes **Chartist petition** to Parliament.
- ➤ **John's frustration turns to bitter class hatred.**
- ➤ Chosen to commit **retaliatory murder** for the union.
- ➤ **Mary helps prove Jem's innocence** after the murder.
- ➤ **Mary, Jem, and friends immigrate** to Canada for a new life.

William Makepeace Thackeray (1811-1863)

- **William Makepeace Thackeray** was born in Calcutta in 1811.
- Thackeray's father died when he was **five**.
- Sent to England, he attended **Charterhouse School**.
- Later joined **Trinity College, Cambridge**, but left early.
- Traveled in Europe, socialized, and gambled extensively.
- Worked as a **freelance journalist** for Punch, Times.
- Many novels were **serialized in magazines**.
- Wrote **travel books** like *The Paris Sketch Book* (1840).
- Famous novels include **Vanity Fair** (1847–48).
- Thackeray's wife struggled with **depression**; he sought cures.
- Raised two children while managing wife's illness.
- First wrote **poetry** as a student at Trinity.
- Known for ballads, **comic poems, and parodies**.
- Set trend for light, **society verse** in *Punch*.
- **Thackeray died unexpectedly** in London in 1863.
- Notable Works:
  - *Catherine (1839–1840)*
  - *The Luck of Barry Lyndon (1844)*
  - *Vanity Fair (1847–1848) – ISBN 0-14-062085-0*
  - *Men's Wives (1852)*
  - *The History of Henry Esmond (1852)*
    - Henry Esmond, a colonel in the service of Queen Anne of England
  - *The Virginians (1857–1859)*
  - *The Book of Snobs (1846–1848)*
  - *Pendennis (1848–1850)*
  - *The Newcomes (1854–1855)*
  - *A Shabby Genteel Story (Unfinished) (1840)*
  - *The Adventures of Philip (1861–1862)*
  - *Thackeray wrote and illustrated five Christmas books as "by Mr M. A. Titmarsh".*
    - *Mrs. Perkins's Ball (1846)*
    - *The Rose and the Ring (Christmas 1854)*

> ✦ **Code Summary:**
>
> 📖 "**Lucky Catherine** became **Men's Wives** AT the **Vanity Fair**.
> ⛏ **History of Henry** in **Virginia** snobs, among **Newcomers**, they are known as **Titmarsh**."

Vanity Fair (1848)

- *Vanity Fair* by **William Makepeace Thackeray**, set post-Napoleonic Wars.
- Follows **Becky Sharp** and **Amelia Sedley's** lives.
- Published as a **19-volume monthly serial** (1847-1848).
- Originally subtitled *Pen and Pencil Sketches* of Society.
- Published in 1848 as *A Novel without a Hero*.
- Satirizes **19th-century British society** and heroism.
- Known as the "principal founder" of the **Victorian novel**.
- Noted for narrative skill, **characterization, and descriptive power**.
- Inspired film adaptations, including **Mira Nair's 2004 version**.
- Central characters: **Amelia Sedley** and **Becky Sharp**.
- Ambitious **Becky Sharp** is the novel's main focus.
- **George Osborne** marries Amelia but admires Becky.
- George dies at the **Battle of Waterloo**.
- Becky marries **Rawdon Crawley** from an aristocratic family.
- **Rawdon** becomes disillusioned and eventually leaves Becky.
- Virtue prevails as Amelia marries **Captain Dobbin**.
- Becky finally settles into **genteel life and charity**.

Question 46

Who among the following edited The Cornhill Magazine?

1. Charles Dickens
2. Lewis Carroll
3. **William Makepeace Thackeray**
4. Anthony Trollope

Correct Explanations:
William Makepeace Thackeray edited The Cornhill Magazine, a monthly literary magazine that ran from 1860 to 1975. During his time as editor,

Thackeray published works by many notable writers, including Elizabeth Gaskell, George Eliot, and Anthony Trollope. He also published some of his own writing in the magazine, including his novel "Lovell the Widower." Thackeray is widely regarded as one of the great Victorian novelists, known for his sharp social commentary and satirical wit. His tenure as editor of The Cornhill Magazine helped to establish the magazine as a leading literary publication of its time.

Arrange the following journals in the chronological order of publication.

- A.   Longman's Magazine
- B.   Cornhill Magazine
- C.   Blackwood's Magazine
- D.   Bentley's Miscellany

Choose the correct answer from the options given below
1.   C, B, A, D
2.   **C, D, B, A**
3.   B, C, D, A
4.   B, C, A, D

Correct Explanations:
Blackwood's Magazine was a British magazine and miscellany printed between 1817 and 1980. It was founded by the publisher William Blackwood and was originally called the Edinburgh Monthly Magazine. The first number appeared in April 1817 under the editorship of Thomas Pringle and James Cleghorn.

Bentley's Miscellany was an English literary magazine started by Richard Bentley. It was **published between 1836 and 1868**. Already a successful publisher of novels, Bentley began the journal in 1836 and invited Charles Dickens to be its first editor. Dickens serialised his second novel Oliver Twist, but soon fell out with Bentley over editorial control, calling him a "Burlington Street Brigand".

The Cornhill Magazine (1860–1975) was a monthly Victorian magazine and literary journal named after the street address of the founding publisher

Smith, Elder & Co. at 65 Cornhill in London. In the 1860s, under editor William Makepeace Thackeray, the paper's large circulation peaked around 110,000.

Longman's Magazine was first published in November 1882] by C. J. Longman, publisher of Longmans, Green & Co. of London. It superseded Fraser's Magazine (published 1830 to 1882). A total of 276 monthly issues had been published when the last number came out in October 1905.

Question 48

Find the chronological order of the writers in terms of their years of birth:

- A. Jane Austen
- B. Henry Fielding
- C. James M. Barrie
- D. Richard Doddridge Blackmore
- E. William Makepeace Thackeray

Choose the correct answer from the options given below:

1. ABCDE
2. **BAEDC**
3. CDABE
4. DBAEC

Explanations:
- ➢ Henry Fielding (1707)
- ➢ Jane Austen (1775)
- ➢ William Makepeace Thackeray (1811)
- ➢ Richard Doddridge Blackmore (1825)
- ➢ James M. Barrie (1860)

Question 49

Match List I with List II

List I	List II
A. George Meredith	I. The Virginians
B. George Eliot	II. Scenes of Clerical Life
C. Charlotte Bronte	III. Evan Harrington
D. William Makepeace Thackeray	IV. The Professor

Choose the correct answer from the options given below:

1. A-III, B-I, C-IV. D-I
2. A-IV. B-III. C-I. D-II
3. A-I. B-II, ONII, D-IV
4. A-II, B-I, C-1V, D-III

Explanations
Answer: 1. A-III, B-I, C-IV. D-I

A. "Evan Harrington" is a glowing Victorian comedy written by George Meredith in 1861. Loosely inspired by his own life, the novel revolves around the social climbing family of the late tailor, Melchisedec Harrington.

B. George Eliot's debut work of fiction, "Scenes of Clerical Life," comprises three short stories first published in Blackwood's Magazine. Released under her famous pseudonym in 1856, Eliot was already a renowned figure in Victorian intellectual circles, known for her contributions to The Westminster Review and translations of theological works.

C. "The Professor, A Tale," Charlotte Brontë's first novel, was written before "Jane Eyre" but faced rejection from several publishing houses. Published posthumously in 1857 with the approval of her widower, Arthur Bell Nicholls, the novel was reviewed and edited by him.

D. William Makepeace Thackeray's historical novel "The Virginians: A Tale of the Last Century" (1857–59) serves as a sequel to his work "Henry Esmond" and is loosely connected to "Pendennis."

Question 50

Arrange the chronological sequence in which the following works were published:

A. Jane Eyre
B. A Tale of Two Cities
C. Middlemarch
D. The Return of the Native
E. The Newcomes

Choose the correct answer from the following options:

1. A. B, C. D, E
2. A. E, B, C. D
3. B. A. C, E, D
4. B, C. A. D. E

Explanations:
Answer: 2. A, E, B, C, D

Jane Eyre is a novel written by Charlotte Brontë and first published in 1847 under the pseudonym Currer Bell. The story follows the life of Jane Eyre and is presented as her autobiography.

The Newcomes is a novel by William Makepeace Thackeray, initially published in 24 instalments from 1853 to 1855 as The Newcomes: Memoirs of a Most Respectable Family. The story is narrated by "Arthur Pendennis, Esq." and revolves around the lives of the Newcome family. It was later released as a book in two volumes in 1854-55.

A Tale of Two Cities is a novel by Charles Dickens, originally published in 1859 both in serial and book form. Set during the French Revolution, the story depicts the social and political turmoil of the late 18th century.

Middlemarch, also known as Middlemarch: A Study of Provincial Life, is a novel by George Eliot (the pseudonym of Mary Ann Evans). It was published in eight parts in 1871-72 and later compiled into four volumes in 1872. The narrative explores various characters and their lives in a provincial town.

The Return of the Native is a novel by Thomas Hardy, published in 1878. It is set on Egdon Heath, a fictional barren moor in Wessex, England. The story revolves around Clym Yeobright, who returns to the area after a career as a jeweller in Paris to become a schoolmaster.

Question 51

Match List - I with List - II.

List - I (Novel)	List - II (Subtitle)
A. The Castle of Otranto	I. A Pure Woman
B. Tess of the d' Urbervilles	II. The Modern Prometheus
C. Frankenstein	III. A Novel without A Hero
D. Vanity Fair	IV. A Gothic Story

Choose the correct answer from the options given below :

    1. (A)-(IV), (B)-(I), (C)-(II), (D)-(III)
    2. (A)-(I), (B)-(II), (C)-(III), (D)-(IV)
    3. (A)-(II), (B)-(I), (C)-(IV), (D)-(III)
    4. (A)-(III), (B)-(IV), (C)-(II), (D)-(I)

Explanations:
Answer: 1. (A)-(IV), (B)-(I), (C)-(II), (D)-(III)

"The Castle of Otranto," written by Horace Walpole and initially released anonymously in 1764, with the first editions dated the following year, is regarded as the pioneering Gothic novel in English literature. **In the second edition, Walpole applied the word 'Gothic' to the novel in the subtitle – A Gothic Story**. In "The Castle of Otranto," Horace Walpole crafts a narrative around the ominous prophecy that the rulership of Otranto would end when the rightful owner became too large for the castle. The story unfolds with Prince Manfred's anticipation of his son Conrad's marriage to Princess Isabella, a union Manfred hopes will secure his lineage and defy the ancient prophecy. However, Conrad's sudden death under a mysterious giant helmet and Manfred's subsequent desperate actions, including his proposal to marry Isabella himself and the wrongful killing of his daughter Matilda, set off a chain of supernatural events. These events lead to the revelation that Theodore, a peasant, is the true heir of Otranto, as he is the grandson of the rightful king Alfonso, whom Manfred's grandfather had murdered to seize the throne. The novel concludes with Manfred's abdication and Theodore's acceptance of Isabella's hand in marriage, despite his mourning for Matilda, marking the fulfillment of the prophecy and the restoration of the rightful rule.

"Tess of the d'Urbervilles: A Pure Woman," authored by Thomas Hardy, first made its appearance through a serialized, edited version in The Graphic, a British illustrated newspaper, in 1891. It was later published in a three-volume book format the same year and eventually in a single-volume edition in 1892. Initially met with mixed critical reception due to its bold critique of the sexual morality of late Victorian England, the novel has since been recognized as a significant 19th-century literary work. Set against the backdrop of Hardy's imagined rural Wessex, the narrative unfolds in an economically struggling England. Tess Durbeyfield, a young woman from an impoverished family, discovers they have noble ancestry and is sent to connect with the wealthy d'Urbervilles. There, she falls victim to Alec d'Urberville's seduction, resulting in a child, Sorrow, who dies young. Tess later finds love and marriage with Angel Clare, who abandons her upon learning of her past. Desperate and alone, Tess eventually returns to Alec. When Angel comes back seeking reconciliation, Tess, driven by a deep sense of injustice, kills Alec and is ultimately arrested and executed for her actions.

Frankenstein; or, The Modern Prometheus is an 1818 novel written by English author Mary Shelley. In Mary Shelley's "Frankenstein," Captain Robert Walton recounts the tragic tale of Victor Frankenstein, a young scientist who discovers the secret to creating life. Victor constructs a creature from dead bodies, but upon witnessing his creation's grotesque appearance, he is filled with horror and abandons it. The creature, longing for companionship and rejected by society, becomes vengeful, leading to the murder of Victor's brother William and friend Henry Clerval, and eventually Victor's wife, Elizabeth, on their wedding night. Victor vows to seek revenge on his creation, leading to a pursuit that ends in the Arctic, where Victor, exhausted and ill, narrates his story to Walton before dying. The creature, expressing remorse and self-loathing over the pain he has caused, vows to end his own life and disappears into the icy darkness, concluding the tale of ambition, responsibility, and the quest for understanding.

"Vanity Fair: A Novel without A Hero," a novel by William Makepeace Thackeray published from 1847 to 1848, marks his first work released under his real name, drawing inspiration from John Bunyan's allegory Pilgrim's Progress to explore the moral corruption at the heart of early 19th-century English society. Without a clear hero, the novel intricately weaves the lives of two contrasting women: the noble but passive Amelia Sedley and the cunning and ambitious Becky Sharp, who emerges as the narrative's central and most unforgettable figure. Through their relationships with men—Amelia's ill-fated marriage to George Osborne, who nearly betrays her for Becky, and Becky's calculated ascent into high society via her marriage to Rawdon Crawley—the story delves into themes of loyalty, betrayal, and the quest for social ascension. Despite Becky's manipulative tactics, the novel concludes with a semblance of moral resolution: Amelia finds happiness with the devoted Captain William Dobbin, and Becky adopts a life of genteel respectability and philanthropy, suggesting a complex interplay between virtue and vice in Thackeray's depiction of Vanity Fair.

Charles Dickens (1812-1870)

- **Charles Dickens** was born near **Portsea**; father worked in Navy Office.
- Second of **eight children**, Charles was a delicate child.
- Read works of **Smollett, Fielding, Le Sage**, inspiring his novels.
- Loved **theater**, a passion that influenced his writing deeply.
- In **1823**, Dickens' family moved to **London**.
- His father, like **Micawber**, had constant **money troubles**.
- Schooling was interrupted; **worked in a blacking factory**.
- Father was imprisoned in **Marshalsea debtors' prison**.
- Schooling resumed; entered an attorney's office in **1827**.
- Became **proficient in shorthand**, leading to reporter work.
- Worked for **Morning Chronicle** and traveled by stagecoach.
- **1833**: Published **Sketches by Boz** in **The Monthly Magazine**.
- In **1836**, began writing **The Pickwick Papers** for publishers.
- Illustrator **Seymour** died; **Phiz** continued illustrations.
- **The Pickwick Papers** was an immediate success.
- Dickens became a **famous, busy, and successful novelist**.
- Achieved fame greater than **Scott**, reaching wider audiences.
- Traveled to **America, Italy, Switzerland, and back to America**.
- Edited **The Daily News** in **1846**.
- Founded **Household Words** in 1849 and **All the Year Round** in 1859.
- Began series of **public readings** in **1858**.
- Readings were intense, **theatrical performances** of his novels.
- The readings earned money but **exhausted him physically**.
- American readings achieved **significant popularity**.
- Dickens's travels and public life influenced his later works.
- Owned **Gad's Hill Place**, a favorite house near Rochester.
- Published many famous novels, cementing his **literary legacy**.
- Dickens's works exposed **social issues** of his time.
- His **humor and memorable characters** captivated readers.

- ➤ **Loved by Victorian audiences**, Dickens became an icon.
- ➤ Died at **Gad's Hill**; buried in **Westminster Abbey**.
- ➤ Dickens remains a celebrated figure in **English literature**.
- ➤ **"The Man who liked Dickens" is a short story written by Evelyn Waugh.**
- ➤ **Notable Work:**
  - o *Sketches by Boz (1833)*
  - o *The Pickwick Papers (1836- 1837)*
  - o *Oliver Twist (1837-1839)*
  - o *Nicholas Nickleby (1838-1839)*
  - o *The Old Curiosity Shop (1840-1841)*
  - o *Barnaby Rudge (1841)*
  - o *A Christmas Carol (1843)*
  - o *Martin Chuzzlewit (1843-1844)*
  - o *Dombey and Son (1846-1848)*
  - o *David Copperfield (1849-1850)*
  - o *Bleak House (1852-1853)*
  - o *Hard Times (1854-1854)*
  - o *Little Dorrit (1855-1857)*
  - o *A Tale of Two Cities (1859-1859)*
  - o *Great Expectations (1860-1861)*
  - o *Our Mutual Friend (1864- 1865)*
  - o *Edwin Drood (1870-1870)*

Code 1
*Picky **Twisty** Nicky found a Curious Christy*
***Barby** and Chose to Dumb her Copy of **Black House**.*
The Hard Door opens Two Cities with Great Expectations,
***Mutual Friend Edwin** stays till the end.*

Code 2
***Pick** and **Twist** Nicky to make Curious Christy Barbecue,*
***Choose to Dumb** in the **Black Copy House**.*
*A **Hard Little Door** opens **Two Cities**,*
*with **Great Expectations** to meet **Mutual Friend Edwin**.*

First Work is The Sketches of Boz.
Last Work is Edwin Drood.

The Pickwick Papers (1836- 1837)

- **The Posthumous Papers of the Pickwick Club**
- Under the pseudonym Boz.
- Caricaturist **Robert Seymour**.
- Naive **Samuel Pickwick** and his friends in the Pickwick Club.
- Samuel Pickwick, **the Esquire**, is a kind and wealthy old gentleman.

Oliver Twist (1837-1839)

- A **three-volume** book in 1838.
- The alternative title, *The Parish Boy's Progress,* alludes to **Bunyan's The Pilgrim's Progress.**
- The orphan **Oliver Twist is sold into apprenticeship** with an undertaker.
- Oliver travels to London, where he meets the "Artful Dodger,"
- **Dodger is a member of a gang of juvenile pickpockets** led by the elderly **criminal Fagin.**
- **Oliver Twist**, an orphan, grows up in a **child farm** with minimal food.
- After **requesting more food, Oliver** is sent as an apprentice.
- **Mistreatment** drives Oliver to **run away to London.**
- Oliver meets the **Artful Dodger** and stays with **Fagin.**
- He learns that Fagin's boys are trained **pickpockets**.
- After a **handkerchief theft**, Mr. Brownlow **arrests Oliver** by mistake.
- **Mr. Brownlow** offers to **care for Oliver** at his home.
- Fagin's group seeks Oliver due to **crime knowledge.**
- **Nancy** retrieves Oliver from **Mr. Brownlow** for Fagin.
- Oliver is forced into a **burglary mission** and gets **injured**.
- **The Maylies** care for Oliver after his **injury.**
- **Fagin** and **Monks** plot to **recapture Oliver.**
- **Nancy** confides to **Rose Maylie** about Fagin's plans.
- Nancy's betrayal leads to **Sikes killing her.**
- **Sikes dies accidentally**, hanging himself soon after.
- The **Maylies** reunite Oliver with **Mr. Brownlow.**
- Mr. Brownlow reveals **Monks is Oliver's half-brother.**
- Oliver learns he's **entitled to a fortune.**
- **Fagin is hanged**, and Oliver's life changes.
- **Oliver, the Maylies, and Mr. Brownlow** settle **peacefully in the countryside.**

Nicholas Nickleby (1838-1839)

- ➤ **Full**: *The Life and Adventures of Nicholas Nickleby, Containing a Faithful Account of the Fortunes, Misfortunes, Uprisings, Downfallings, and Complete Career of the Nickleby Family*
- ➤ It was Dickens's **third** novel.
- ➤ The story centers on the life and adventures of **Nicholas Nickleby**.
- ➤ A young man who must **support his mother and sister** after his father dies.
- ➤ **Ralph Nickleby: The book's principal antagonist,** Nicholas's uncle.
- ➤ **Smike: A poor drudge living in Squeers's "care".**

The Old Curiosity Shop (1840-1841)

- ➤ One of two novels **(Barnaby Rudge)** that Charles Dickens published along with short stories in his weekly serial *Master Humphrey's Clock,* from 1840 to 1841.
- ➤ The plot follows the life of **Nell Trent** and her grandfather
- ➤ They both residents of The Old Curiosity Shop in London.
- ➤ **Nell Trent**, an orphan, lives with **Grandfather**.
- ➤ They run a **curiosity shop in London**.
- ➤ Grandfather **gambles** away their limited savings.
- ➤ They **fall into debt** to **Daniel Quilp**.
- ➤ Quilp, a cruel moneylender, **seizes the shop**.
- ➤ Nell and Grandfather **flee from Quilp**.
- ➤ They endure **poverty, hardship, and illness**.
- ➤ **Friends search** for them but **fail**.
- ➤ Nell eventually **dies from exhaustion**.
- ➤ Grandfather, grief-stricken, **dies by her side**.

Barnaby Rudge (1841)

- ➤ **Full**: *Barnaby Rudge: A Tale of the Riots of' Eighty.*
- ➤ A historical novel.
- ➤ Set in the late 18th century and presents the spectacle of large-scale mob violence.
- ➤ **Barnaby Rudge** lives in **18th-century England**.
- ➤ The **Gordon Riots** cause widespread violence.
- ➤ Barnaby, a naive boy, joins the rioters.
- ➤ His mother tries to save him.
- ➤ Barnaby eventually finds **peace and redemption**.

A Christmas Carol (1843)

- **Full**: *A Christmas Carol, in Prose: Being a Ghost Story of Christmas.*
- Short novel by Charles Dickens, originally published in 1843.
- The story, suddenly conceived and written in a few weeks.
- It is one of modern literature's most outstanding Christmas stories.
- **Scrooge** is a wealthy, **miserly old man**.
- **Despises Christmas** and rejects holiday cheer.
- **Marley's ghost** warns him of consequences.
- Three **spirits visit**: Past, Present, Future.
- **Ghost of Past** shows his lost love.
- **Ghost of Present** reveals others' hardships.
- **Tiny Tim** symbolizes innocence and generosity.
- **Future spirit** shows Scrooge's lonely death.
- **Scrooge repents**, embracing kindness and generosity.
- Celebrates Christmas, helping others with joy.

Martin Chuzzlewit (1843-1844)

- The Life and Adventures of Martin Chuzzlewit.
- Characters in this novel gained fame, including Pecksniff and Mrs. Gamp.
- **Young Martin** Chuzzlewit quarrels with **his grandfather**.
- He seeks fortune in **America**, facing **hardship**.
- **Mark Tapley**, his friend, joins him **loyally**.
- They return, discovering **fraud within family**.
- Martin reconciles with **grandfather**, inheriting **fortune**.

Dombey and Son (1846-1848)

- **Full**: *Dealings with the Firm of Dombey and Son, Wholesale, Retail, and for Exportation.*
- **Mr. Dombey** is obsessed with having a son.
- **Paul Dombey Jr.** is born, bringing pride.
- **Mrs. Dombey** dies shortly after Paul's birth.
- Dombey neglects his daughter, **Florence**.
- Paul grows sickly and goes to **boarding school**.
- Paul dies young, devastating **Mr. Dombey**.
- **Dombey remarries** a woman named Edith.
- **Edith and Dombey's marriage** is unhappy.
- Edith elopes with **Mr. Carker**, Dombey's employee.

- Carker eventually meets his tragic **death**.
- Dombey's business collapses, leaving him **bankrupt**.
- Florence, neglected, finds **family love** elsewhere.
- Dombey finally seeks **forgiveness from Florence**.
- Father and daughter **reunite and reconcile**.
- **Florence cares for him** in his final years.

David Copperfield (1849-1850)

- **Full**: *The Personal History of David Copperfield*.
- Dickens's most popular novels and was his own **"favourite child."**
- The work is **semiautobiographical**.
- **The Künstlerroman Novel**.
- **David** is born after his father's death.
- His mother marries cruel **Mr. Murdstone**.
- **David** faces harsh treatment and isolation.
- Sent to **boarding school**, meets **Steerforth**.
- Mother dies, **David** works in **London**.
- Lives with kind **Mr. Micawber**, in poverty.
- Runs away to **Aunt Betsey Trotwood**.
- Receives a good education, becomes **law clerk**.
- Falls in love with **Dora Spenlow**.
- **Steerforth** ruins **Emily**, tragic consequences ensue.
- Marries **Dora**, who soon passes away.
- **David** matures, dedicates himself to writing.
- Learns **Uriah Heep** is manipulating **Mr. Wickfield**.
- Exposes **Heep**, restores **Mr. Wickfield**'s honor.
- **David** finds love with **Agnes Wickfield**, lives happily.

Bleak House (1852-1853)

- Heroine, **Esther Summerson**, and partly by an **omniscient narrator**.
- Bleak House is a long-running legal case in the Court of *Chancery, Jarndyce, and Jarndyce.*
- The **Jarndyce vs. Jarndyce case** spans generations.
- **Esther Summerson**, orphan, raised by **Miss Barbary**.
- Esther lives with **John Jarndyce** at **Bleak House**.
- She befriends **Ada Clare** and **Richard Carstone**.
- **Richard** obsessed with inheritance, ruins finances.
- **Lady Dedlock** hides her connection to Esther.
- **Lawyer Tulkinghorn** uncovers Lady Dedlock's secret.

- ➤ Tulkinghorn is **murdered**, shocking everyone involved.
- ➤ **Inspector Bucket** investigates the **murder mystery**.
- ➤ **Jo the street-sweeper** offers crucial evidence.
- ➤ Lady Dedlock **flees**, overcome with guilt.
- ➤ Esther finds **Lady Dedlock's body**, heartbroken.
- ➤ **Richard dies**, obsessed with Jarndyce case.
- ➤ **Case resolves**, inheritance drained by legal costs.
- ➤ Esther marries **Allan Woodcourt**, finds peace.

Hard Times (1854-1854)

- ➤ Published in serial form (as *Hard Times: For These Times*) in the periodical *Household Words*.
- ➤ The novel is a **bitter indictment of industrialization**.
- ➤ **Mr. Gradgrind** values **facts over imagination** in life.
- ➤ He raises **Louisa and Tom** under strict rules.
- ➤ **Sissy Jupe**, a circus girl, joins their home.
- ➤ **Mr. Bounderby**, a wealthy industrialist, woos Louisa.
- ➤ Louisa reluctantly **marries Bounderby** for her father.
- ➤ **Tom** works at Bounderby's bank, grows bitter.
- ➤ **Stephen Blackpool**, a mill worker, faces hardship.
- ➤ Stephen loves Rachael but **stuck in marriage**.
- ➤ Stephen refuses **strike**, alienating fellow workers.
- ➤ Bank is **robbed**, and Stephen framed.
- ➤ **Tom** is the true thief, escapes guilt.
- ➤ Louisa realizes **lack of love** in life.
- ➤ **Sissy and Rachael** support Louisa emotionally.
- ➤ Mr. Gradgrind sees **value beyond facts**.
- ➤ **Tom** flees, **Louisa rebuilds life independently**.

Little Dorrit (1855-1857)

- ➤ **Amy Dorrit**, born in **Marshalsea Debtors' Prison**.
- ➤ **Her father**, William Dorrit, **imprisoned for debt**.
- ➤ **Arthur Clennam** returns from China, questioning family secrets.
- ➤ Arthur meets Amy, becomes **curious about her life**.
- ➤ **Amy cares** for her father with **selflessness**.
- ➤ Arthur discovers hidden **family wealth** for Dorrits.
- ➤ **The Dorrit family is freed** and becomes wealthy.
- ➤ Arthur, financially ruined, **lands in Marshalsea**.
- ➤ Amy remains **devoted to Arthur** during hardship.

> ➤ **Arthur and Amy marry**, finding peace together.

A Tale of Two Cities (1859-1859)

> ➤ **Set in the late 18th century** during **French Revolution**.
> ➤ **Dickens drew inspiration from Carlyle's** *The French Revolution*.
> ➤ The novel emphasizes **drama over historical accuracy**.
> ➤ Large-scale mob violence is **vivid but superficial**.
> ➤ Tale of **London** and revolutionary **Paris**.
> ➤ *Changing Places* (1975) is David Lodge's first "campus novel."
> ➤ The subtitle, *A Tale of Two Campuses*, alludes to *A Tale of Two Cities*.
> ➤ Inspired by the play *The Dead Heart* by Watts Phillips.
> ➤ Similar storyline led to **talk of plagiarism**.
> ➤ Other influences: *The French Revolution: A History* by Carlyle.
> ➤ *Zanoni* by **Bulwer-Lytton** and *The Castle Spectre* by **Lewis**.
> ➤ *Travels in France* by **Arthur Young** contributed.
> ➤ **Parisian life** insights from *Tableau de Paris* by Mercier.
> ➤ Prison and **trial accounts** from *The Annual Register*.
> ➤ **Set in London and Paris during revolution**
> ➤ Dr. Manette is freed from prison.
> ➤ Lucie Manette reunites with her father.
> ➤ Charles Darnay, a French aristocrat, relocates to London.
> ➤ Darnay is tried in England, acquitted later.
> ➤ **Sydney Carton**, lawyer, secretly loves **Lucie**.
> ➤ Darnay returns to France, faces imprisonment.
> ➤ **Carton sacrifices himself** to save Darnay.
> ➤ Carton dies at the guillotine, nobly redeemed.
> ➤ Lucie and family escape to England safely.

Great Expectations (1860-1861)

> ➤ It is the thirteenth novel.
> ➤ A serial in Dickens's weekly **periodical *All the Year Round***.
> ➤ Thomas **Carlyle** referred to it disparagingly as ***"that Pip nonsense,"***
> ➤ Carlyle nevertheless reacted to each fresh installment with "**roars of laughter.**"
> ➤ **George Bernard Shaw** praised the novel as "***All of one piece and consistently truthful.***"
> ➤ **Kathy Acker** wrote a postmodern **reworking of Great Expectations without altering the original title.**

- ➢ **Peter Carey** did write a novel called **"Jack Maggs,"** which is a **reworking of "Great Expectations."**
- ➢ **Pip**, an orphan, lives with **sister and Joe.**
- ➢ He meets an **escaped convict, Magwitch.**
- ➢ **Pip helps** Magwitch, giving **food and file.**
- ➢ Miss **Havisham invites Pip to Satis House.**
- ➢ Pip meets **Estella, Havisham's beautiful ward.**
- ➢ **Pip falls** in love with **cold-hearted Estella.**
- ➢ Pip's **aspirations shift to becoming a gentleman.**
- ➢ A **mysterious benefactor funds Pip's education.**
- ➢ **Pip believes** Havisham sponsors him for **Estella.**
- ➢ Pip **moves to London** for his **upbringing.**
- ➢ Pip's **expectations increase** along with his **wealth.**
- ➢ Pip discovers **Magwitch is his benefactor.**
- ➢ **Magwitch returns** to London, risking **capture.**
- ➢ **Pip plans** to help Magwitch **escape.**
- ➢ Estella **marries Drummle, breaking Pip's heart.**
- ➢ **Magwitch is captured**, Pip loses **fortune.**
- ➢ Pip **grows humbler** after losing **expectations.**
- ➢ Joe and Biddy **nurse Pip back** to health.
- ➢ **Pip reconciles** with Joe, finds **contentment.**
- ➢ Pip and **Estella meet, finding closure** together.

Our Mutual Friend (1864- 1865)

- ➢ **The last completed novel.**
- ➢ A body is found in the Thames.
- ➢ John Harmon's inheritance depends on marriage.
- ➢ Harmon, believed dead, assumes new identity.
- ➢ He returns as John Rokesmith, incognito.
- ➢ Bella Wilfer learns about her inheritance.
- ➢ Rokesmith becomes secretary to Boffins.
- ➢ Love triangle develops between Bella, Rokesmith.
- ➢ Social critique of wealth and class divisions.
- ➢ Harmon reveals true identity to Bella.
- ➢ They marry, inheriting fortune and peace.

Edwin Drood (1870-1870)

- ➢ *The Mystery of Edwin Drood,* an **unfinished novel** by Charles Dickens.

> Edwin Drood disappears under mysterious circumstances.
> **John Jasper,** his uncle, harbors secret feelings.
> Rosa Bud, Edwin's fiancée, suspects Jasper.
> Jasper struggles with opium addiction and jealousy.
> Novel remains unfinished, mystery unsolved due to Dickens's death.

Questions

Question 52

Harold Skimpole is a character in:

1. Bleak House
2. Dombey and Son
3. Great Expectations
4. Oliver Twist

Explanations:

Answer: 1. Bleaks House.

Harold Skimpole is a character in Charles Dickens' novel "Bleak House." He is a charming and affable man who presents himself as a childlike innocent, and he is often described as "childlike" or "childish." Skimpole is a self-proclaimed man of leisure who lives off the generosity of others, and he claims to have no concept of money or responsibility. He is often portrayed as being carefree and irresponsible, with no concern for the consequences of his actions. However, it eventually becomes clear that Skimpole is not the innocent he appears to be, and he is revealed to be a manipulative and self-centered individual who takes advantage of those around him. The character of Harold Skimpole has been interpreted as a critique of the Victorian ideal of the "gentleman," and a commentary on the dangers of idleness and irresponsibility.

Extra Perk:

"Bleak House" by Charles Dickens:
> **Esther Summerson**: the main protagonist of the novel, who serves as a narrator and central character in the story
> **John Jarndyce:** a wealthy and generous man who takes Esther and other young wards under his care
> **Lady Dedlock:** a noblewoman who harbors a dark secret from her past
> **Mr. Tulkinghorn:** a lawyer who is determined to uncover Lady Dedlock's secret

> - **Richard Carstone and Ada Clare:** two young people who are also under Jarndyce's care and who become caught up in a legal case that spans decades

"Dombey and Son" by Charles Dickens:
> - **Paul Dombey:** the young heir to the Dombey family business
> - **Florence Dombey:** Paul's older sister, who cares for him deeply
> - **Walter Gay:** a young man who becomes involved with the Dombey family
> - **Edith Granger:** Dombey's second wife, who has a complicated relationship with her husband
> - **James Carker:** a scheming employee of the Dombey business

"Great Expectations" by Charles Dickens:
> - **Pip (Philip Pirrip):** the main protagonist of the novel, who is brought up by his abusive sister and her husband
> - **Miss Havisham:** an eccentric woman who has been jilted on her wedding day and now lives in seclusion
> - **Estella:** Miss Havisham's ward, who is trained to be a heartbreaker and who becomes the object of Pip's affections
> - **Abel Magwitch:** a convict whom Pip helps early in the novel, and who becomes an unlikely benefactor to Pip later on
> - **Jaggers:** a lawyer who is involved in Pip's life in various ways, including the revelation of his secret benefactor

"Oliver Twist" by Charles Dickens:
> - **Oliver Twist:** The titular character and protagonist of the novel. He is an orphan who is raised in a workhouse and later becomes a member of a gang of pickpockets.
> - **Fagin:** The leader of the gang of pickpockets who takes Oliver under his wing. He is a cunning and manipulative man who is known for his skill in training young thieves.
> - **Nancy:** A member of Fagin's gang who befriends Oliver and tries to help him. She is a tragic character who is caught between her loyalty to the gang and her conscience.
> - **Bill Sikes:** A brutal and violent criminal who is also a member of Fagin's gang. He is involved in several violent crimes throughout the novel.
> - **Mr. Brownlow:** A kindly gentleman who takes an interest in Oliver and tries to help him. He is one of the few characters in the novel who is genuinely kind and compassionate.
> - **Mr. Bumble:** The pompous and self-important beadle of the workhouse where Oliver is raised. He is a cruel and heartless man who mistreats the orphans in his care.

> ➤ **Monks:** A mysterious and sinister figure who is revealed to be one of Oliver's relatives. He is involved in a plot to harm Oliver and to claim his inheritance.

Read the given passage and answer the questions that follow:

*The surgeon deposited it in her arms. She imprinted her cold. white lips passionately on its forehead: passed her hands over her face: gazed wildly around; shuddered: fell back — and died. They chafed her breast. hands, temples; but the blood had stopped forever. They talked of hope and comfort. They had been strangers too long. 'It's all over, Mrs Thingummy!', said the surgeon at last. – **Dickens, Oliver Twist***

Question 53

In the expression, "passed her hands over her face", the 'face' is of:

1. the lady surgeon
2. the child
3. the nurse
4. the patient

Explanations:

Answer: 4. the patient

In the given passage, the pronoun "her" refers to the woman who just gave birth to a child. After the surgeon deposited the child in her arms, she kissed the child's forehead and passed her hands over her own face, which suggests that she was overwhelmed with emotion. Therefore, the 'face' in the expression "passed her hands over her face" refers to the face of the patient, who died soon after giving birth.

Question 54

The implication of they had been strangers too long' is:

1. Those who spoke of 'hope and comfort' had been strangers too long.
2. 'Hope' had been stranger to 'comfort' for too long.
3. 'Hope and comfort' had been stranger to the patient too long.
4. 'Hope and comfort' had been strangers to the surgeon, nurse and the patient too long.

Explanations:

Answer: 3. 'Hope and comfort' had been stranger to the patient too long.

The line "They had been strangers too long" suggests that the patient had been deprived of hope and comfort for a prolonged period of time, possibly due to her illness or the circumstances of her life. This deprivation may have contributed to her intense emotional response to holding her child, as well as her sudden and tragic death. The implication is that if she had experienced more hope and comfort in her life, she may have been more resilient and able to survive her illness or cope with her emotional distress. Overall, the line highlights the importance of hope and comfort in promoting physical and emotional well-being.

Question 55

Match List I vrith List II

List I (Novel)	List II (Character)
A. Barnaby Rudge	(i) Miss La Creevy
B. Little Dorrit	(ii) Miss Dolly
C. Nicholas Nickleby	(iii) Mrs Boffin
D. Our Mutual Friend	(iv) Mrs. Flintwinch

Choose the correct answer fro1n the options given below:

1. (a)-(i), (b)-(iii) (c)-(ii), (d)-(iv)
2. (a)-(ii), (b)-(iv), (c)-(i), (d)-(iii)
3. (a)-(iii), (b)-(ii), (c)-(iv) (d)-(i)
4. (a)-(iv),. (b)-(i). (c)-(iii), (d)-(ii)

Explanations:
Answer: 3. (a)-(ii), (b)-(iv), (c)-(i), (d)-(iii)

In Charles Dickens' novels, the matching of List I (Novel) with List II (Character) is as follows:

A. Barnaby Rudge - (ii) Miss Dolly
B. Little Dorrit - (iv) Mrs. Flintwinch
C. Nicholas Nickleby - (i) Miss La Creevy
D. Our Mutual Friend - (iii) Mrs. Boffin

Extra Perk:

(i) Miss La Creevy (Nicholas Nickleby): Miss La Creevy is a kind-hearted portrait painter who befriends and supports the characters in their times of need, providing a source of comfort and guidance throughout the story.

(ii) Miss Dolly (Barnaby Rudge): Miss Dolly is a gentle and compassionate young woman who shows unwavering loyalty and love for her father, even in the face of adversity, displaying resilience and strength of character.

(iii) Mrs. Boffin (Our Mutual Friend): Mrs. Boffin is a generous and warm-hearted woman who undergoes a transformation from humble origins to wealth, remaining genuine and down-to-earth, and using her newfound resources to help others.

(iv) Mrs. Flintwinch (Little Dorrit): Mrs. Flintwinch is a complex and mysterious character, portrayed as manipulative and scheming, often keeping secrets and exerting control over others, adding intrigue and tension to the unfolding plot of the novel.

Question 56

Mr Pumblechook is a character in

1. Little Dorret
2. Hard Times
3. Nicholas Nickleby
4. Great Expectations

Explanations:

Answer: 4. Great Expectation

Mr. Pumblechook is a character in Charles Dickens's novel "Great Expectations." He is a pompous and self-important character who is a relative of the protagonist, Pip. Mr. Pumblechook is portrayed as a wealthy corn merchant and a condescending figure in Pip's life. He often takes credit for Pip's achievements and seeks personal gain from his association with Pip. Mr. Pumblechook serves as a satirical representation of social climbing and false importance in the Victorian era.

Extra Perk:

Major characters in "Little Dorrit":

➤ Amy Dorrit (Little Dorrit): The kind-hearted and self-sacrificing protagonist, who grows up in the Marshalsea debtor's prison and later becomes a source of support and strength for her family.
➤ Arthur Clennam: The main male protagonist who returns to England to uncover his family's past and becomes involved with the Dorrit family, particularly Little Dorrit.
➤ William Dorrit: Amy's father, known as the "Father of the Marshalsea," who undergoes a transformation from being a long-term

prisoner to inheriting a fortune and becoming a snobbish gentleman.
- ➢ Mrs. Clennam: Arthur's strict and cold-hearted mother, who holds dark secrets from the past and plays a significant role in the story's mysteries.

Major characters in "Hard Times":

- ➢ **Thomas Gradgrind**: A wealthy and utilitarian businessman and father who prioritizes facts and practicality over emotions, leading to the unhappiness and disillusionment of his family.
- ➢ **Louisa Gradgrind:** Thomas Gradgrind's eldest daughter, who struggles with the emotional and imaginative deprivation of her upbringing.
- ➢ **Josiah Bounderby:** A wealthy factory owner and self-made man who presents himself as a success story but is revealed to be full of lies and hypocrisy.
- ➢ **Sissy Jupe:** A circus girl who becomes a student and friend to the Gradgrind family, offering a contrast to the utilitarian values and representing warmth, compassion, and imagination.

Major characters in "Nicholas Nickleby":

- ➢ **Nicholas Nickleby:** The young protagonist who is forced to support his mother and sister after the death of his father, embarking on a journey that leads him through various trials and encounters.
- ➢ **Smike**: A physically and emotionally abused young man who becomes a loyal companion to Nicholas and experiences personal growth and redemption.
- ➢ **Ralph Nickleby:** Nicholas' uncle, a cold and ruthless businessman who manipulates and exploits others for his own gain.
- ➢ **Kate Nickleby**: Nicholas' younger sister, who faces her own challenges and finds herself pursued by unsavory characters while trying to maintain her integrity.

Major characters in "Great Expectations":

- ➢ **Pip (Philip Pirrip):** The protagonist who narrates the story, tracing his journey from humble beginnings to becoming a gentleman, driven by his desires for advancement and love.
- ➢ **Estella Havisham**: Adopted by Miss Havisham, Estella is the object of Pip's affection and embodies the coldness and aloofness instilled in her by her adoptive mother.
- ➢ **Miss Havisham:** A wealthy and eccentric spinster who has been living in her decaying mansion for decades, wearing her wedding dress and fostering bitterness and revenge.

> ➤ **Abel Magwitch**: A convict whom Pip encounters in his childhood and who later becomes Pip's anonymous benefactor, playing a significant role in Pip's life and expectations.

Which two of the following were published in the year 1859?

(A) On the Origin of Species
(B) A Tale of Two Cities
(C) Alice in Wonderland
(D) Silas Marner

Choose the correct answer from the options given below:

1. (A) and (B) Only
2. (B) and (C) Only
3. (A) and (C) Only
4. (B) and (D) Only

Explanations:
Answer: 1. (A) and (B) Only
(A) On the Origin of Species: Written by Charles Darwin, this groundbreaking scientific work was published in 1859. It presented the theory of evolution through natural selection, revolutionizing our understanding of the natural world and human origins.

(B) A Tale of Two Cities: Penned by Charles Dickens, this historical novel was published in 1859. Set against the backdrop of the French Revolution, it explores themes of sacrifice, love, and social injustice, becoming one of Dickens' most celebrated works.

(C) Alice in Wonderland: Written by Lewis Carroll (pseudonym of Charles Lutwidge Dodgson), this whimsical and imaginative novel was published in 1865. It takes readers on a surreal journey through a fantastical world, captivating both children and adults with its nonsensical characters and surreal adventures.

(D) Silas Marner: Authored by George Eliot (pen name of Mary Ann Evans), this novel was published in 1861. It tells the story of a reclusive weaver and his transformation through love and the arrival of a young child, exploring themes of redemption, community, and human connections.

Read the following and then answer the questions that follow

He went to work in this preparatory lesson, not unlike Morgiana in the Forty Thieves: looking into all the vessels ranged before him, one after another, to see what they contained. Say, good MChoakumchild. When from thy boiling store, thou shalt fill each jar brim full by-and-by; dost thou think that thou wilt always kill outright the robber Fancy lurking within - or sometimes only maim him and distort him. - **Dickens Hard Times**

Question 58

In the expression *".... looking into all the vessels ranged before him."*.

Which one of the following devices are used?

1. Synecdoche
2. Metonymy
3. Metaphor
4. Simile

Explanations:
Answer: 3. Metaphor

In the expression "....looking into all the vessels ranged before him," the device used is a metaphor. The act of looking into the vessels is compared to Morgiana in the story of the Forty Thieves, who looks into the vessels to see what they contain. The metaphorical comparison enhances the reader's understanding of the character's actions and creates vivid imagery by drawing a parallel between the two situations.

Question 59

'Fancy' is opposed to which two of the following?

A. Emotion
B. Reason
C. Fact
D. Imagination

Choose the correct answer from the options given below

1. (B) and (C) Only
2. (C) and (D) Only
3. (A) and (C) Only
4. (B) and (D) Only

Explanations:
Answer: 1. (B) and (C) Only

In the passage, "Fancy" is being contrasted with "Fact" and "Reason." The speaker questions whether the act of filling the vessels with knowledge and information will completely eliminate or destroy the imaginative and creative aspect represented by "Fancy," or if it will only suppress and distort it. This implies that "Fancy" is seen as the opposite or in opposition to the more logical and factual aspects of "Reason" and "Fact." Therefore, the correct answer is (B) and (C) Only.

Question 60

Who among the following Dickens characters appears as a ghost?

1. Daniel Quilp
2. Dora Spenlow
3. Esther Summerson
4. **Jacob Marley**

Correct Explanations:
Jacob Marley, a business partner of Ebenezer Scrooge, appears as a ghost in Charles Dickens' novel "A Christmas Carol." Marley's ghost warns Scrooge about the consequences of his selfish and greedy ways and foretells the visitations of three spirits that will help to reform him. The character has become an iconic figure in popular culture, often depicted with chains and a ghostly pallor, and has appeared in numerous adaptations of the novel, including films, television shows, and stage productions.

Other Explanations:
Daniel Quilp is a character from Charles Dickens' novel "The Old Curiosity Shop," who is a cunning and grotesque dwarf who becomes obsessed with destroying the life of the novel's protagonist, Nell Trent.

Dora Spenlow is a character from Dickens' novel "David Copperfield," who is the titular character's first wife. She is portrayed as a childlike and somewhat naive woman who is ill-suited to the demands of married life.

Esther Summerson is a central character in Dickens' novel "Bleak House," who is raised as an orphan and later discovers her true parentage. She is portrayed as a kind and virtuous young woman who becomes embroiled in the complex legal case at the center of the novel.

Read the following extract and answer the questions that follow:

The earth was made for Dombey and Son to trade in, and the sun and moon were made to give them light. Rivers and seas were formed to float their ships; rainbows gave them the promise of fair weather; winds blew for or against their enterprises; stars and planets circled in their orbits to preserve inviolate a system of which they were the centre. Common abbreviations took new meanings in his eyes and had sole reference to them: A. D. had no concern with anno Domini, but stood for anno Dombey—and Son. **— Charles Dickens, *Dombey and Son***

Question 61

The whole description is an example of:

1. Aporia.
2. Image.
3. **Analogy**.
4. Sarcasm.

Correct Explanation:
The whole description is an example of an extended metaphor, an analogy that compares two things in detail over several lines or sentences. **Therefore, the correct option is Analogy.**

Other Explanations:
Aporia: It is a rhetorical device that refers to a moment of uncertainty or doubt in a text, often expressed as a question or a series of questions. It is used to create a sense of confusion or highlight a topic's complexity without necessarily providing a clear resolution or answer. Aporia can be used in various genres, including poetry, philosophy, and rhetoric, and is often used to challenge traditional ways of thinking and provoke deeper reflection or inquiry.

Image: It refers to using language to create vivid mental pictures or sensory impressions in the reader's mind. It is a literary device that appeals to the reader's imagination and helps to convey the writer's meaning more effectively.

Analogy: It is a comparison between two things that are similar in some respects but are otherwise different. It is a literary device that helps to clarify or explain a concept or idea by comparing it to something else that is more familiar or concrete.

Sarcasm: It is the use of language to convey a meaning that is the opposite of what is said, often with the intention of mocking or ridiculing someone or something. It is a form of verbal irony that can be used for humorous effect or to express contempt or disdain.

Question 62

What is the 'system' of which Dombey and Son were the centres?

1. The British political system
2. The country's commerce
3. **The family business**
4. The workings of nature

Correct Explanations:

The "system" of which Dombey and Son were the centre refers to the economic and commercial system of the time, particularly the trading and shipping industry in which they operated. It is not related to the British political system, the country's commerce in general, or the workings of nature. **Therefore, the correct option is the family business.**

Question 63

Who wrote a postmodern reworking of Charles Dickens's Great Expectations without altering the original title?

1. Shirley Jackson
2. **Kathy Acker**
3. Angela Carter
4. Peter Carey

Correct Explanations:

"Great Expectations" is a classic novel by Charles Dickens that was first published in 1860-61. The novel tells the story of a young orphan named Pip and his journey from poverty to wealth, and his experiences with love, ambition, and social class in Victorian England.

While there have been many adaptations and reworkings of "Great Expectations" over the years, including film, television, and stage adaptations. **Kathy Acker wrote a postmodern reworking of Charles Dickens's Great Expectations without altering the original title.**

However, British author Peter Carey did write a novel called "Jack Maggs," which is a reworking of "Great Expectations." The novel was published in 1997 and tells the story of a former convict named Jack Maggs who returns to London in the 1830s to seek revenge on a wealthy family who wronged him in the past. The novel explores many of the same themes as "Great Expectations," including ambition, love, social class, and identity, but it is not a postmodern reworking of the original novel, and the title is not the same as "Great Expectations."

Question 64

Which among the following are examples of the Künstlerroman?

    A.   The Portrait of a Lady
    B.   David Copperfield
    C.   Tom Jones
    D.   A Portrait of the Artist as a Young Man

Choose the correct answer from the options given below:

    1.   A and C only
    2.   **B and D only**
    3.   A and B only
    4.   C and D only

Correct Explanations:
Both "A Portrait of the Artist as a Young Man" by James Joyce and "David Copperfield" by Charles Dickens are considered examples of the Künstlerroman, a type of novel that focuses on the growth and development of an artist or writer.

In "A Portrait of the Artist as a Young Man," Joyce presents the story of Stephen Dedalus, a young man who struggles to find his artistic voice in the face of societal pressures and religious expectations. The novel follows Stephen's journey as he grapples with his identity, eventually leading him to embrace his vocation as a writer.

Similarly, "David Copperfield" chronicles the life of the titular character, who starts out as a young boy with a passion for reading and writing. Throughout the novel, David faces numerous challenges as he strives to become a successful writer, ultimately finding success and fulfillment in his artistic pursuits.

Other Explanations:

"The Portrait of a Lady" by Henry James and "Tom Jones" by Henry Fielding are not typically considered examples of Künstlerroman, although they do feature protagonists who undergo personal growth and transformation throughout the course of the narrative.

"The Portrait of a Lady" follows the story of Isabel Archer, an independent and spirited young woman who travels to Europe to explore the world and find her place in society. The novel focuses on Isabel's personal relationships and her struggle to reconcile her desire for independence with her social obligations and expectations.

"Tom Jones," on the other hand, **is a picaresque novel** that follows the adventures of the titular character as he travels through England in search of love and fortune. While the novel does feature Tom's personal growth and development, it is primarily focused on his experiences and exploits as he navigates the complexities of 18th century society.

Question 65

Match List I with List II

List I	List II
A. "The Lion's Skin"	I. Washington Irving
B. "The Man who liked Dickens"	II. W. Somerset Maugham
C. "Rip Van Winkle"	III. Stephen Crane
D. "The Bride tomes to Yellow Sky"	IV. Evelyn Waugh

Choose the correct answer from the options given below:

1. A - I. B - II. C - IV. D - III
2. A - III, B - IV, C - I, D - I
3. **A - II. B - IV. C - I. D - III**
4. A - IV, B - I, C - III, D - I

Correct Explanations:

A. "The Lion's Skin" is actually a short story written by W. Somerset Maugham, a British playwright, novelist, and short story writer. The story tells the tale of a British diplomat who is sent to a remote posting in a small Middle Eastern country. While there, he becomes embroiled in local politics and is forced to resort to subterfuge in order to protect his position and his life. The title of the story refers to a local legend about a lion who terrorizes the countryside, and the diplomat's decision to use this legend to his advantage.

B. "The Man who liked Dickens" is a short story written by Evelyn Waugh, a British writer known for his satirical and darkly comedic works. The story follows a man who becomes obsessed with the writings of Charles Dickens and begins to model his life after the characters in his books.

C. "Rip Van Winkle" is a short story written by Washington Irving, an American author best known for his humorous and satirical works. The story tells the tale of a man who falls asleep in the Catskill Mountains and wakes up 20 years later to find that the world around him has changed.

D. "The Bride Comes to Yellow Sky" is a short story written by Stephen Crane, an American writer known for his naturalistic and impressionistic style. The story tells the tale of a lawman who returns to his small Texas town with his new bride, only to find that the town's sense of order has been disrupted by his absence.

E. "The Lion's Skin" is a short story written by Saki (H.H. Munro), a British writer known for his wit and satire. The story tells the tale of a mischievous young man who decides to play a trick on his aunt by pretending to be a wild animal.

Find the chronological order of publication of Charles Dickens's novels:

A. *Oliver Twist*
B. *Dombey and Sons*
C. *Pickwick Papers*
D. *Bleak House*
E. *David Copperfield*

Choose the correct answer from the options given below:

1. A, D, C, B) E
2. D, E, B, C) A
3. B, D, C, A, E
4. C, A, B, D, E

Explanations:
Ans: C, A, B, D, E

The following is the chronological order of publication of Charles Dickens's novels:

➢ *The Pickwick Papers (1836)*
➢ *Oliver Twist (1837-39)*
➢ *Nicholas Nickleby (1838-39)*
➢ *The Old Curiosity Shop (1840-41)*
➢ *Barnaby Rudge (1841)*
➢ *Martin Chuzzlewit (1843-44)*
➢ *Dombey and Son (1846-48)*
➢ *David Copperfield (1849-50)*
➢ *Bleak House (1852-53)*
➢ *Hard Times (1854)*
➢ *Little Dorrit (1855-57)*
➢ *A Tale of Two Cities (1859)*
➢ *Great Expectations (1860-61)*
➢ *Our Mutual Friend (1864-65)*
➢ *The Mystery of Edwin Drood (unfinished, 1870)*

> **Code 1**
> *Picky **Twisty** Nicky found a Curious Christy*
> ***Barby** and Chose to Dumb her Copy of **Black House**.*
> *The Hard Door opens Two Cities with Great Expectations,*
> ***Mutual Friend Edwin** stays till the end.*
>
> **Code 2**
> ***Pick** and **Twist** Nicky to make Curious Christy Barbecue,*
> ***Choose to Dumb** in the **Black Copy House**.*
> *A **Hard Little Door** opens **Two Cities**,*
> *with **Great Expectations** to meet **Mutual Friend Edwin**.*
>
> *First Work is The Sketches of Boz.*
>
> *Last Work is Edwin Drood.*

Question 67

Find the chronological order of publication of Charles Dickens's novels:

- A. Oliver Twist
- B. Dombey and Sons
- C. Pickwick Papers
- D. Bleak House
- E. David Copperfield

Choose the correct answer from the options given below:

1. ADCEB
2. DEBCA
3. BDCAE
4. CABDE
5. **DROP**

Question 68

From which novel by Charles Dickens are the following lines exist?

"I took her hand in mine, and we went out of the ruined place; and, as the morning mists had risen long ago when I first left the forge, so, the evening mists

were rising now; and in all the broad expanse of tranquil light they showed to me, I saw no shadow of another parting from her."

1. Great Expectations
2. David Copperfield
3. Nicholas Nickleby
4. Bleak House

Explanations
Answer: 1. Great Expectations

The passage is from Charles Dickens' novel "Great Expectations." It occurs towards the end of the novel when Pip and Estella, the two main characters, reunite after a long period of separation. The imagery of leaving the ruined place and the rising mists symbolises a fresh start and the potential for a brighter future. The narrator, Pip, expresses his hope and relief that there will be no more partings between them, suggesting a newfound sense of optimism and the possibility of a lasting connection.

Question 69

In a novel of Charles Dickens, a high spirited boy of 19 is left penniless along with his mother and sister Kate on the death of his father. Which of the following is the novel?

1. Oliver Twist
2. David Copperfield
3. Nicholas Nickleby
4. Hard Times

Explanations:
Answer: 3. Nicholas Nickleby

3. Nicholas Nickleby: Nicholas Nickleby's father dies unexpectedly after losing all of his money in a poor investment. Nicholas, his mother and his younger sister, Kate, are forced to give up their comfortable lifestyle in Devonshire and travel to London to seek the aid of their only living relative, Nicholas's uncle, Ralph Nickleby.

1. Oliver Twist: A young orphan named Oliver Twist navigates the harsh streets of London, encounters a cast of colourful characters, and becomes entangled in a web of crime and deception as he seeks to uncover the truth about his past.

2. David Copperfield: From his tumultuous childhood to his journey towards adulthood, David Copperfield faces various trials and tribulations, including the loss of loved ones, financial struggles, and complicated relationships, as he strives to find his place in the world and discover true happiness.

4. Hard Times: Set in an industrial town, Hard Times explores the lives of individuals affected by the harsh realities of the Victorian era. The story delves into themes of social inequality, the impact of industrialization, and the struggles faced by characters such as Thomas Gradgrind and Sissy Jupe as they navigate a rigid and unforgiving society.

Question 70

Arrange the chronological sequence in which the following works were published:

    A. Jane Eyre
    B. A Tale of Two Cities
    C. Middlemarch
    D. The Return of the Native
    E. The Newcomes

Choose the correct answer from the following options:

    1. A. B, C. D, E
    2. A. E, B, C. D
    3. B. A. C, E, D
    4. B, C. A. D. E

Explanations:
Answer: 2. A, E, B, C, D

Jane Eyre is a novel written by Charlotte Brontë and first published in 1847 under the pseudonym Currer Bell. The story follows the life of Jane Eyre and is presented as her autobiography.

The Newcomes is a novel by William Makepeace Thackeray, initially published in 24 instalments from 1853 to 1855 as The Newcomes:

Memoirs of a Most Respectable Family. The story is narrated by "Arthur Pendennis, Esq." and revolves around the lives of the Newcome family. It was later released as a book in two volumes in 1854-55.

A Tale of Two Cities is a novel by Charles Dickens, originally published in 1859 both in serial and book form. Set during the French Revolution, the story depicts the social and political turmoil of the late 18th century.

Middlemarch, also known as Middlemarch: A Study of Provincial Life, is a novel by George Eliot (the pseudonym of Mary Ann Evans). It was published in eight parts in 1871-72 and later compiled into four volumes in 1872. The narrative explores various characters and their lives in a provincial town.

The Return of the Native is a novel by Thomas Hardy, published in 1878. It is set on Egdon Heath, a fictional barren moor in Wessex, England. The story revolves around Clym Yeobright, who returns to the area after a career as a jeweller in Paris to become a schoolmaster.

Question 71

Of which of the following was Charles Dickens the founding editor?

    A. North and South
    B. The Newcomes
    C. Household Words
    D. The Way We Live Now
    E. All the Year Round

Choose the correct answer from the options given below

    1. A and C
    2. B and D
    3. C and E
    4. D and E

Explanations:
Answer: 3. C and E

Household Words was an English weekly magazine edited by Charles Dickens in the 1850s. It took its name from the line in Shakespeare's Henry V: "Familiar in his mouth as household words."

All the Year Round was a Victorian periodical, being a British weekly literary magazine founded and owned by Charles Dickens, published between 1859 and 1895 throughout the United Kingdom. Edited by Dickens, it was the direct successor to his previous publication Household Words, abandoned due to differences with his former publisher.

Other Explanations:
The Way We Live Now is a satirical novel by Anthony Trollope, published in London in 1875 after first appearing in serialised form. It is one of the last significant Victorian novels to have been published in monthly parts.

North and South is a social novel published in 1854–55 by English writer Elizabeth Gaskell. With Wives and Daughters (1865) and Cranford (1853), it is one of her best-known novels and was adapted for television three times (1966, 1975 and 2004). Initially, Gaskell wanted the novel to be titled after the heroine, **Margaret Hale, but Charles Dickens, the editor of Household Words**, the magazine in which the novel was serialised, insisted on North and South.

The Newcomes: Memoirs of a Most Respectable Family is a novel by William Makepeace Thackeray, first published in 1854 and 1855.

Question 72

What is the correct order of publication of the novels of Charles Dickens?

    A. Great Expectations
    B. Hard Times
    C. Oliver Twist
    D. David Copperfield
    E. A Tale of Two Cities

Choose the correct answer from the options given below:

    1. (E),(C), (A),(B), (D)
    2. (C),(D),(B), (E), (A)

    3. (B),(A), (D),(C),(E)
    4. (D),(B), (C), (A),(E)

Explanations:
Answer: 2. (C),(D),(B), (E), (A)

List of Dicken's Works
- *The Pickwick Papers (April 1836 to November 1837)*
- ***Oliver Twist (February 1837 to April 1839)***
- *Nicholas Nickleby (April 1838 to October 1839)*
- *The Old Curiosity Shop (April 1840 to November 1841)*
- *Barnaby Rudge (February to November 1841)*
- *A Christmas Carol (1843)*
- *Martin Chuzzlewit (January 1843 to July 1844)*
- *Dombey and Son (October 1846 to April 1848)*
- *The Haunted Man (1848)*
- ***David Copperfield (May 1849 to November 1850)***
- *Bleak House (March 1852 to September 1853)*
- ***Hard Times (1 April 1854 to 12 August 1854)***
- *Little Dorrit (December 1855 to June 1857)*
- ***A Tale of Two Cities (30 April 1859 to 26 November 1859)***
- ***Great Expectations (1 December 1860 to 3 August 1861)***
- *Our Mutual Friend (May 1864 to November 1865)*
- *The Mystery of Edwin Drood (April 1870 to September 1870)*

Code 1
*Picky **Twisty** Nicky found a Curious Christy*
***Barby** and Chose to Dumb her Copy of **Black House**.*
The Hard Door opens Two Cities with Great Expectations,
***Mutual Friend Edwin** stays till the end.*

Code 2
***Pick** and **Twist** Nicky to make Curious Christy Barbecue,*
***Choose to Dumb** in the **Black Copy House**.*
*A **Hard Little Door** opens **Two Cities**,*
*with **Great Expectations** to meet **Mutual Friend Edwin**.*

First Work is The Sketches of Boz.
Last Work is Edwin Drood.

Question 73

Which two cities are referred in Charles Dickens' A Tale of Two Cities?

1. Paris and Venice
2. Venice and Florence
3. London and Paris
4. London and Birmingham

Explanations:
Answer: 3. London and Paris

Charles Dickens' "A Tale of Two Cities" was released in both serialized form and as a complete book in 1859, immersing readers in the tumultuous era of the French Revolution during the late 18th century. Drawing inspiration from **Thomas Carlyle's "The French Revolution"** for its expansive narrative **across London and Paris,** the novel emphasizes drama over historical precision. The narrative is renowned for its depiction of mob violence, albeit with a limited grasp of the historical intricacies.

Question 74

Which among the following are the titles of the periodicals?

A. Dickens' Household Words
B. S.T. Coleridge' Friend
C. Richard Steele's Guardian
D. Franz Kafka's The Metamorphosis
E. Leigh Hunt's Indicator

Choose the correct answer from the options given below:

1. (A) and (B) Only
2. (B) and (C) Only
3. (A), (B), (C) and (E) Only
4. (C), (D) and (E) Only

Explanations:
Answer: 3. (A), (B), (C) and (E) Only

Charles Dickens, in the 1850s, took on the role of editor for the English weekly magazine _Household Words_, named after a phrase from Shakespeare's Henry V. Throughout its conception, Dickens considered various titles such as The Robin, The Household Voice, The Comrade, The Lever, and The Highway of Life before settling on Household Words.

In 1809, Samuel Taylor Coleridge embarked on his second venture into publishing with _The Friend,_ a weekly journal showcasing his broad spectrum of interests from law to literary criticism. Coleridge's disorganization and poor business acumen led to financial difficulties, necessitating loans from affluent friends to continue the publication. Despite initial support, including subscriptions from members of Parliament, The Friend faced an inevitable decline due to Coleridge's financial mismanagement.

Sir Richard Steele, in collaboration with Joseph Addison, co-founded _The Spectator_, following their initial project, **_The Tatler_**. Launched on 12 April 1709, The Tatler was published three times a week under the pseudonym Isaac Bickerstaff. Steele aimed to critique societal pretenses and advocate for simplicity in life through The Tatler, which predominantly featured his writings. The magazine was discontinued in 1711 to escape political backlash, leading Steele and Addison to start The Spectator and later **_The Guardian_**.

Leigh Hunt, an influential English critic and poet, co-founded **_The Examiner_,** a radical journal, becoming a nexus for the "Hunt circle" which included notable figures like William Hazlitt and Charles Lamb. Hunt played a crucial role in introducing poets like John Keats and Percy Bysshe Shelley to the public. Aside from _The Examiner_, Hunt edited **_The Reflector_,** a quarterly magazine, and **_The Indicator_,** a weekly publication that he likely filled with his literary contributions. He also briefly managed **_The Companion_**, a weekly that focused on literature and the arts.

The Metamorphosis, a profound allegorical narrative by the esteemed Austrian author Franz Kafka, was first made available to the public in the German language as Die Verwandlung in the year 1915.

Question 75

Match List I with List II

List I (Work)	List II (Character)
A. Charles Dickens' Martin Chuzzlewit	I. Abraham Durbeyfield -
B. G.B. Shaw's The Doctor's Dilemma	II. Harry
C. Thomas Hardy's Tess of d' Urbervilles	III. Sir Ralph Bloomfield Bonnington
D. T.S. Eliot's The Family Reunion	IV. Mrs Gamp

Choose the correct answer from the options given below:

1. A - IV, B - III, C - II, D - I
2. A - III, B -II, C -IV, D - I
3. A - III, B - II, C - I, D - IV
4. A - IV, B -III, C - I, D- II

Explanations:
Answer: 4. A - IV, B -III, C - 1, D- II

***Martin Chuzzlewit* is a novel by Charles Dickens,** released in parts from 1843 to 1844 and as a complete book in 1844. **Using the pseudonym "Boz,"** Dickens tells the tale of Martin Chuzzlewit, a young architect betrayed by Seth Pecksniff and cut off by his rich but peculiar grandfather. Martin, alongside servant Mark Tapley, ventures to America, facing fraud and misadventures but returns to England disillusioned. The story ends with Martin mending fences with his grandfather and securing his marriage to Mary Graham. A notable character, **<u>Sarah Gamp, provides dark humor as a drunken midwife and nurse.</u>**

***The Doctor's Dilemma* by George Bernard Shaw** is a four-act drama with an epilogue, debuted in London in 1906 and published in 1911. This work critiques the medical field and public misconceptions about moral character and professional success. It centers on a moral question faced by Dr. Colenso Ridgeon, who must decide between saving the life of Louis Dubedat, a charming but unethical artist, or aiding a destitute but dedicated doctor. Complications arise when Ridgeon falls for Dubedat's loyal wife, Jennifer, introducing a twisted layer of personal and professional ethics, highlighted by characters like **<u>Sir Ralph Bloomfield Bonington</u>**.

***Tess of the d'Urbervilles* by Thomas Hardy,** first serialized in 1891, tells the tragic story of Tess **<u>Durbeyfield</u>**, portrayed as a pure and virtuous woman crushed by the harsh morals of Victorian society. Hardy's narrative diverges from typical Victorian novels by focusing on the rural lower class and candidly discussing sexuality and religion. Tess, a naive young woman from an impoverished family, discovers they have noble ancestors and is sent to connect with the wealthy d'Urbervilles. Seduced by the libertine Alec d'Urberville, she gives birth to a child, Sorrow, who dies young. Tess later marries Angel Clare, who abandons her upon learning of her past, driving Tess back into Alec's arms. In a final act of desperation and perceived justice, Tess murders Alec, leading to her eventual arrest and execution.

The Family Reunion, a play by T. S. Eliot, combines elements of Greek tragedy and contemporary detective stories, using mostly blank verse to explore themes of guilt and redemption. The narrative centers around characters such as Amy, Lady Monchensey; Violet; Ivy; Charles and Gerald; Agatha; The Late Lord Monchensey; **Harry**; and Mary, detailing the protagonist's journey from overwhelming guilt towards a semblance of redemption.

Bronte Sisters

- ➢ **Charlotte Brontë** (1816–55) was the **most important** Brontë sister.
- ➢ **Emily** (1818–48) and **Anne Brontë** (1820–49) were her sisters.
- ➢ Their father, an **Irish clergyman**, held a position in **Yorkshire**.
- ➢ **Financial issues** led Charlotte to become a **schoolteacher** and **governess**.
- ➢ She visited **Brussels** with Emily in **1842**, then returned home.
- ➢ Success from her books relieved **financial stress** later on.
- ➢ **Married in 1854**, Charlotte died the **next year**.
- ➢ The sisters used **pen names: Currer, Ellis, and Acton Bell**.
- ➢ Their **poems** (1846) were fine, especially **Emily's pieces**.
- ➢ **Charlotte's first novel, *The Professor*,** saw **no success** initially.
- ➢ **Jane Eyre** (1847) created a **stir** for its **candor** and **passion**.
- ➢ **Charlotte** acknowledged **Thackeray** as her **Master** in fiction.
- ➢ Her other novels include **Shirley** (1849) and **Villette** (1853).
- ➢ **Charlotte's work** had **truth and intensity**, yet lacked **humor**.
- ➢ Her **plots were** often **based on personal experiences**.
- ➢ She brought **energy** and **romantic beauty** to **commonplace**.
- ➢ **Emily's novel, *Wuthering Heights*** (1847), was a **tragic romance**.
- ➢ **Emily's tragic emphasis** often reached a **sublime** level.
- ➢ However, *Wuthering Heights* was too **uneven to be very great**.

- ➤ **Anne Brontë's novels** include *Agnes Grey* and *The Tenant of Wildfell Hall.*
- ➤ Her novels (both **1847**) are **less intense** than her sisters' works.
- ➤ Anne's work **lacks power** and **intensity** compared to Charlotte and Emily.
- ➤ **Overall**, the **Brontë sisters** brought **passion and intensity** to fiction.
- ➤ *A Literature of Their Own: British Women Novelists from Brontë to Lessing (1978)* by Elain Showalter.

Charlotte Bronte's Jane Eyre (1847)

- ➤ **Jane Eyre** was written by **Charlotte Brontë** as "Currer Bell."
- ➤ **Published on 16 October 1847** by Smith, Elder & Co.
- ➤ The first **American edition** was published in 1848.
- ➤ The novel follows **Jane Eyre's growth** and love for Mr. Rochester.
- ➤ Lacks the **power and intensity** of her sisters' novels.
- ➤ Jane Eyre is **raised by her cruel aunt**.
- ➤ Sent to **Lowood School,** faces harsh conditions there.
- ➤ Jane befriends **Helen Burns, who later dies.**
- ➤ Education at Lowood builds Jane's resilience and character.
- ➤ Jane **becomes a teacher at Lowood** upon graduation.
- ➤ Accepts a **governess position at Thornfield Hall.**
- ➤ **Meets Mr. Rochester,** Thornfield's mysterious master.
- ➤ Jane and Rochester form a close, intense bond.
- ➤ Jane **hears strange sounds in Thornfield's attic.**
- ➤ Falls deeply in love with Mr. Rochester.
- ➤ Rochester proposes marriage; Jane happily agrees.
- ➤ Wedding halted **due to Rochester's hidden wife.**
- ➤ Rochester's wife, **Bertha, is mentally unstable.**
- ➤ Heartbroken, Jane leaves Thornfield in despair.
- ➤ Jane finds **refuge with St. John Rivers' family**.
- ➤ Learns of her **newfound family inheritance.**
- ➤ **St. John proposes**, urging her to join him.
- ➤ Jane declines; her heart belongs to Rochester.
- ➤ Jane **returns to find Thornfield destroyed by fire.**
- ➤ **Reunited with Rochester, now blind**, they marry happily.

Emily Bronte's Wuthering Heights (1847)

- Published under **Ellis Bell's pseudonym in 1847**.
- Two gentry families living on the West Yorkshire moors, the **Lintons the Earnshaws**.
- Depicts their turbulent relationships with Earnshaw's adopted son, **Heathcliff**.
- **Romanticism and Gothic fiction** influenced the novel.
- Publisher Thomas Newby.
- **Lockwood** acts as an **outsider**, learning about the families.
- **Nelly** is depicted as the **main character** and servant.
- <u>**Zillah: Heathcliff's servant at Heights post-Catherine, dislikes Cathy.**</u>
- Lockwood, narrator of *Wuthering Heights*, **recounts narratives** of main characters.
- He rents **Thrushcross Grange** in **Yorkshire** and learns family histories.
- Lockwood uncovers histories of **two local families** gradually.
- A housekeeper tells him **vital details** about the families.
- **The opening line** "*1801—I have just returned from a visit to my landlord—the solitary neighbor that I shall be troubled with*".
- Heathcliff, an orphan, is adopted by Mr. Earnshaw.
- He grows close to Earnshaw's daughter, **Catherine**.
- Heathcliff faces **mistreatment** from Earnshaw's son, Hindley.
- **Hindley inherits** Wuthering Heights after Earnshaw's death.
- **Heathcliff's social position** and treatment worsen.
- Catherine and Heathcliff share a **passionate bond**.
- Catherine chooses **Edgar Linton**, a wealthy neighbor, to marry.
- **Heathcliff leaves**, hurt by Catherine's choice of Edgar.
- Heathcliff returns **wealthy** and seeks **revenge**.
- Heathcliff buys Wuthering Heights from **a broke Hindley**.
- He marries **Isabella Linton** to spite Edgar.
- Isabella soon realizes Heathcliff's **vindictive nature**.
- Catherine becomes ill after a **confrontation** with Heathcliff.
- Catherine **dies after childbirth**, leaving Heathcliff devastated.
- Heathcliff becomes **obsessed with Catherine's memory**.
- **Catherine's daughter, Cathy**, grows up at Thrushcross Grange.
- Heathcliff controls **Hareton**, Hindley's neglected son.
- **Heathcliff plans Cathy's marriage** to his son, Linton.
- Cathy marries **Linton**, who soon **dies**, leaving her alone.

- ➤ Heathcliff begs Catherine, *"Be with me always –take any form—drive me mad! Only do not leave me in this abyss where I cannot find you."*
- ➤ **Heathcliff dies** haunted by Catherine, ending his revenge
- ➤ Heathcliff is brought up alongside Cathy, and she loves and cares for him so much that she tells Nelly, *"He's more myself than I am."*

Anne Brontë's The Tenant of Wildfell Hall (1848)

- ➤ The Tenant of Wildfell Hall is the second and final novel written by Anne Brontë.
- ➤ It was first published in 1848 under the **pseudonym Acton Bell**.
- ➤ **May Sinclair,** in 1913, said that *"the slamming of [Helen's] bedroom door against her husband reverberated throughout Victorian England."*
- ➤ Helen Graham arrives at **Wildfell Hall** with her son.
- ➤ Her mysterious past intrigues **local farmer Gilbert Markham**.
- ➤ Through Helen's diary, her **troubled marriage is revealed**.
- ➤ She escaped her abusive husband to **protect her son**.
- ➤ Helen and Gilbert's love **blooms after her husband's death**.

Questions

Question 76

Which of the following statements is not true about Jean Rhys's Wide Sargasso Sea?

1. It was first published in 1966.
2. It takes its theme and main character from the novel Jane Eyre by Charlotte Bronte
3. Action of the novel takes place in South Africa
4. Name of Antoinette's mother is Annette

Explanations:
Answer: 3. Action of the novel takes place in South Africa.

Wide Sargasso Sea is a **1966 novel by Jean Rhys.**
- ➤ It serves as a **postcolonial, feminist prequel to Jane Eyre**.
- ➤ The novel, initially **set in Jamaica.**
- ➤ Opens a short while after the **Slavery Abolition Act 1833**.

- ➢ It explores **Mr. Rochester's marriage from Antoinette Cosway's** perspective.
- ➢ **Antoinette Cosway** mirrors Brontë's **"madwoman in the attic"**.
- ➢ Name of Antoinette's mother is **Annette**.
- ➢ The novel traces her **youth in Jamaica to her marriage**.
- ➢ Mr. Rochester **renames her Bertha and declares her mad**.
- ➢ **Themes include race, Caribbean history, and assimilation**.
- ➢ **Antoinette feels isolated** between Europe and Jamaica.

Question 77

In the 1985 essay, "Three Women's Texts and a critique of Imperialism", Gayatri Spivak shows the development of the white liberal feminist subject. Which are the texts referred in the title of the essay ?

A. The Wide Sargasso Sea by Jean Rhys
B. Jane Eyre by Charolotte Bronte
C. Frankenstein by Mary Shelley
D. Pride and Prejudice by Jane Austen
E. The Mill on the Floss by George Eliot

Choose the correct answer from the options given below :

(1) A, B and D only
(2) C, D and A only
(3) A, B and C only
(4) E, B and D only

Explanations:
Answer: (3) A, B and C only

"Three Women's Texts and a Critique of Imperialism" is an essay by **Gayatri Spivak** that analyzes three works by women and the role of women in imperialist society:

1. **Jane Eyre: By Charlotte Brontë**
2. **Wide Sargasso Sea: By Jean Rhys**
3. **Frankenstein: By Mary Shelley**

In the essay, Spivak focuses on the "imperialist narrativization of history" in the works and how contemporary Anglo-American feminist literary criticism privileges it. She also highlights the importance of "childbearing and soul-making" for feminist individualism in the age of imperialism.

Question 78

Arrange the following women novelists in chronological order (by date of birth):

A. Anne Bronte
B. Jane Austen
C. Ann Radcliffe
D. Fanny Burney
E. Maria Edgeworth

Choose the correct answer from the options given below:

1. B, A, D, C, E
2. C, D, B, E, A
3. D, C, E, B, A
4. A, B, C, E, D

Explanations:
Answer: 3. D, C, E, B, A

Fanny Burney (1752-1840): Major works: "Evelina" (1778), "Cecilia" (1782), "Camilla" (1796), "The Wanderer" (1814)

Maria Edgeworth (1768-1849): Major works: "Castle Rackrent" (1800), "Belinda" (1801), "The Absentee" (1812)

Ann Radcliffe (1764-1823): Major works: "The Castles of Athlin and Dunbayne" (1789), "The Mysteries of Udolpho" (1794), "The Italian" (1797)

Jane Austen (1775-1817): Major works: "Sense and Sensibility" (1811), "Pride and Prejudice" (1813), "Mansfield Park" (1814), "Emma" (1815), "Persuasion" (1818), "Northanger Abbey" (1818)

Anne Bronte (1820-1849): "Agnes Grey" (1847), "The Tenant of Wildfell Hall" (1848)

Question 79

To which of these boarding schools is Jane Eyre sent by her aunt Mrs.

Reed?

1. Lowood School
2. Abbey Mount
3. Hailsham school
4. Greyfriars School

Explanations:
Answer: 1. Lowood School

In Charlotte Brontë's novel "Jane Eyre," Jane is indeed sent to Lowood School, a boarding school, by her aunt, Mrs. Reed. After the death of Jane's parents, she is taken in by her maternal uncle, Mr. Reed. However, upon his death, Jane's aunt, Mrs. Reed, becomes her guardian but treats her with cruelty and disdain. Eventually, Mrs. Reed decides to send Jane away to Lowood School, a charitable institution for orphaned girls. At Lowood, Jane faces strict discipline, challenging conditions, and encounters influential figures who shape her experiences and contribute to her personal growth throughout the novel.

Question 80

Which of the following are representative texts of "Gynocriticism"?

A. Patricial Meyer Spacks' The Female Imagination
B. Mary Ellman's Thinking About Women
C. Sandra Gilbert and Susan Gubar's The Madwoman in the Attic
D. Ellen Moer's Literary Women
E. Kate Millett's Sexual Politics

Choose the correct answer from the options given below;
1. A and B only
2. A, B, and C only
3. B, D and E only
4. **A, C and D only**

Correct Explanations:
Gynocriticism or gynocritics is the term coined in the seventies by Elaine Showalter to describe a new literary project intended to construct **"a female framework for the analysis of women's literature"**. By expanding the historical study of women writers as a distinct literary tradition, gynocritics

sought to develop new models based on the study of female experience to replace male models of literary creation and so "map the territory" left unexplored in earlier literary criticisms.

Patricia Ann Meyer Spacks (born 1929) is an American literary scholar. She specializes in eighteenth-century English Literature and writes cultural criticism on varied subjects such as boredom, gossip, and feminism. "With remarkable breadth of reference, Spacks has written more extensively than any other feminist critic on eighteenth- and nineteenth-century English narrative."

The Madwoman in the Attic: The Woman Writer and the Nineteenth-Century Literary Imagination is a 1979 book by Sandra Gilbert and Susan Gubar. **They examine Victorian literature from a feminist perspective.** Gilbert and Gubar draw their title from Charlotte Brontë's Jane Eyre, in which Rochester's wife (née Bertha Mason) is locked secretly in an attic apartment by her husband.

Ellen Moers (1928–1978) was an American academic and literary scholar. She is best known for her pioneering contribution to gynocriticism, Literary Women (1976).

Other Explanations:

Thinking About Women by Mary Ellman is a scathingly witty attack on literary misperceptions of women and prejudice against women in letters by an Oxonian critic and writer.

Sexual Politics is the debut book by American writer and activist Kate Millett, based on her PhD dissertation at Columbia University. It was published in 1970 by Doubleday. It is regarded as a classic of feminism and one of radical feminism's key texts, a formative piece in shaping the intentions of the second-wave feminist movement. In Sexual Politics, an explicit focus is placed on the omnipresence of male dominance throughout prominent 20th-century art and literature.

Question 81

Who, among the following, wrote about Charlotte Bronte that her mind contained nothing but hunger, rebellion, and rage"?

1. Elizabeth Gaskell
2. Matthew Arnold
3. Charles Dickens
4. Mary Shelley

Explanations:
Answer: 2. Matthew Arnold

Jane Eyre, published within seven weeks of submission under the pseudonym Currer Bell, was an instant success. With its emphasis on the gothic and romantic, it was considered coarse by some of Charlotte's contemporaries, as was Wuthering Heights (though it has a strong moral dimension). Praised by Queen Victoria as "really a wonderful book", it is often pointed out these days that in plot it is indistinguishable from a Mills & Boon. During her lifetime, Charlotte was the best-known and most celebrated of the Brontë sisters, moving in literary circles with greats such as WM Thackeray and Elizabeth Gaskell. **Matthew Arnold and Virginia Woolf caught on the violent aspects of Brontë's work when the former complained that her mind "contained nothing but hunger, rebellion, and rage"** and the latter asserted that "All her force, and it is the more tremendous for being constricted, goes into the assertion, 'I love,' 'I hate,' 'I suffer.'"

Question 82

Match List I with List II

List I	List II
A. George Meredith	I. The Virginians
B. George Eliot	II. Scenes of Clerical Life
C. Charlotte Bronte	III. Evan Harrington
D. William Makepeace Thackeray	IV. The Professor

Choose the correct answer from the options given below:

1. A-III, B-I, C-IV. D-I
2. A-IV. B-III. C-I. D-II

3. A-I. B-II, ONII, D-IV
4. A-II, B-I, C-1V, D-III

Explanations
Answer: 1. A-III, B-I, C-IV. D-I

A. "Evan Harrington" is a glowing Victorian comedy written by George Meredith in 1861. Loosely inspired by his own life, the novel revolves around the social climbing family of the late tailor, Melchisedec Harrington.

B. George Eliot's debut work of fiction, "Scenes of Clerical Life," comprises three short stories first published in Blackwood's Magazine. Released under her famous pseudonym in 1856, Eliot was already a renowned figure in Victorian intellectual circles, known for her contributions to The Westminster Review and translations of theological works.

C. "The Professor, A Tale," Charlotte Brontë's first novel, was written before "Jane Eyre" but faced rejection from several publishing houses. Published posthumously in 1857 with the approval of her widower, Arthur Bell Nicholls, the novel was reviewed and edited by him.

D. William Makepeace Thackeray's historical novel "The Virginians: A Tale of the Last Century" (1857–59) serves as a sequel to his work "Henry Esmond" and is loosely connected to "Pendennis."

Question 83

Which of the novelists have been correctly matched with their works?

A. Thomas Hardy - The Return of the Native
B. Charles Dickens - The History of Henry Esmond
C. Virginia Woolf - Mrs. Dalloway
D. George Eliot - Northanger Abbey
E. Charlotte Bronte - The Professor

Choose the correct answer from the options given below:

1. C, D and B
2. A. C and E
3. B. C and D

4. C, D and E

Explanations:
Answer: 4. A. C and E

"The Return of the Native" by Thomas Hardy (1878): A tragic novel set in Wessex, exploring themes of love, desire, and the clash between nature and society.

"The History of Henry Esmond" by William Makepeace Thackeray (1852): A historical novel tracing the life of the eponymous protagonist through the late 17th and early 18th centuries in England.

"Mrs. Dalloway" by Virginia Woolf (1925): A modernist novel set in a single day in post-World War I London, delving into the thoughts and experiences of its characters, particularly the titular Mrs. Dalloway.

"Northanger Abbey" by Jane Austen (1817): A satirical novel following the adventures of Catherine Morland as she navigates her way through society and the pitfalls of Gothic literature.

"The Professor" by Charlotte Bronte (1857): Bronte's debut novel, originally written before "Jane Eyre," tells the story of William Crimsworth, a young Englishman who becomes a professor in Brussels and experiences love and adversity.

Question 84

Arrange the chronological sequence in which the following works were published:

A. Jane Eyre
B. A Tale of Two Cities
C. Middlemarch
D. The Return of the Native
E. The Newcomes

Choose the correct answer from the following options:

1. A. B, C. D, E

2. A. E, B, C. D
3. B. A. C, E, D
4. B, C. A. D. E

Explanations:
Answer: 2. A, E, B, C, D

Jane Eyre is a novel written by Charlotte Brontë and first published in 1847 under the pseudonym Currer Bell. The story follows the life of Jane Eyre and is presented as her autobiography.

The Newcomes is a novel by William Makepeace Thackeray, initially published in 24 instalments from 1853 to 1855 as The Newcomes: Memoirs of a Most Respectable Family. The story is narrated by "Arthur Pendennis, Esq." and revolves around the lives of the Newcome family. It was later released as a book in two volumes in 1854-55.

A Tale of Two Cities is a novel by Charles Dickens, originally published in 1859 both in serial and book form. Set during the French Revolution, the story depicts the social and political turmoil of the late 18th century.

Middlemarch, also known as Middlemarch: A Study of Provincial Life, is a novel by George Eliot (the pseudonym of Mary Ann Evans). It was published in eight parts in 1871-72 and later compiled into four volumes in 1872. The narrative explores various characters and their lives in a provincial town.

The Return of the Native is a novel by Thomas Hardy, published in 1878. It is set on Egdon Heath, a fictional barren moor in Wessex, England. The story revolves around Clym Yeobright, who returns to the area after a career as a jeweller in Paris to become a schoolmaster.

Question 85

Which among the following statements are true about Emily Bronte's Wuthering Heights?

A. This novel was published in 1847.
B. Emily Bronte published this novel under the pseudonym Ellis Bell.
C. Lockwood and Catherine Linton are the main narrators of the story.

D. The novel is unique for its abstention from authorial intrusion, unusual structure
and narrative technique.

E. Wuthering Heights was the third novel of Emily Bronte.

Choose the correct answer from the options given below:

1. (B), (C) and (D) Only
2. (A), (B) and (C) Only
3. (A), (B) and (D) Only
4. (C), (D) and (E) Only

Explanations:
Answer: 3. (A), (B) and (D) Only

Published in 1847 under the alias Ellis Bell, "Wuthering Heights" is Emily Brontë's intensely vivid and uniquely structured novel. Set apart from its contemporaries by its dramatic and poetic flair, the novel notably avoids direct author commentary, offering an immersive storytelling experience.

Narrated primarily through **Lockwood,** an external observer, the plot unfolds via the recollections of **Ellen Dean,** the housekeeper, providing a layered narrative perspective. The tale centers on the turbulent effect of Heathcliff, an adopted orphan, on the Earnshaw and Linton families in a secluded Yorkshire area during the late 18th century. Heathcliff's deep-seated resentment, fueled by mistreatment and the heartache of **Cathy Earnshaw's marriage to the kind-hearted Edgar Linton, propels him toward vengeance against both lineages, a vendetta spanning generations. Despite Cathy's death during childbirth, Heathcliff** remains haunted by his unyielding affection for her until his own demise. The eventual union of the remaining Earnshaw and Linton descendants heralds a resolution and reconciliation.

Emily Brontë, a prominent figure in English literature, is best known for her novel "Wuthering Heights." Unlike her sisters Charlotte and Anne Brontë, who both produced multiple works, Emily's published works are limited. **Here's a list of her notable works:**

Wuthering Heights (1847): Emily Brontë's only novel, published under the pseudonym Ellis Bell, is a masterpiece that explores themes of passion, revenge, and the supernatural.

Poetry: Emily, along with her sisters, published a collection of poems under the pseudonyms Currer, Ellis, and Acton Bell. **The collection, titled "Poems by Currer, Ellis, and Acton Bell (1846),"** includes several of Emily's poems. Some of her well-known poems include:

- "No Coward Soul Is Mine"
- "Remembrance"
- "The Prisoner"
- "Last Lines"

Question 86

Match List - I with List - II.

List - I (Character)	List - II (Work)
A. Christophine	I. Wuthering Heights
B. Zillah	II. Wide Sargasso Sea
C. Estella	III. Things Fall Apart
D. Ekwefi	IV. Great Expectations'

Choose the correct answer from the options given below :

1. (A)-(IV), (B)-(III), (C)-(II), (D)-(I)
2. (A)-(I), (B)-(II), (C)-(III), (D)-(IV)
3. (A)-(II), (B)-(I), (C)-(IV), (D)-(III)
4. (A)-(III), (B)-(IV), (C)-(I), (D)-(II)

Explanations:
Answer: 3. (A)-(II), (B)-(I), (C)-(IV), (D)-(III)

Jean Rhys's novel "Wide Sargasso Sea," published in 1966, is celebrated for its creative reimagining of Charlotte Brontë's "Jane Eyre." It tells the backstory of Bertha Mason, here named Antoinette Mason, a West Indian woman who becomes the tragic first wife of Mr. Rochester. The narrative, set mainly in the West Indies, unfolds Antoinette's transition from Jamaica to an unwelcoming England, where she finds herself in a deteriorating, loveless marriage. Mr.

Rochester, her husband, confines her to Thornfield's attic, known only to him and her caretaker, Grace Poole, as she descends into madness. The story is shared through the perspectives of Antoinette in the first and third parts, and Mr. Rochester in the middle, offering a profound exploration of her life before "Jane Eyre."

Summary of Wide Sargasso Sea:

Part One: Coulibri, Jamaica
- Set in Coulibri, Jamaica after slavery's abolition in 1834.
- Narrator Antoinette, a child, describes family's fall to poverty.
- Annette, her mother, remarries wealthy Englishman Mr. Mason.
- Coulibri estate burned by emancipated slaves; brother Pierre killed.
- Annette's mental health worsens, eventually leading to her death.
- Antoinette visits Annette, who refuses to see or speak.
- Annette abused by caretakers, Antoinette leaves without speaking to her.

Part Two: Honeymoon in Dominica
- Honeymoon in Dominica, narrated by Antoinette and Mr. Rochester.
- Marriage strains from mutual suspicions and external machinations.
- Daniel, alleged half-brother, tarnishes Antoinette's reputation, demands money.
- **Christophine, Antoinette's nurse, distrusts Mr. Rochester.**
- Mr. Rochester unfaithful, emotionally abusive, renames Antoinette Bertha.
- Antoinette seeks Christophine's help, gets obeah love potion.
- Potion poisons relationship further; Mr. Rochester plans to leave Granbois.

Part Three: Life in England
- Antoinette, now Bertha, confined to Thornfield Hall's attic.
- Describes life in England, guarded by servant Grace Poole.
- Her relationship with Mr. Rochester disintegrates; he neglects her.
- Writes to stepbrother Richard; he cannot legally help.
- Bertha attacks Rochester, later forgets the encounter.
- Dreams of flames and freedom, fulfills destiny by setting fire.

***Wuthering Heights*, penned by Emily Brontë in 1847** using the pseudonym Ellis Bell, distinguishes itself from its contemporaries through its potent, vivid imagination, the exclusion of authorial commentary, and its unconventional narrative structure. Narrated by Lockwood, an external observer, his account frames the deeply reflective tales told by Ellen Dean, the housekeeper. The central theme revolves around the tumultuous effect of Heathcliff, an orphan brought into the Earnshaw and Linton families, set against the backdrop of a secluded Yorkshire region during the late 18th century. Heathcliff's life is marked by resentment, stemming from mistreatment and the marriage of his passionate love, Cathy Earnshaw, to the kind and affluent Edgar Linton. This fuels his desire for vengeance against both clans, a vendetta that spans generations. Despite Cathy's death during childbirth, Heathcliff remains haunted by his love for her until his own demise. Ultimately, tranquility is restored through the union of the remaining descendants of the Earnshaw and Linton lineages.

Characters in "Wuthering Heights":

- **Heathcliff**: Foundling from Liverpool, becomes vengeful lover and master at Heights.
- **Catherine** Earnshaw: Heathcliff's love, marries Edgar, dies after birthing Cathy Linton.
- **Edgar Linton:** Catherine's husband, contrasts Heathcliff, dotes on family, eventually dies.
- **Ellen (Nelly) Dean:** Narrator, servant to Earnshaws and Lintons, observes and reports.
- **Isabella Linton:** Edgar's sister, Heathcliff's wife, escapes abuse, dies in London.
- **Hindley Earnshaw:** Catherine's brother, mistreats Heathcliff, succumbs to despair and death.
- **Hareton Earnshaw:** Hindley's son, uneducated, inherits nothing, eventually loves Cathy.
- **Cathy Linton:** Catherine and Edgar's daughter, marries Linton then loves Hareton.
- **Linton Heathcliff:** Heathcliff and Isabella's son, marries Cathy, dies young.
- **Joseph**: Longtime servant, devout Christian, lacks kindness, speaks dialect.
- **Mr Lockwood:** First narrator, rents Grange, finds society preferable to isolation.
- **Frances**: Hindley's wife, dies soon after Hareton's birth, considered silly.

- ➢ **Mr and Mrs Earnshaw:** Catherine's and Hindley's parents; Mr favors Heathcliff.
- ➢ **Mr and Mrs Linton**: Educate Edgar and Isabella in manners, Mr is magistrate.
- ➢ **Dr Kenneth:** Gimmerton doctor, friend to Hindley, present during illnesses.
- ➢ **<u>Zillah: Heathcliff's servant at Heights post-Catherine, dislikes Cathy.</u>**
- ➢ **Mr Green**: Edgar's lawyer, betrays him to aid Heathcliff's inheritance.

Great Expectations, **novel by Charles Dickens,** first published serially in All the Year Round in 1860–61 and issued in book form in 1861. The classic novel was one of its author's greatest critical and popular successes. It chronicles the coming of age of the orphan Pip while also addressing such issues as social class and human worth.

Summary of *Great Expectations*:
- ➢ Pip narrates his life's story from an unspecified future.
- ➢ Raised in Kent marshlands with sister and Joe Gargery.
- ➢ Encounters escaped convict Abel Magwitch in the churchyard.
- ➢ Pip aids Magwitch with food and a file secretly.
- ➢ Magwitch and his enemy Compeyson are eventually captured.
- ➢ Visits Miss Havisham, jilted on her wedding day.
- ➢ **<u>Meets Estella at Satis House, falls in love.</u>**
- ➢ Ashamed of humble origins, aspires to be a gentleman.
- ➢ Becomes Joe's apprentice, dreams of higher social standing.
- ➢ Lawyer Jaggers reveals Pip has an anonymous benefactor.
- ➢ Goes to London, assumes Miss Havisham is benefactor.
- ➢ Educated as a gentleman with Herbert Pocket's help.
- ➢ Discovers benefactor is actually Abel Magwitch, not Havisham.
- ➢ Plans to leave England with Magwitch to avoid arrest.
- ➢ Confronts Miss Havisham about misleading him on patronage.
- ➢ Professes love to Estella, who plans to marry Drummle.
- ➢ Learns Magwitch is Estella's father; Compeyson was Havisham's lover.
- ➢ Grows close to Magwitch, gains respect for him.
- ➢ Magwitch fights Compeyson in Thames; Compeyson drowns.
- ➢ Magwitch is arrested, convicted, dies before execution.
- ➢ Pip falls ill, arrested for debts, Joe nurses him.

- ➢ Learns Miss Havisham died, Joe paid his debts.
- ➢ Pip works in Cairo for Herbert's firm, finds contentment.
- ➢ Returns to England after over ten years.
- ➢ Visits ruins of Satis House, encounters widowed Estella.
- ➢ Believes they will not part again, hinting at reunion.
- ➢ Pip's journey from innocence to experience and maturity.
- ➢ Themes of social class, justice, and redemption explored.
- ➢ Estella's transformation from cold to more human shown.
- ➢ Ends on a note of hopeful ambiguity for Pip and Estella.

***Things Fall Apart*, authored by Chinua Achebe and published in 1958,** was instrumental in igniting the Nigerian literary renaissance of the 1960s. This seminal work delineates the saga of Okonkwo, a prominent figure within his Igbo community, tracing his fall from grace following an inadvertent homicide that leads to his exile. Over the span of seven years in banishment, followed by his return, the novel meticulously examines the profound disruptions within tribal Igbo society wrought by the encroachment of European missionaries and colonial governance in the 1890s. Adhering to traditional narrative structures and enriched with Igbo aphorisms, the narrative adeptly explores the concurrent disintegration of both its central character, Okonkwo, and the fabric of his village. The novel has been lauded for its insightful and nuanced portrayal of indigenous beliefs and the psychological unraveling that accompanies societal collapse.

Character in *Things Fall Apart*:
- ➢ **Okonkwo:** Leader in Umuofia, embodies traditional masculinity, fears failure.
- ➢ **<u>Ekwefi: Second wife to Okonkwo, often rebels against him.</u>**
- ➢ **Unoka:** Okonkwo's father, seen as weak and unmasculine.
- ➢ **Nwoye:** Okonkwo's son, rejects father's masculinity for Christianity.
- ➢ **Ikemefuna:** Adopted by Okonkwo, tragically killed by village decree.
- ➢ **Ezinma:** Okonkwo's favored daughter, defies traditional female roles.
- ➢ **Obierika:** Okonkwo's thoughtful friend, questions cultural practices.
- ➢ **Chielo:** Priestess of Agbala, leads a dual life.
- ➢ **Ogbuefi** Ezeudu: Elder of Umuofia, provides wisdom and guidance.
- ➢ **Mr. Brown:** Compassionate English missionary, seeks understanding with Igbo.
- ➢ **Mr. Smith:** Strict missionary, contrasts with predecessor Mr. Brown.

Arrange the following texts chronologically on the basis of their publication:

    A.   A Literature of Their Own: Brtish Women Noveliss from Bronte to Lessing by Elaine Showalter
    B.   In Search of Our Mother's Gardens by Alice Walker
    C.   The Mad Woman in the Attic: The Woman Witer and the Nineteenth Century Imagination by Sandra Gilbert and Susan Guban
    D.   Sexual Politics by Kate Millett
    E.   The Second Sex by Simone De Beauvoir

Choose the correct answer from the options given below:

    1. E,C,B,D,A
    2. E,C,B,A,D
    3. E,D,B,A,C
    4. E,D,B,C,A

Explanations:
Answer: 3. E,D,B,A,C

The Second Sex, penned by French existentialist philosopher Simone de Beauvoir in **1949**, delves into women's roles and perceptions throughout history and contemporary society. Developed over 14 months from 1946 to 1949, the book is divided into two parts: "Facts and Myths," and "Lived Experience," with some sections initially published in Les Temps modernes. This seminal work examines the enduring inequalities faced by women.

"Sexual Politics," authored by Kate Millett and originating from her PhD dissertation at Columbia University, made its **debut in 1970,** published by Doubleday. This groundbreaking work is celebrated as a foundational text in feminist literature and stands as a cornerstone of radical feminism. It played a pivotal role lin defining the goals of the second-wave feminist movement. Millett's analysis critically examines how male dominance is embedded within the fabric of 20th-century Western art and literature, highlighting the perpetuation of patriarchal norms and societal heteronormativity. She **contends that the power dynamics favoring men over women stem from**

societal constructs, challenging the notion that such dominance is rooted in biological determinism.

In Search of Our Mothers' Gardens: Womanist Prose, published in 1983, is a compilation of Alice Walker's 36 writings, including essays, articles, and speeches, spanning from 1966 to 1982. These works reflect her interpretation of "**womanist**" theory, a term she explains as a black feminist or feminist of color, emphasizing a love and appreciation for women's culture and the commitment to the survival and wholeness of all people. Walker's collection illustrates the depth and diversity of womanist thought, paralleling feminist shades as purple does to lavender.

Elaine Showalter, born on January 21, 1941, has been a pivotal figure in American literary and feminist discourse, particularly through her development of "**gynocritics**," which focuses on the study of women as writers. In her seminal work "**Towards a Feminist Poetics,**" Showalter outlines the evolution of women's literature into three distinct phases:

1.   **The Feminine phase from 1840–1880,**
2.   **The Feminist phase from 1880–1920, and**
3.   **The Female phase from 1920 onwards.**

Her Ph.D. thesis, "The Double Critical Standard: Criticism of Women Writers in England, 1845–1880," expanded into **"A Literature of Their Own: British Women Novelists from Brontë to Lessing" in 1978**, offers an in-depth exploration of these phases with a notable analysis of Virginia Woolf.

***The Madwoman in the Attic: The Woman Writer and the Nineteenth-Century Literary Imagination* is a 1979** book by Sandra Gilbert and Susan Gubar, in which they examine Victorian literature from a feminist perspective. Gilbert and Gubar draw their title from Charlotte Brontë's Jane Eyre, in which Rochester's wife (née Bertha Mason) is kept secretly locked in an attic apartment by her husband.

George Eliot (1819-1880)

> **George Eliot** was the pen name of **Mary Ann Evans**.
> Known for **realism** and **psychological insights** in novels.
> Born **22 November 1819** in **Warwickshire**, England.

- ➤ Left school in **1836** after her mother's death.
- ➤ Moved to **Coventry** in **1841** with her father.
- ➤ After his death in **1849**, she traveled in **Europe**.
- ➤ Became editor of the **Westminster Review** in **1850**.
- ➤ Met **George Henry Lewes**, lived with him till his death.
- ➤ Their relationship caused a **scandal**; friends shunned her.
- ➤ Encouraged by **Lewes**, she began **writing fiction**.
- ➤ **'Scenes of Clerical Life'** (1856) published in **Blackwood's Magazine**.
- ➤ *Scenes of Clerical Life* is George Eliot's first published work of fiction, is an 1858 collection of three short stories
- ➤ First novel, **'Adam Bede'** (1859), achieved great success.
- ➤ Used **male pen name** for literary credibility.
- ➤ Other novels: **'The Mill on the Floss'** (1860), **'Silas Marner'** (1861).
- ➤ **'Romola'** (1863), **'Middlemarch'** (1872), **'Daniel Deronda'** (1876).
- ➤ **Popularity** brought **social acceptance** among intellectuals.
- ➤ After **Lewes' death**, she married **John Cross**.
- ➤ Cross was **20 years younger** than Eliot.
- ➤ Eliot died on **22 December 1880** in London.
- ➤ Buried at **Highgate Cemetery**, north London.
- ➤ **Novels:**
  - ○ *Adam Bede, 1859*
  - ○ *The Mill on the Floss, 1860*
  - ○ *Silas Marner, 1861*
  - ○ *Romola, 1863*
  - ○ *Felix Holt, the Radical, 1866*
  - ○ *Middlemarch, 1871–72*
  - ○ *Daniel Deronda, 1876*

Adam Bede, 1859

- ➤ Published in **three volumes** in 1859.
- ➤ The title character, **a carpenter, is in love** with an unmarried woman
- ➤ **She bears a child by another man.**
- ➤ Eliot described the work as *"a country story—full of the breath of cows and the scent of hay."*
- ➤ Derbyshire dialect.
- ➤ Follows **four characters** in the fictional community of **Hayslope**.
- ➤ The novel revolves around a love "rectangle"
- ➤ The beautiful but self-absorbed **Hetty Sorrel;**

- ➤ Captain **Arthur Donnithorne**, the young squire who seduces her;
- ➤ **Adam Bede**, her **unacknowledged suitor;**
- ➤ **Dinah Morris, Hetty's cousin**, a fervent, virtuous and lay preacher.
- ➤ **Adam Bede**, a skilled carpenter, loves **Hetty Sorrel** deeply.
- ➤ **Hetty**, vain and beautiful, dreams of **wealth and status**.
- ➤ **Arthur Donnithorne**, a squire's grandson, attracts Hetty's attention.
- ➤ Hetty becomes **pregnant** by Arthur, leading to tragedy.
- ➤ Abandoned by Arthur, **Hetty faces severe consequences**.
- ➤ **Dinah Morris**, a Methodist preacher, comforts Hetty compassionately.
- ➤ **Adam and Dinah** eventually fall in love and marry.

The Mill on the Floss, 1860

- ➤ Published in **three volumes** in 1860.
- ➤ **Maggie Tulliver** to adapt to her provincial world.
- ➤ Her brother **Tom Tulliver**.
- ➤ Spanning a period of 10 to 15 years.
- ➤ Set in **Dorlcote Mill on the River Floss**.
- ➤ Near the village of **St Ogg's in Lincolnshire**, England.
- ➤ The story follows siblings **Maggie and Tom Tulliver**.
- ➤ Their father, Mr. Tulliver, owns **Dorlcote Mill**.
- ➤ Mr. Tulliver's lawsuit causes **financial ruin** for the family.
- ➤ Maggie and Tom lose **Dorlcote Mill** due to debts.
- ➤ Tom, a strict and practical person, resents Maggie.
- ➤ Maggie, imaginative and passionate, struggles with **society's rules**.
- ➤ "Childhood has no forebodings; but then, it is soothed by no memories."
- ➤ Maggie forms a bond with **Philip Wakem**, Mr. Tulliver's enemy's son.
- ➤ Tom forbids Maggie from seeing **Philip Wakem**.
- ➤ Mr. Tulliver dies after a bitter struggle with bankruptcy.
- ➤ Maggie finds herself torn between **duty and love**.
- ➤ She briefly considers a relationship with **Stephen Guest**.
- ➤ Stephen's influence conflicts with **Maggie's moral ideals**.
- ➤ "I am not resigned: I am not sure that life is long enough to learn that lesson."
- ➤ Maggie chooses to honor her family over **personal happiness**.
- ➤ Tom and Maggie reunite after **family disputes**.
- ➤ A massive flood overtakes **St. Ogg's** and the river.
- ➤ Maggie rows to save Tom; both perish in the flood.

- ➤ "In their death they were not divided."
- ➤ *The Mill on the Floss* explores **family, sacrifice, and social conflict.**

Silas Marner, 1861

- ➤ **Full**: *Silas Marner: The Weaver of Raveloe.*
- ➤ Title character is a **friendless weaver** who cares only for his **cache of gold.**

Romola, 1863

- ➤ Set in the **fifteenth century.**
- ➤ It is *"a deep study of life in the city of Florence from an intellectual, artistic, religious, and social point of view".*
- ➤ The novel first appeared in **fourteen parts published in Cornhill Magazine.**

Felix Holt, the Radical, 1866

- ➤ **A social novel.**
- ➤ Political disputes in a small English town during the **First Reform Act of 1832.**
- ➤ The novel is set in England in the early 1830s.

Middlemarch, 1871–72

- ➤ *Middlemarch, A Study of Provincial Life.*
- ➤ Set in Middlemarch, a fictional **English Midland town**, from 1829 to 1832.
- ➤ **Set in provincial town of Middlemarch, England** – explores social dynamics.
- ➤ **Dorothea Brooke**, idealistic, desires purpose and meaningful work. *"It is a narrow mind which cannot look at a subject from various points of view."*
- ➤ Marries **Reverend Casaubon**, hoping for intellectual partnership.
- ➤ **Casaubon is cold, controlling**, leaving Dorothea unfulfilled. *"Marriage, which should be a state of peace, is full of care."*
- ➤ **Tertius Lydgate**, ambitious doctor, struggles with town's conservative values.
- ➤ Lydgate marries **Rosamond Vincy**, who is shallow and materialistic.

- ➤ **Money and ambition** strain Lydgate and Rosamond's marriage. *"People glorify all sorts of bravery except the bravery they might show on behalf of their nearest neighbors."*
- ➤ **Bulstrode**, banker, hides a dark past, leading to his downfall.
- ➤ Dorothea, after Casaubon's death, finds love with **Will Ladislaw**.
- ➤ **Themes of morality, ambition, and social change** throughout. *"For the growing good of the world is partly dependent on unhistoric acts."*

Daniel Deronda, 1876

- ➤ Published in **eight parts in 1876**.
- ➤ Notable for exposing **Victorian anti-Semitism** and societal biases.
- ➤ Contrasts **Mirah Cohen**, a poor Jew, with **Gwendolen Harleth**.
- ➤ **Daniel**, after learning he's Jewish, marries Mirah.
- ➤ **Daniel departs for Palestine** to support Jewish homeland efforts.
- ➤ The **Cohen family portrayal** received praise from Jewish readers.
- ➤ **Gwendolen's character analysis** is Eliot's critical triumph.

Questions

Question 88

Match List - I with List - II.

List - I (Original name)	List - II (Penname / Pseudonym)
A. Charles Lutwidge Dodgson	I. George Eliot
B. Mary Ann Evans	II. Mark Twain
C. Eric Arthur Blair	III. George Orwell
D. Samuel Langhorne Clemens	IV. Lewis Carroll

Choose the correct answer from the options given below :

    (1) A-IV, B-I, C-III, D-II.
    (2) A-III, B-IV, C-II, D-I
    (3) A-I, B-II, C-III, D-IV
    (4) A-II, B-I, C-III, D-IV

Explanations:
Answer: (1) A-IV, B-I, C-III, D-II.

A. Charles Lutwidge Dodgson → IV. Lewis Carroll
(Lewis Carroll is the pseudonym of Charles Lutwidge Dodgson, famous for *Alice's Adventures in Wonderland*.)

B. Mary Ann Evans → I. George Eliot
(George Eliot is the pen name of Mary Ann Evans, known for *Middlemarch* and *Silas Marner*.)

C. Eric Arthur Blair → III. George Orwell
(George Orwell is the pen name of Eric Arthur Blair, known for *1984* and *Animal Farm*.)

D. Samuel Langhorne Clemens → II. Mark Twain
(Mark Twain is the pen name of Samuel Langhorne Clemens, known for *The Adventures of Tom Sawyer* and *The Adventures of Huckleberry Finn*.)

Which two of the following were published in the year 1859?

    (A) On the Origin of Species
    (B) A Tale of Two Cities
    (C) Alice in Wonderland
    (D) Silas Marner

Choose the correct answer from the options given below:

1. (A) and (B) Only
2. (B) and (C) Only
3. (A) and (C) Only
4. (B) and (D) Only

Explanations:
Answer: 1. (A) and (B) Only
(A) On the Origin of Species: Written by Charles Darwin, this groundbreaking scientific work was published in 1859. It presented the theory of evolution through natural selection, revolutionizing our understanding of the natural world and human origins.

(B) A Tale of Two Cities: Penned by Charles Dickens, this historical novel was published in 1859. Set against the backdrop of the French Revolution, it explores themes of sacrifice, love, and social injustice, becoming one of

Dickens' most celebrated works.

(C) Alice in Wonderland: Written by Lewis Carroll (pseudonym of Charles Lutwidge Dodgson), this whimsical and imaginative novel was published in 1865. It takes readers on a surreal journey through a fantastical world, captivating both children and adults with its nonsensical characters and surreal adventures.

(D) Silas Marner: Authored by George Eliot (pen name of Mary Ann Evans), this novel was published in 1861. It tells the story of a reclusive weaver and his transformation through love and the arrival of a young child, exploring themes of redemption, community, and human connections.

Question 90

Which one is correctly matched?

1.   Heathcliff — Mansfield Park
2.   **Maggie Tulliver — The Mill on the Floss**
3.   Josiah Bounderby — Wuthering Height
4.   Fanny Price — Hard Times

Correct Explanations:
1. Heathcliff is a fictional character in Emily Brontë's 1847 novel Wuthering Heights. Owing to the novel's enduring fame and popularity, he is often regarded as an archetype of the tortured antihero whose all-consuming rage, jealousy and anger destroy both him and those around him; in short, the Byronic hero.

2. The Mill on the Floss, novel by George Eliot, published in three volumes in 1860. It sympathetically portrays the vain efforts of Maggie Tulliver to adapt to her provincial world. The tragedy of her plight is underlined by the actions of her brother Tom, whose sense of family honour leads him to forbid her to associate with the one friend who appreciates her intelligence and imagination. When she is caught in a compromising situation, Tom renounces her altogether, but brother and sister are reconciled in the end as they try in vain to survive a climactic flood.

3. Josiah Bounderby, fictional character, a wealthy businessman in Charles Dickens's novel Hard Times (1854). Bounderby uses everyone around him to further his own interests. He keeps the existence of his mother a secret as he perpetuates the myth that he began life as an orphan who had to struggle to survive and to establish himself.

4. Frances "Fanny" Price (named after her mother) is the heroine in Jane Austen's 1814 novel, Mansfield Park. The novel begins when Fanny's overburdened, impoverished family--where she is both the second-born and the eldest daughter out of 10 children--sends her at the age of ten to live in the household of her wealthy uncle, Sir Thomas Bertram, and his family at Mansfield Park. The novel follows her growth and development, concluding in early adulthood.

Question 91

Adam in Adam Bede of George Eliot is a

1. Mason
2. Teacher
3. Carpenter
4. Doctor

Explanations
Answer: 3. Carpenter

Adam Bede is a novel written **by George Eliot** and published in three volumes in 1859. Set in the countryside, the story revolves around the title character, **a skilled carpenter,** who falls in love with an unmarried woman. Despite his efforts to support her when she becomes pregnant with another man's child, he ultimately loses her. However, Adam Bede eventually discovers happiness with another person.

Regarded as George Eliot's first major novel, Adam Bede is a vivid portrayal of rural life. Eliot's attention to detail, including the authentic depiction of the Derbyshire dialect, introduced a new level of realism to English fiction. The novel exemplifies a unique blend of profound empathy for its characters and a firm moral stance, reflecting Eliot's ability to combine compassion with rigorous moral judgement.

Other Explanations

Jude the Obscure is a novel by Thomas Hardy, which began as a magazine serial in December 1894 and was first published in book form in 1895 (though the title page says 1896). It is Hardy's last completed novel. **The protagonist, Jude Fawley, is a working-class young man; he is a stonemason who dreams of becoming a scholar.** The other main character is his cousin, Sue Bridehead, who is also his central love interest. The novel is concerned in particular with issues of class, education, religion, morality and marriage.

Question 92

Match List I with List II

List I	List II
A. George Meredith	I. The Virginians
B. George Eliot	II. Scenes of Clerical Life
C. Charlotte Bronte	III. Evan Harrington
D. William Makepeace Thackeray	IV. The Professor

Choose the correct answer from the options given below:

1. A-III, B-I, C-IV. D-I
2. A-IV. B-III. C-I. D-II
3. A-I. B-II, ONII, D-IV
4. A-II, B-I, C-1V, D-III

Explanations
Answer: 1. A-III, B-I, C-IV. D-I

A. "Evan Harrington" is a glowing Victorian comedy written by George Meredith in 1861. Loosely inspired by his own life, the novel revolves around the social climbing family of the late tailor, Melchisedec Harrington.

B. George Eliot's debut work of fiction, "Scenes of Clerical Life," comprises three short stories first published in Blackwood's Magazine. Released under her famous pseudonym in 1856, Eliot was already a renowned figure in Victorian intellectual circles, known for her contributions to The Westminster Review and translations of theological works.

C. "The Professor, A Tale," Charlotte Brontë's first novel, was written before "Jane Eyre" but faced rejection from several publishing houses. Published posthumously in 1857 with the approval of her widower, Arthur Bell Nicholls, the novel was reviewed and edited by him.

D. William Makepeace Thackeray's historical novel "The Virginians: A Tale of the Last Century" (1857–59) serves as a sequel to his work "Henry Esmond" and is loosely connected to "Pendennis."

Arrange the chronological sequence in which the following works were published:

> A. Jane Eyre
> B. A Tale of Two Cities
> C. Middlemarch
> D. The Return of the Native
> E. The Newcomes

Choose the correct answer from the following options:

> 1. A. B, C. D, E
> 2. A. E, B, C. D
> 3. B. A. C, E, D
> 4. B, C. A. D. E

Explanations:
Answer: 2. A, E, B, C, D

Jane Eyre is a novel written by Charlotte Brontë and first published in 1847 under the pseudonym Currer Bell. The story follows the life of Jane Eyre and is presented as her autobiography.

The Newcomes is a novel by William Makepeace Thackeray, initially published in 24 instalments from 1853 to 1855 as The Newcomes: Memoirs of a Most Respectable Family. The story is narrated by "Arthur Pendennis, Esq." and revolves around the lives of the Newcome family. It was later released as a book in two volumes in 1854-55.

A Tale of Two Cities is a novel by Charles Dickens, originally published in 1859 both in serial and book form. Set during the French Revolution, the story depicts the social and political turmoil of the late 18th century.

Middlemarch, also known as Middlemarch: A Study of Provincial Life, is a novel by George Eliot (the pseudonym of Mary Ann Evans). It was published in eight parts in 1871-72 and later compiled into four volumes in 1872. The narrative explores various characters and their lives in a provincial town.

The Return of the Native is a novel by Thomas Hardy, published in 1878. It is set on Egdon Heath, a fictional barren moor in Wessex, England. The story revolves around Clym Yeobright, who returns to the area after a career as a jeweller in Paris to become a schoolmaster.

Question 94

Arrange the following literary texts in the chronological sequence:

    A. Middlemarch
    B. The Good Soldier
    C. Night and Day
    D. A Passage to India
    E. Heart of Darkness

Choose the correct answer from the options given below:

    1.   A,E,D,B,C
    2.   A,C,D,B,E
    3.   A,B,C,D,E
    4.   A,D,B,C,E

Explanations:
Answer: 3. A,B,C,D,E

Middlemarch, by George Eliot, was serialized in 1871–72 and bound in four volumes in 1872, becoming Eliot's most lauded novel. This realist narrative dissects societal classes in Middlemarch, focusing especially on Dorothea Brooke and Tertius Lydgate, whose lofty aspirations lead to disastrous marriages.

Heart of Darkness, a 1899 novella by Joseph Conrad, narrates Charles Marlow's assignment as a steamer captain in the African interior for a Belgian company, critiquing European colonialism in Africa and exploring power and morality. The Congo River setting reflects the exploitation under King Leopold II's rule, centering on the enigmatic ivory trader Kurtz.

The Good Soldier, a 1915 novel by Ford Madox Ford, portrays the tragic tale of John Dowell and his wife Florence, whose heart condition necessitates a life spent at European health resorts, unraveling the complexities of their relationship and the illusions of their social circle.

Night and Day, Virginia Woolf's 1919 novel set in Edwardian London, contrasts Katharine Hilbery and Mary Datchet's lives and romantic entanglements, delving into themes of love, marriage, happiness, and the quest for fulfillment.

A Passage to India, published in 1924 by E.M. Forster, critically examines the underpinnings of racism and colonialism in British India, alongside Forster's recurring motif of the dichotomy between living a life connected to the earth versus one of intellectualism.

Thomas Hardy (1840-1928)

- **Thomas Hardy** was born in **Dorset** in 1840 and died in 1928.
- Hardy's **father** was a **fiddler and stonemason**, and his **mother** was influential.
- Dorset's **rural life** influenced Hardy's **fiction** and **poetry** deeply.
- Hardy identified with **Dorset** and saw himself as a successor to **William Barnes**.
- His novels, called **Wessex Novels**, use a map of fictional **Wessex**.
- Hardy was drawn to **history** and explored **ancient ruins** and **Napoleonic Wars**.
- His **poetical drama** _The Dynasts_ reflects his lifelong interest in history.
- Many writers visited Hardy, including **Yeats, Sassoon, and Woolf**.
- Hardy's **war poems** addressed the **Boer War** and **World War I**.
- His work influenced **war poets** like **Sassoon** and **Rupert Brooke**.

- Hardy's life spanned **Victorian** and **modern** eras; he held a **bleak worldview**.
- Hardy's novels often met with **criticism** for their **sexual themes** and **bleak outlook**.
- Key novels include **Tess of the D'Urbervilles** and **Jude the Obscure**.
- Hardy turned to **poetry** in 1898 after facing **negative reviews** for his novels.
- He published around **one thousand poems** in his lifetime.
- His poetic drama, *The Dynasts*, explored **"evolutionary meliorism"**.
- Hardy's **lyric poetry** is his most famous and enduring work.
- **Influential** poets like **Frost** and **Auden** admired his poetry.
- Hardy's poetry often reflects **fatalism** and **bleak themes**.
- His **Emma poems** were inspired by the death of his wife.
- These **Emma poems** are regarded as celebrations of **loss and grief**.
- Hardy had **relationships** with younger women; remarried **Florence Dugdale**.
- Critics often describe Hardy's **poetry** as **gloomy and intense**.
- Hardy's **musical language** is noted for its **transcendence**.
- Scholars now appreciate Hardy's **poetry** as part of **Modernism**.
- His works remain **controversial**, needing constant **reassessment**.
- **Virginia Woolf** saw Hardy's work as a **visionary exploration** of life.
- Hardy's **ashes** rest in **Westminster Abbey**; his **heart** at Stinsford Church.

Notable Works

- *The Poor Man and the Lady (1867, unpublished and lost)*
- *Under the Greenwood Tree: A Rural Painting of the Dutch School (1872)*
- *Far from the Madding Crowd (1874)*
- *Desperate Remedies: A Novel (1871)*
- *A Pair of Blue Eyes: A Novel (1873)*
- *The Hand of Ethelberta: A Comedy in Chapters (1876)*
- *The Return of the Native (1878)*
- *A Laodicean: A Story of To-day (1881)*
- *The Trumpet-Major (1880)*
- *Two on a Tower: A Romance (1882)*
- *The Mayor of Casterbridge: The Life and Death of a Man of Character (1886)*
- *The Woodlanders (1887)*

- *Wessex Tales (1888, a collection of short stories)*
- *Tess of the d'Urbervilles: A Pure Woman Faithfully Presented (1891)*
- *Life's Little Ironies (1894, a collection of short stories)*
- *Jude the Obscure (1895)*
- *Wessex Poems (1898)*
  - *Valenciennes*
- *Poems of the Past and the Present in 1901*
  - *The Darkling Thrush (originally titled "The Century's End")*
  - *The Dead Drummer*

Far From the Madding Crowd (1874)

- Hardy's **fourth** novel and his first major literary success.
- Monthly serial in **Cornhill Magazine**.
- The novel is set in Thomas Hardy's **Wessex** in rural southwest England.
- **Bathsheba Everdene** inherits her uncle's large farm.
- She captures **Gabriel Oak's heart,** but **rejects** him.
- Bathsheba later meets and attracts **Sergeant Troy**.
- Troy, charming but unreliable, **wins Bathsheba's affection**.
- Her other admirer, **William Boldwood, proposes unsuccessfully.**
- **Troy marries Bathsheba, then gambles and leaves her.**
- Troy is presumed dead, but reappears unexpectedly.
- **Boldwood**, distraught over **Troy, kills him** impulsively.
- **Boldwood is imprisoned; Gabriel supports Bathsheba** throughout.
- **Bathsheba realizes her love for Gabriel and marries him.**

The Return of the Native (1878)

- Thomas Hardy's **sixth** published novel.
- It first appeared in **Belgravia**.
- **Set on Egdon Heath**, the novel explores nature's power.
- **Clym Yeobright returns home**, seeking a meaningful life.
- **Eustacia Vye**, passionate and restless, dreams of escape.
- **Tragic misunderstandings and fate** lead to suffering and loss.
- Hardy presents themes of **love, isolation, and destiny**.

The Mayor of the Casterbridge (1886)

- First serially (in the periodical **The Graphic**) and later that year in book form.

- ➤ **Michael Henchard drunkenly sells wife and child at a fair**.
- ➤ Henchard **becomes a successful grain merchant in Casterbridge**.
- ➤ He swears an oath to **avoid alcohol for 21 years**.
- ➤ His wife, **Susan, and daughter, Elizabeth-Jane**, return years later.
- ➤ Henchard's past mistakes and rival **Farfrae haunt him**.
- ➤ **Farfrae** gains popularity and eventually **replaces Henchard as mayor**.
- ➤ Henchard's life spirals, leading to isolation and poverty.
- ➤ **He dies alon**e, with his only request unfulfilled.

Tess of the D'Urbervilles (1891)

- ➤ *Tess of the d'Urbervilles: A Pure Woman Faithfully Presented*.
- ➤ Published in *The Graphic* in 1891.
- ➤ Thomas Hardy's fictional Wessex.
- ➤ **Tess Durbeyfield** learns she may be **nobility**.
- ➤ Her father's discovery of **D'Urberville ancestry** sparks hope.
- ➤ Tess meets **Alec D'Urberville**, who **seduces her**.
- ➤ **Alec's betrayal** leaves Tess feeling **shamed and isolated**.
- ➤ She returns home, bearing **guilt and sorrow**.
- ➤ Tess gives birth to a **child**, who soon dies.
- ➤ Child's name **was Sorrow**.
- ➤ **To escape her past**, Tess seeks work as a **dairymaid**.
- ➤ She meets **Angel Clare** at **Talbothays Dairy**.
- ➤ Angel falls in love with Tess's **innocence** and **beauty**.
- ➤ **Tess and Angel** marry, but she reveals her **past**.
- ➤ **Angel rejects her**, blaming her for **Alec's sin**.
- ➤ After rejecting Tess, **Angel Clare** turns to **Izz Huett**.
- ➤ **Izz stays loyal, reminding Angel of Tess's love**.
- ➤ Tess faces hardship, as Angel leaves **for Brazil**.
- ➤ **Alec reappears** and persuades Tess to **return to him**.
- ➤ Angel returns, realizing his **mistake and love**.
- ➤ Tess, devastated, **kills Alec** in a fit of **rage**.
- ➤ She reunites with Angel and **flees with him**.
- ➤ Tess and Angel hide at an **ancient stone circle**.
- ➤ **Police arrest Tess**, who peacefully **surrenders**.
- ➤ Tess is tried and **sentenced to death**.
- ➤ She is **executed**; Angel mourns her **tragic fate**.

Jude the Obscure (1895)

- ➢ Hardy's **last** completed novel.
- ➢ **An abridged form in Harper's New Monthly**
- ➢ **Jude Fawley, is a working-class young man, a stonemason who dreams of becoming a scholar.**
- ➢ **Jude Fawley**, a poor stonemason, dreams of **higher education.**
- ➢ His ambitions lead him to **Christminster** (based on Oxford).
- ➢ Jude marries **Arabella** but later separates from her.
- ➢ He meets and falls for **cousin Sue Bridehead.**
- ➢ Jude and Sue struggle against **societal norms** and restrictions.
- ➢ Tragedy strikes when **Jude's children** face a horrific fate.
- ➢ The novel critiques **class, marriage, and social oppression.**

The Darkling Thrush

- ➢ **"The Darkling Thrush"** is a poem by **Thomas Hardy.**
- ➢ Originally titled **"By the Century's Deathbed,"** first published in 1900.
- ➢ Later published in **London Times** on **1 January 1901.**
- ➢ Manuscript suggests it may have been written in **1899.**
- ➢ Included in **Poems of the Past and Present (1901).**
- ➢ First two stanzas depict a **bleak winter landscape** at dusk.
- ➢ Describes the **lifelessness** felt in the **winter setting.**
- ➢ In stanza three, an **"aged thrush"** sings joyfully.
- ➢ The bird's song is an **"evensong of joy illimited."**
- ➢ Final stanza ponders bird's **"blessed Hope"** unknown to speaker.
- ➢ **"Darkling"** recalls **Matthew Arnold's "Dover Beach"** on faith loss.
- ➢ The poem contrasts **despair** with the **thrush's hopeful song.**

Questions

Read the following extract and answer the questions:

"Justice' was done, and the President of the Immortals, in Aeschylean phrase, had ended his sport with Tess. And the D'Urberville knights and dames slept on in their tombs, unknowing. The two speechless gazers bent themselves down to the earth as if in prayer and remained thus a long time, absolutely motionless; the flag continued to wave silently. As soon as they had enough strength, they arose, joined hands again, and went on."

Thomas Hardy, *Tess of the D'Urbervilles*

Question 95

How did the 'sport with Tess' end?

1. **She was hanged.**
2. She was expelled from Wintoncester.
3. The tormentor married her.
4. She died an untimely death.

Correct Explanations:
The extract suggests that the 'sport with Tess' has ended because 'Justice' has been done by someone referred to as the President of the Immortals. It is not specified how Tess met her end, but it can be inferred that she has died.

Question 96

Who are the 'two speechless gazers'?

1. Reverend James Clare and Mrs Brooks
2. **'Liza Lu and Angel Clare**
3. Tess's two parents
4. Parson Tringham and Mrs. d'Urberville

Correct Explanations:
The extract refers to the 'two speechless gazers' who are not explicitly named. However, based on the context of the novel, it is likely that they are Angel Clare and Liza-Lu, Tess's younger sister.

Question 97

"So the baby was carried in a small deal box, under an ancient woman's shawl, to the churchyard that night, and buried by lantern-light, at the cost of a shilling, and a pint of beer to the sexton, in that shabby corner of God's allotment where He lets the nettles grow, and where all unbaptized infants, notorious drunkard, suicides and others of the conjecturally damned are laid."

From which novel is this excerpt taken?

1. Wuthering Heights by Emily Bronte
2. Tess by Thomas Hardy
3. Great Expectations by Charles Dickens
4. Mill on the Floss by George Eliot

Explanations:
Ans: Tess by Thomas Hardy.

This passage from Thomas Hardy's *Tess of the d'Urbervilles* describes the tragic fate of Tess's unnamed child, who is born out of wedlock and dies soon after birth. The child is buried in a pauper's grave in a neglected corner of the churchyard, where the grass is allowed to grow wild and the graves are unmarked. The passage highlights the social stigma attached to illegitimacy in Victorian England, as well as the callousness with which the poor and marginalized were often treated by society. It also reflects Hardy's preoccupation with the themes of fate, tragedy, and the harsh realities of life in rural England.

Extra Perk:

All of the novels mentioned have prominent child characters:

In "Wuthering Heights," the sickly child is named Linton Heathcliff, the son of Isabella Linton and Heathcliff. He is depicted as weak, selfish, and cowardly, in contrast to the wild and passionate characters of his parents, Catherine and Heathcliff.

In "Tess of the d'Urbervilles," Tess's son, Sorrow, is a major character who has a significant impact on Tess's life and the novel's plot.

In "Great Expectations," the protagonist Pip is a child at the beginning of the novel, and his experiences as a young boy shape his later life and relationships.

In "The Mill on the Floss," the main character, Maggie Tulliver, is a child at the beginning of the novel, and her childhood experiences and relationships with her family members are central to the story's themes of family, education, and societal expectations.

Important Quotes

***Wuthering Heights* by Emily Bronte:**

➤ *"Whatever our souls are made of, his and mine are the same."*
➤ *"He's more myself than I am. Whatever our souls are made of, his and mine are the same."*
➤ *"I have not broken your heart - you have broken it; and in breaking it, you have broken mine."*

Tess by Thomas Hardy:

➤ *"Why didn't you tell me there was danger? Why didn't you warn me? Ladies know what to guard against, because they read novels that tell them of these tricks."*
➤ *"I have heard that women love men even for their vices," he said. "But I think they love them best for their virtues: they forgive everything when they love."*
➤ *"It is difficult for a woman to define her feelings in language which is chiefly made by men to express theirs."*

***Great Expectations* by Charles Dickens:**

➤ *"I loved her against reason, against promise, against peace, against hope, against happiness, against all discouragement that could be."*
➤ *"Suffering has been stronger than all other teaching, and has taught me to understand what your heart used to be. I have been bent and broken, but - I hope - into a better shape."*
➤ *"We need never be ashamed of our tears."*

Mill on the Floss by George Eliot:

➤ *"Life seems to go on without effort when I am filled with music."*
➤ *"I think I should have no other mortal wants, if I could always have plenty of music. It seems to infuse strength into my limbs and ideas into my brain. Life seems to go on without effort, when I am filled with music."*
➤ *"A difference of taste in jokes is a great strain on the affections."*

Question 98

Arrange the correct chronological sequence in which the following texts were published:

A. Tess of the D'Urbervilles
B. Kim
C. The Old Wives Tale
D. The Time Machine.
E. A Portrait of the Artist as a Young Man

Choose the correct answer from the options given below

1. A, D, B, C, E
2. D, A, C, B, E
3. B, D, A, C, E
4. A, C, B, E, D

Explanations
Answer: 1. A, D, B, C, E

A. *Tess of the d'Urbervilles* **is a novel by Thomas Hardy, first published in serialised form in the Graphic from July to December 1891** and later in book form in the same year. The novel was subtitled "A Pure Woman Faithfully Presented" as Hardy believed its protagonist to be a virtuous victim of the strict Victorian moral code.

D. *The Time Machine* **is the first novel by H. G. Wells, published in book form in 1895.** Regarded as one of the earliest works of science fiction, it is considered the progenitor of the "time travel" subgenre.

B. *Kim* **is a novel by Rudyard Kipling, published in 1901.** It follows the adventures of an Irish orphan in India who becomes a disciple of a Tibetan monk while learning espionage from the British secret service. The book stands out for its vivid and nostalgic portrayal of Indian culture, particularly the exotic aspects of street life.

C. *The Old Wives' Tale* **is a novel by Arnold Bennett, published in 1908.** A masterpiece of literary realism, it delves into the changes that time brings to the lives of two English sisters during the 19th century.

E. *A Portrait of the Artist as a Young Man* is an autobiographical novel by James Joyce, serialised in The Egoist in 1914–15 and published in book form in 1916. Widely regarded as one of the greatest bildungsromans in the English language, the novel depicts the early years of Stephen Dedalus, who reappears as a key character in Joyce's later work, Ulysses (1922).

Question 99

Which of the novelists have been correctly matched with their works?

A. Thomas Hardy - The Return of the Native
B. Charles Dickens - The History of Henry Esmond
C. Virginia Woolf - Mrs. Dalloway
D. George Eliot - Northanger Abbey
E. Charlotte Bronte - The Professor

Choose the correct answer from the options given below:

1. C, D and B
2. A. C and E
3. B. C and D
4. C, D and E

Explanations:
Answer: 4. A. C and E

"The Return of the Native" by Thomas Hardy (1878): A tragic novel set in Wessex, exploring themes of love, desire, and the clash between nature and society.

"The History of Henry Esmond" by William Makepeace Thackeray (1852): A historical novel tracing the life of the eponymous protagonist through the late 17th and early 18th centuries in England.

"Mrs. Dalloway" by Virginia Woolf (1925): A modernist novel set in a single day in post-World War I London, delving into the thoughts and experiences of its characters, particularly the titular Mrs. Dalloway.

"Northanger Abbey" by Jane Austen (1817): A satirical novel following the adventures of Catherine Morland as she navigates her way through society and the pitfalls of Gothic literature.

"The Professor" by Charlotte Bronte (1857): Bronte's debut novel, originally written before "Jane Eyre," tells the story of William Crimsworth, a young Englishman who becomes a professor in Brussels and experiences love and adversity.

Question 100

Find the chronological order of Thomas Hardy's poetry publications:

    A. "Channel Firing"
    B. "The Darkling Thrush"
    C. "In Time of the Breaking of Nations"
    D. "He Never Expected Much"
    E. "A Trampwoman's Tragedy"

Choose the correct answer from the options given below:

    1. A, B.C, D, E
    2. B, E, A, C, D
    3. C, D, E, B, A
    4. D, B. C. A, E

Explanations:
Answer: 2. B, E, A, C, D

"The Darkling Thrush" is a poem by Thomas Hardy, originally titled "By the Century's Deathbed." It was published in The Graphic on 29 December **1900** and later in the London Times on 1 January 1901. The poem may have been written in 1899. It was included in the collection Poems of the Past and the Present (1901).

"A Trampwoman's Tragedy" is a narrative poem of 104 lines, published in 1903. Hardy held this poem in high regard and considered it one of his most successful works.

"Channel Firing," published in May 1914, shortly before World War I, is regarded as one of Hardy's best and most popular poems. Inspired by gunnery practice on the south coast of England during the war preparations, the poem accurately predicts the devastation of the upcoming conflict.

Hardy also wrote significant war poems related to the Boer Wars and World War I, including "Drummer Hodge," "In Time of 'The Breaking of Nations'," and "The Man He Killed." These poems had a profound influence on other war poets such as Rupert Brooke and Siegfried Sassoon.

"He Never Expected Much" was published in The Daily Telegraph on 19 March 1928, after Hardy's death. It was included in the posthumous volume Winter Words. The poem reflects on the ups and downs of life and the inevitability of its end, allowing readers to find their own experiences and truths within its words.

Question 101

Arrange the following novels in chronological order of publication:

    A. Jude the Obscure
    B. Tess of the D'Urbervilles
    C. Under the Greenwood Tree
    D. A Pair of Blue Eyes
    E. Far From the Madding Crowd

Choose the correct answer from the options given below:

    1. C, D, E. B and A
    2. D, E, A, C and B
    3. E. A, C. D and B
    4. A. B. C, D and E

Explanations:
Answer: 1. C, D, E. B and A

Here is the list of novels by Thomas Hardy arranged in chronological order:

    ➢ Desperate Remedies: A Novel (1871)

> **Under the Greenwood Tree: A Rural Painting of the Dutch School (1872)**
> **A Pair of Blue Eyes: A Novel (1873)**
> **Far from the Madding Crowd (1874)**
> The Hand of Ethelberta: A Comedy in Chapters (1876)
> The Return of the Native (1878)
> The Trumpet-Major (1880)
> A Laodicean: A Story of To-day (1881)
> Two on a Tower: A Romance (1882)
> The Mayor of Casterbridge: The Life and Death of a Man of Character (1886)
> The Woodlanders (1887)
> Wessex Tales (1888, a collection of short stories)
> **Tess of the d'Urbervilles: A Pure Woman Faithfully Presented (1891)**
> A Group of Noble Dames (1891, a collection of short stories)
> **Jude the Obscure (1895)**

Please note that "The Poor Man and the Lady" is listed as unpublished and lost, so it is not included in the chronological order.

Question 102

Arrange the chronological sequence in which the following works were published:

A. Jane Eyre
B. A Tale of Two Cities
C. Middlemarch
D. The Return of the Native
E. The Newcomes

Choose the correct answer from the following options:

1. A. B, C. D, E
2. A. E, B, C. D
3. B. A. C, E, D
4. B, C. A. D. E

Explanations:

Answer: 2. A, E, B, C, D

Jane Eyre is a novel written by Charlotte Brontë and first published in 1847 under the pseudonym Currer Bell. The story follows the life of Jane Eyre and is presented as her autobiography.

The Newcomes is a novel by William Makepeace Thackeray, initially published in 24 instalments from 1853 to 1855 as The Newcomes: Memoirs of a Most Respectable Family. The story is narrated by "Arthur Pendennis, Esq." and revolves around the lives of the Newcome family. It was later released as a book in two volumes in 1854-55.

A Tale of Two Cities is a novel by Charles Dickens, originally published in 1859 both in serial and book form. Set during the French Revolution, the story depicts the social and political turmoil of the late 18th century.

Middlemarch, also known as Middlemarch: A Study of Provincial Life, is a novel by George Eliot (the pseudonym of Mary Ann Evans). It was published in eight parts in 1871-72 and later compiled into four volumes in 1872. The narrative explores various characters and their lives in a provincial town.

The Return of the Native is a novel by Thomas Hardy, published in 1878. It is set on Egdon Heath, a fictional barren moor in Wessex, England. The story revolves around Clym Yeobright, who returns to the area after a career as a jeweller in Paris to become a schoolmaster.

Question 103

Which of the following novels of Thomas Hardy was first published in an abridged form as Hearts Insurgent?

1. The Mayor of Casterbridge
2. Jude the Obscure
3. Far From the Madding Crowd
4. The Return of the Native

Explanations:
Answer: 2. Jude the Obscure

Jude the Obscure, novel by Thomas Hardy, published in 1894–95 in an abridged form in Harper's New Monthly as Hearts Insurgent; published in book form in 1895.

The Mayor of Casterbridge: The Life and Death of a Man of Character (1886) by Thomas Hardy: Published by **Smith, Elder & Co.**, this novel set in the fictional Wessex, inspired by Dorchester in Dorset, delves into the life of a man marked by an impulsive act in his youth. First serialized in 1886, it's a profound exploration of fate, character, and the English rural landscape.

Far from the Madding Crowd (1874) by Thomas Hardy: Hardy's breakthrough novel was serialized anonymously in **The Cornhill Magazine** and later published under his name by Smith, Elder & Co. in the same year. It tells the story of Bathsheba Everdene and her three suitors against the backdrop of the English countryside, offering insight into various forms of love.

The Return of the Native (1878) by Thomas Hardy: Published in Belgravia Magazine, this story unfolds on the fictional Egdon Heath, reflecting the somber beauty of Wessex's moorlands. It follows Clym Yeobright's return from Paris to his native land, aiming to educate and uplift his community, and wrestles with themes of ambition, nature, and belonging.

Henry James (1843-1916)

- Major **nineteenth-century realism** writer.
- **The Portrait of a Lady** and **Daisy Miller** are his best-known works.
- His writing reflects **European culture** and **upper-class traditions**.
- James wrote **22 novels, 100+ short stories,** and **plays**.
- Born into a **wealthy, intellectual family** in **New York**.
- His father, Henry James Sr., was an **intellectual clergyman**.
- James' siblings also achieved recognition in **philosophy** and **writing**.
- **Travels between America and Europe** shaped his worldview.
- Educated in **Geneva, London, Paris, Bologna, and Bonn**.
- Attended **Harvard Law School** briefly, then pursued **literature**.
- Critics divide his work into **three distinct phases**.
- First phase: **simple, direct writing** style.
- Second phase: focus on **drama and short stories**.
- Third phase: **long, complex novels**.

- **Daisy Miller (1879)**: an American struggling in **European society**.
- **The Portrait of a Lady (1881)**: about an American woman in Europe.
- **The Bostonians (1886)**: explores the **feminist movement**.
- **What Maisie Knew (1897)**: a young girl choosing between parents.
- **The Wings of the Dove (1902)**: a significant **love story**.
- **The Ambassadors (1903)**: considered his **best work**.
- **The Turn of the Screw**: a renowned **ghost story novella**.
- Several novels, like **The Wings of the Dove**, adapted into films.
- Movies based on his novels include **Washington Square**.
- Died on **February 28, 1916**, from **pneumonia** and **stroke**.
- Known for **detailed prose and psychological insight**.

Works:

Novels

- *Watch and Ward (1871)*
- *Roderick Hudson (1875)*
- *The American (1877)*
- *The Europeans (1878)*
- *Confidence (1879)*
- *Washington Square (1880)*
- *The Portrait of a Lady (1881)*
  - **Isabel Archer**, a spirited American, inherits wealth unexpectedly.
  - She travels to **Europe** seeking freedom and self-discovery.
  - Falls into a troubled marriage with **Gilbert Osmond**.
  - Discovers **Osmond's manipulative nature** and hidden motives.
  - Struggles with choices between **freedom and duty** in life.
- *The Bostonians (1886)*
- *The Princess Casamassima (1886)*
- *The Reverberator (1888)*
- *The Tragic Muse (1890)*
- *The Other House (1896)*
- *The Spoils of Poynton (1897)*
- *What Maisie Knew (1897)*
- *The Awkward Age (1899)*
- *The Sacred Fount (1901)*
- *The Wings of the Dove (1902)*
- *The Ambassadors (1903)*

- ➢ ***The Golden Bowl (1904)***
- ➢ *The Whole Family (collaborative novel with eleven other authors, 1908)*
- ➢ *The Outcry (1911)*
- ➢ *The Ivory Tower (unfinished, published posthumously 1917)*
- ➢ ***The Sense of the Past (unfinished, published posthumously 1917)***

Short stories and novellas

- ➢ *"A Tragedy of Error" (1864)*
- ➢ *"The Story of a Year" (1865)*
- ➢ *"The Romance of Certain Old Clothes" (1868)*
- ➢ *A Passionate Pilgrim (1871)*
- ➢ *Madame de Mauves (1874)*
- ➢ ***Daisy Miller (1878)***
  - o A novella
  - o In The Cornhill Magazine.
  - o **Daisy Miller**, a young American, visits **Europe**.
  - o She meets **Winterbourne**, who admires her charm.
  - o Daisy's **free-spirited nature** defies **European social norms**.
  - o Her behavior leads to **social rejection** and **gossip**.
  - o **Daisy dies** from malaria, symbolizing **innocence misunderstood**.
- ➢ ***The Turn of the Screw (1898)***
  - o **Governess** is hired to care for **Miles** and **Flora**.
  - o **Governess sees ghosts** of **Peter Quint** and **Miss Jessel**.
  - o She believes the **children** are influenced by spirits.
  - o **Miles's odd behavior** and **Flora's fear** increase tension.
  - o **Story ends ambiguously**, leaving **Governess's sanity** in question.

Plays

- ➢ *Pyramus and Thisbe (1869)*
- ➢ *Still Waters (1871)*
- ➢ *A Change of Heart (1872)*
- ➢ *Daisy Miller (1882)*
- ➢ *The American (1890)*

Essays and criticism

- ➢ *French Poets and Novelists (1878)*
- ➢ *Picture and Text (1893)*
- ➢ *Notes on Novelists (1914)*
- ➢ ***The Art of the Novel: Critical Prefaces (1934)***

Questions:

Question 104

Arrange the following essays in chronological order of publication.

A. T. S. Eliot, "The Function of Criticism"
B. Edgar Allan Poe, "The Philosophy of Composition"
C. Henry James, "The Art of Fiction"
D. Virginia Woolf, "Modern Fiction"

Choose the correct answer from the options given below

1. C, B, A, D
2. C, B, D, A
3. B, C, D, A
4. **B, C, A, D**

Correct Explanations:

Edgar Allan Poe's "The Philosophy of Composition" was published in 1846, and it offers a highly structured and detailed account of his creative process in writing his poem "The Raven." Poe discusses how he arrived at the idea of writing the poem, how he developed its theme and tone, and how he constructed the various components of the poem, such as the stanza form and the refrains.

Henry James's "The Art of Fiction" was published in 1884, and it is a response to Walter Besant's lecture "Fiction as One of the Fine Arts." James argues that the novel is an independent art form and that the writer's primary goal should be to create a "felt life" for the reader. He also discusses the importance of character, plot, and dialogue, and offers advice to aspiring writers.

T. S. Eliot's "The Function of Criticism" was published in 1923, and it is an exploration of the relationship between the poet, the critic, and the reader. Eliot argues that the critic's role is to understand and evaluate the work of the poet, and that this evaluation should be based on an objective and historical understanding of literary tradition.

Virginia Woolf's "Modern Fiction" was published in 1925, and it is a critique of the traditional Victorian novel and an argument for a new form of fiction. Woolf argues that the novel should reflect the complexity and uncertainty of modern life, and that it should abandon the rigid conventions of plot and character development in favor of a more fluid and experimental form.

In chronological order, Poe's "The Philosophy of Composition" was published first in 1846, followed by James's "The Art of Fiction" in 1884, Eliot's "The Function of Criticism" in 1923, and finally Woolf's "Modern Fiction" in 1925.

Other Novelists

Wilkie Collins (1824-1889)

- ➢ William Wilkie Collins, was an **English sensation novelist**.
- ➢ An early master of the mystery story, and **a pioneer of detective fiction**.
- ➢ Collins was born in London, and was a son of a famous painter.
- ➢ He was a versatile man, dabbling much in journalism and play-writing.
- ➢ **Works:**
  - ○ *Antonina, or The Fall of Rome (1850)*
  - ○ ***Basil (1852)***
  - ○ *"Gabriel's Marriage" (1853), short story*
  - ○ *Hide and Seek (1854)*
  - ○ *The Dead Secret (1856)*
  - ○ *After Dark (1856), short story collection*
  - ○ *The Frozen Deep (1857), play co-written with Charles Dickens*
  - ○ *"A House to Let" (1858), short story co-written with Charles Dickens, Elizabeth Gaskell and Adelaide Anne Procter*
  - ○ *"The Haunted House", short story co-written with Charles Dickens, Elizabeth Gaskell, Adelaide Anne Proctor, George Sala and Hesba Stretton*
  - ○ ***The Woman in White (1860)***
  - ○ *No Name (1862)*
  - ○ *Armadale (1866)*
  - ○ *No Thoroughfare (1867), story and play co-written with Charles Dickens*
  - ○ ***The Moonstone (1868)***

- o *Man and Wife (1870)*
- o *Poor Miss Finch (1872), dedicated to Frances Minto Elliot*
- o *The Law and the Lady (1875)*
- o *The Haunted Hotel (1878)*
- o *The Fallen Leaves (1879)*
- o *Jezebel's Daughter (1880)*
- o *The Black Robe (1881)*
- o *Heart and Science (1882–1883)*
- o *The Evil Genius (1885)*

The Woman in White (1860)

- ➤ Fifth published novel, written in 1859 and set from 1849 to 1850.
- ➤ It is a mystery novel and falls under **"sensation novels."**
- ➤ Walter Hartright meets mysterious **woman in white** at night.
- ➤ He becomes a **drawing master** at Limmeridge House.
- ➤ Walter falls in love with **Laura Fairlie**, his student.
- ➤ Laura is engaged to **Sir Percival Glyde**, a sinister man.
- ➤ Anne Catherick, **woman in white**, warns about Glyde.
- ➤ Sir Percival and **Count Fosco** plot for Laura's fortune.
- ➤ Laura is sent to an **asylum** in Anne's place.
- ➤ Walter and **Marian** uncover Percival's **forged documents**.
- ➤ Percival dies trying to **hide his secret**.
- ➤ Walter marries Laura, and **justice prevails**.

The Moonstone (1868)

- ➤ The Moonstone, one of the first **English detective novels**.
- ➤ Moonstone, a sacred gem, from India.
- ➤ It brings bad luck to each of its English possessors.
- ➤ The **Moonstone** is a **mysterious diamond from India**.
- ➤ Given to **Rachel Verinder** as a birthday gift.
- ➤ The diamond is **stolen that very night**, causing chaos.
- ➤ **Detective Cuff** investigates the theft with suspicion on guests.
- ➤ **Rachel's servant Rosanna** becomes a suspicious figure.
- ➤ **Franklin Blake** reveals his role under drug influence.
- ➤ **Godfrey Ablewhite**, a respected man, is the actual thief.
- ➤ **Diamond is traced** to London, returned to India.
- ➤ Explores themes of **greed, colonialism, and superstition**.
- ➤ Known as **one of the first detective novels**.

Which of the following novels are written by Wilkie Collins?

A. Basil
B. A Tale of a Tub
C. The Woman in White
D. Lapsing
E. A School for Lovers

Choose the correct answer from the options given below:

1. A and B
2. C and D
3. A and C
4. B, C, and D

Explanations:

Answer: 3. A and C

Charles Kingsley (1810-1875)

- ➤ Devonshire man, being born at Holne and brought up at Clovelly.
- ➤ He completed his education at Oxford (1842),
- ➤ He was very successful as a student, and took orders.
- ➤ His first novel, **Yeast** (printed in Fraser's Magazine, 1848; in book form, 1851)
- ➤ **Alton Locke (1850)**, is the story of a tailor-poet who rebels against the ignominy of sweated labor and becomes a leader of the Chartist movement.
- ➤ **Carlyle** is introduced as one of the personages.
- ➤ **Hypatia (1853)** is a luridly erotic story set in early Christian Egypt.
- ➤ **Westward Ho! (1855)** is an imperialist and anti-Roman Catholic adventure set in the Elizabethan period.
- ➤ **Hereward the Wake (1866)** is about Anglo-Saxon England and the Norman Conquest.
- ➤ The didactic children's fantasy **The Water-Babies (1863)**.
- ➤ Memorable **ballads ("Airly Beacon," "The Sands of Dee," "Young and Old")**.

RD Blackmore (1825-1900)

- ➤ English Victorian novelist whose novel *Lorna Doone (1869)* won a secure place among English historical romances.
- ➤ Lorna Doone, a historical romance.
- ➤ Set in the wilds of **Exmoor (northern Devonshire, Eng.)**
- ➤ During the late 17th century,
- ➤ The novel concerns the adventurous life of the yeoman **John Ridd** and the circuitous course of his love for **Lorna Doone**, a beautiful maiden.

Question 106

Find the chronological order of the writers in terms of their years of birth:

- A. Jane Austen
- B. Henry Fielding
- C. James M. Barrie
- D. Richard Doddridge Blackmore
- E. William Makepeace Thackeray

Choose the correct answer from the options given below:

1. ABCDE
2. **BAEDC**
3. CDABE
4. DBAEC

Explanations:
- ➤ Henry Fielding (1707)
- ➤ Jane Austen (1775)
- ➤ William Makepeace Thackeray (1811)
- ➤ Richard Doddridge Blackmore (1825)
- ➤ James M. Barrie (1860)

George Meredith (1828-1909)

- ➤ English Victorian poet and novelist.

- ➤ His best-known works are *The Ordeal of Richard Feverel (1859)* and *The Egoist (1879)*.
- ➤ **Novels**
  - ○ *The Shaving of Shagpat (1856)*
  - ○ *Farina (1857)*
  - ○ ***The Ordeal of Richard Feverel (1859)***
    - ■ *The Ordeal of Richard Feverel: A History of Father and Son (1859)*
    - ■ **Richard Feverel's father**, Sir Austin, raises him strictly.
    - ■ Richard falls in love with **Lucy, a farmer's niece.**
    - ■ Their love clashes with **Sir Austin's rigid principles.**
    - ■ **Family conflicts and heartbreak** lead Richard to mature.
  - ○ ***Evan Harrington (1861)***
  - ○ *Emilia in England (1864), republished as Sandra Belloni in 1887*
  - ○ *Rhoda Fleming (1865)*
  - ○ *Vittoria (1867)*
  - ○ ***The Adventures of Harry Richmond (1871)***
    - ■ It is believed to be strongly autobiographical in some sections.
    - ■ **Harry Richmond's life** unfolds through adventure and romance.
    - ■ His **relationship with his father** shapes his journey.
    - ■ **Pursuit of true love** leads him across Europe.
    - ■ Story highlights **class, identity, and self-discovery themes.**
  - ○ *Beauchamp's Career (1875)*
  - ○ *The House on the Beach (1877)*
  - ○ *The Case of General Ople and Lady Camper (1877)*
  - ○ *The Tale of Chloe (1879)*
  - ○ ***The Egoist (1879)***
  - ○ *The Tragic Comedians (1880)*
  - ○ ***Diana of the Crossways (1885)***
  - ○ *One of our Conquerors (1891)*
  - ○ *Lord Ormont and his Aminta (1894)*
  - ○ *The Amazing Marriage (1895)*

The Egoist (1879)

- **Sir Willoughby Patterne** is a wealthy, self-centered man.
- **He proposes to Constantia Durham**, who later abandons him.
- Humiliated, he quickly **seeks another fiancée, Clara Middleton**.
- Clara grows disillusioned with Willoughby's controlling nature.
- Willoughby's selfishness strains his relationship with Clara deeply.
- Clara struggles to break free from Willoughby's hold.
- Friends and family begin to see Willoughby's egoism.
- Clara eventually finds courage to end the engagement.
- Willoughby remains self-centered, failing to learn humility.

Diana of the Crossways (1885)

- It is an account of an intelligent and forceful woman trapped in a miserable marriage.
- *Diana of the Crossways* explores love, betrayal, and society.
- Diana Warwick faces scandal after selling political secrets.
- Inspired by real-life writer Caroline Norton's struggles.
- Themes of *independence* and *gender roles* in Victorian England.
- Meredith critiques societal expectations and female autonomy.

Question 107

Match List I with List II

List I	List II
A. George Meredith	I. The Virginians
B. George Eliot	II. Scenes of Clerical Life
C. Charlotte Bronte	III. Evan Harrington
D. William Makepeace Thackeray	IV. The Professor

Choose the correct answer from the options given below:

1. A-III, B-I, C-IV. D-I
2. A-IV. B-III. C-I. D-II
3. A-I. B-II, ONII, D-IV
4. A-II, B-I, C-1V, D-III

Explanations
Answer: 1. A-III, B-I, C-IV. D-I

A. "Evan Harrington" is a glowing Victorian comedy written by George Meredith in 1861. Loosely inspired by his own life, the novel revolves around the social climbing family of the late tailor, Melchisedec Harrington.

B. George Eliot's debut work of fiction, "Scenes of Clerical Life," comprises three short stories first published in Blackwood's Magazine. Released under her famous pseudonym in 1856, Eliot was already a renowned figure in Victorian intellectual circles, known for her contributions to The Westminster Review and translations of theological works.

C. "The Professor, A Tale," Charlotte Brontë's first novel, was written before "Jane Eyre" but faced rejection from several publishing houses. Published posthumously in 1857 with the approval of her widower, Arthur Bell Nicholls, the novel was reviewed and edited by him.

D. William Makepeace Thackeray's historical novel "The Virginians: A Tale of the Last Century" (1857–59) serves as a sequel to his work "Henry Esmond" and is loosely connected to "Pendennis."

Question 108

Which one of these is not a literary journal/ magazine?

1. The Egoist
2. The Criterion
3. The English Review
4. The Hundred and One Dalmatians

Explanations:
Answer: The Hundred and One Dalmatians

The Hundred and One Dalmatians: A children's novel:
"The Hundred and One Dalmatians" is a beloved 1956 children's novel by Dodie Smith, which captures the thrilling adventures of Pongo and Missis. This tale, initially serialized in Woman's Day as "The Great Dog Robbery," unfolds the daring rescue of their Dalmatian puppies from a fur farm. The saga continues with the 1967 sequel, "The Starlight Barking," picking up from the novel's conclusion.

The Egoist by George Meredith

Published in three volumes in 1879, "The Egoist" is a comic novel by George Meredith that delves into the life of Sir Willoughby Patterne. Meredith weaves a narrative around Patterne's conceited nature and his journey through rejection and self-discovery, following his pursuit of love amidst his egotistical traits.

The Egoist: Magazine

Operating from 1914 to 1919, "The Egoist" emerged as a pivotal London literary magazine, heralding the modernist movement. With a manifesto that embraced no taboos, it published groundbreaking works, including excerpts from "Ulysses," securing its place as England's foremost Modernist periodical.

The Criterion

Founded by T.S. Eliot, "The Criterion" was a literary beacon from October 1922 to January 1939, aspiring to uphold literary standards and foster a unified European intellectual community. Despite mixed reviews, it showcased contributions from literary giants like Virginia Woolf and Ezra Pound, marking its legacy as an exemplary literary journal.

The English Review

Initiated by Ford Madox Hueffer in 1908, "The English Review" sought to provide a platform for eminent writers like Thomas Hardy and Henry James. Despite its editorial excellence and contributions from notable authors, the magazine struggled financially, yet it remains celebrated for its literary contributions.

Lewis Carrol (1832-1898)

- **Charles Lutwidge Dodgson**, better known by his pen name Lewis Carroll.
- His most notable works are *Alice's Adventures in Wonderland (1865)* and *its sequel, Through the Looking-Glass (1871)*.
- **Literary Works:**
- *La Guida di Bragia, a Ballad Opera for the Marionette Theatre (around 1850)*
- *"Miss Jones," comic song (1862)*
- *Alice's Adventures in Wonderland (1865)*

- o **Alice falls through a rabbit hole into a fantasy world**.
- o It is seen as an example of the **literary nonsense genre**.
- ➢ *Phantasmagoria and Other Poems (1869)*
- ➢ ***Through the Looking-Glass, and What Alice Found There (includes "Jabberwocky" and "The Walrus and the Carpenter") (1871)***
  - o Written as a sequel to Alice's Adventures in Wonderland.
  - o **Alice steps through a mirror** into a strange world.
  - o She encounters **living chess pieces** and talking creatures.
  - o **Alice becomes a pawn** in a life-sized chess game.
  - o **Meeting strange characters** like Tweedledum and Tweedledee.
  - o **Alice reaches the end** and becomes a queen.
  - o *Jabberwocky:*
    - The poem's **nonsense language** builds vivid, imaginative imagery.
    - **A young hero is warned of the Jabberwock.**
    - He's told of creatures like the Jubjub bird.
    - He ventures bravely, weapon in hand, prepared.
    - The hero confronts and defeats the Jabberwock.
    - Victorious, he returns to his father's joy.
- ➢ *The Hunting of the Snark (1876)*
- ➢ *Rhyme? And Reason? (1883) – shares some contents with the 1869 collection, including the long poem "Phantasmagoria."*
- ➢ *A Tangled Tale (1885)*
- ➢ *Sylvie and Bruno (1889)*
- ➢ *The Nursery "Alice" (1890)*
- ➢ *Sylvie and Bruno Concluded (1893)*
- ➢ *Pillow Problems (1893)*
- ➢ *What the Tortoise Said to Achilles (1895)*
- ➢ *Three Sunsets and Other Poems (1898)*
- ➢ *The Manlet (1903)*

Question 109

Match List - I with List - II.

List - I (Original name)	List - II (Penname / Pseudonym)
A. Charles Lutwidge Dodgson	I. George Eliot
B. Mary Ann Evans	II. Mark Twain
C. Eric Arthur Blair	III. George Orwell
D. Samuel Langhorne Clemens	IV. Lewis Carroll

Choose the correct answer from the options given below :

> (1) A-IV, B-I, C-III, D-II.
> (2) A-III, B-IV, C-II, D-I
> (3) A-I, B-II, C-III, D-IV
> (4) A-II, B-I, C-III, D-IV

Explanations:
Answer: (1) A-IV, B-I, C-III, D-II.

A. Charles Lutwidge Dodgson → IV. Lewis Carroll
(Lewis Carroll is the pseudonym of Charles Lutwidge Dodgson, famous for *Alice's Adventures in Wonderland*.)

B. Mary Ann Evans → I. George Eliot
(George Eliot is the pen name of Mary Ann Evans, known for *Middlemarch* and *Silas Marner*.)

C. Eric Arthur Blair → III. George Orwell
(George Orwell is the pen name of Eric Arthur Blair, known for *1984* and *Animal Farm*.)

D. Samuel Langhorne Clemens → II. Mark Twain
(Mark Twain is the pen name of Samuel Langhorne Clemens, known for *The Adventures of Tom Sawyer* and *The Adventures of Huckleberry Finn*.)

Samuel Butler (1835-1902)

> - English novelist, essayist, and critic wrote a satire, **Erewhon *(1872)*.**
> - His autobiographical novel, ***The Way of All Flesh (1903)*.**
> - **Notable Works:**
> - *Erewhon, or Over the Range (1872)*
>   - A satirical novel.
>   - **Erewhon** is a fictional country with unique customs.
>   - **Illness is treated as a crime in Erewhon.**
>   - Crime, however, is seen as a disease.
>   - Erewhonians avoid machines, fearing their takeover.
>   - The novel critiques Victorian society's norms and beliefs.
> - *Luck or Cunning as the Main Means of Organic Modification? (1887)*

- *Erewhon Revisited Twenty Years Later: Both by the Original Discoverer of the Country and by His Son (1901)*
- *The Way of All Flesh (1903)*
    - An **autobiographical** novel.
    - Published **posthumously** in 1902.
    - **John Pontifex** was a **carpenter**;
    - His son George rises in the world to become a publisher;
    - Follows **Ernest Pontifex** and his struggles with family.
    - Critiques **Victorian society, hypocrisy, and oppressive religion**.
    - Ernest's journey explores **personal growth and self-identity**.
    - Ends with Ernest finding **freedom and self-acceptance**.
- *God the Known and God the Unknown (1909).*
- *A First Year in Canterbury Settlement With Other Early Essays (1914)*

RL Stevenson (1850-1894)

- Scottish novelist, essayist, poet, and travel writer.
- He is best known for works such as:
- *Treasure Island (1883)*
    - Originally titled *The Sea Cook: A Story for Boys.*
    - *Stevenson, telling a story of "buccaneers and buried gold."*
    - **Young Jim Hawkins finds pirate map** in an inn.
    - **Jim, Dr. Livesey, and others plan** a treasure hunt.
    - **They hire a ship, Hispaniola**, led by Captain Smollett.
    - **Long John Silver**, a one-legged cook, joins the crew.
    - **Jim discovers Silver's plan to steal** the treasure.
    - **Jim overhears pirates' mutiny plot** against Captain Smollett.
    - **Battle ensues between Jim's group and pirates** for treasure.
    - **Jim faces danger and courageously foils Silver's plot.**
    - **Treasure is found, but some pirates flee** with Silver.
    - **Jim and friends return home safely** with their treasure.
- *Prince Otto (1885)*
- *Strange Case of Dr Jekyll and Mr Hyde (1886)*
    - **Gothic novella.**
    - Gabriel John Utterson, a London legal practitioner.
    - **Dr. Jekyll creates a potion** that transforms him.
    - **He becomes Mr. Hyde**, his dark alter ego.
    - Hyde commits crimes, **revealing Jekyll's hidden desires**.

- o Jekyll loses control, **Hyde begins taking over**.
- o Jekyll's inner conflict ends **in tragic self-destruction**.
- ➤ *Kidnapped (1886)*
- ➤ *The Black Arrow (1888)*
  - o A historical adventure novel and romance set during the Wars of the Roses.
- ➤ *The Master of Ballantrae (1889)*
  - o A tale of revenge set in Scotland, America and India.
- ➤ *The Wrong Box (1889)*
- ➤ *The Ebb-Tide (1894)*
- ➤ *A Child's Garden of Verses.*

Question 110

Find the chronological order of publication of the given works:

- A.   Darwin's Origin of Species
- B.   Macaulay's "Essay on Milton"
- C.   Stevenson's Treasure Island
- D.   Browning's "Pauline"
- E.   Arnold Bennet's Old Wives Tale

Choose the correct answer from the options given below:

1. ABCDE
2. **BDACE**
3. CDABE
4. DEACB

Explanations:
1. Browning's "Pauline" (1833)
2. Darwin's Origin of Species (1859)
3. Macaulay's "Essay on Milton" (1859)
4. Stevenson's Treasure Island (1883)
5. Arnold Bennet's Old Wives Tale (1908)

Question 111

In which year was R. L. Stevenson's Treasure Island published?

1. 1893

2. 1886
3. **1883**
4. 1896

Explanations:
Treasure Island is an adventure novel written by Robert Louis Stevenson and first published in book form in 1883. The story follows a young boy named Jim Hawkins who discovers a treasure map and sets sail on a perilous journey to find the hidden treasure with a group of pirates led by the infamous Long John Silver. The novel is set in the 18th century and is known for its vivid and realistic descriptions of pirate life and nautical adventure.

Jerome K Jerome (1859-1927)

- Jerome Klapka Jerome, was an English novelist and playwright.
- Jerome left school at 14, working first as a railway clerk.
- Then as a schoolteacher, an actor, and a journalist.
- His first book, *On the Stage—and Off (1885)*.
- *The Idle Thoughts of an Idle Fellow (1886)*
- *Three Men in a Boat (1889)*
  - *Three Men in a Boat (To Say Nothing of the Dog),* published in 1889.
  - Three friends—**J., George, and Harris**—plan a boating trip.
  - They seek a **break from stressful urban life**.
  - **Montmorency, the dog**, joins them on the journey.
  - Their adventures include **mishaps and comical misunderstandings**.
  - They struggle with **packing, navigation, and cooking**.
  - The trip highlights **friendship and English countryside beauty**.
  - The trio often **complains but also jokes together**.
  - J. reflects on **life's humor and simple joys**.
  - Weather, illness, and mistakes **test their patience**.
  - Ultimately, they **abandon the trip, choosing comfort**.
- *Three Men on the Bummel (1900)*
- *Paul Kelver (1902),* an autobiographical novel.
- He also wrote several plays.
- A book of Jerome's memoirs, *My Life and Times*, was published in 1926.

Question 112

Given below are two statements:

Statement I: Jerome K. Jerome's Three Men in a Boat (1889) is humorous and journalistic in form.
Statement II: It is about three young men and their dog on a holiday.

In light of the above statements, choose the correct answer from the options given below:

1. **Both Statement I and Statement II are true**
2. Both Statement I and Statement II are false
3. Statement I is true, but Statement II is false
4. Statement I is false, but Statement II is true

Correct Explanations:
Statement I: The statement is partially correct. Jerome K. Jerome's Three Men in a Boat (1889) **is a humorous travelogue that employs journalistic style**.

Statement II: The statement is partially correct. **The book is about three friends - J, George, and Harris - and their dog, Montmorency, taking a boating trip on the Thames in England, and is not limited to their holiday.**

James Barrie (1860-1937)

➢ Sir James Matthew Barrie, 1st Baronet, **was a Scottish novelist** and playwright
➢ Best remembered as the creator of **Peter Pan**.
➢ Born and educated in Scotland and then moved to London.
➢ **Llewelyn Davies boys inspired** Barrie's imaginative stories.
➢ Barrie wrote of a magical baby in *Kensington Gardens*.
➢ This story first appeared in *The Little White Bird* (1902).
➢ He then created *Peter Pan*, the boy who wouldn't grow up.
➢ *Peter Pan* features adventures in Neverland with Wendy.
➢ *Peter Pan; or, The Boy Who Would Not Grow Up (1904)*
    o It is a play.
    o **Peter Pan**, a boy who never grows up, visits **London**.
    o **Wendy Darling** and her brothers follow Peter to **Neverland**.

- o They encounter **mermaids, fairies**, and fight **pirates** led by **Captain Hook**.
- o Peter's bravery helps him defeat **Captain Hook**.
- o The **Darlings return home**, leaving Peter in **Neverland**.

VICTORIAN PROSE WRITERS

Walter Savage Landor (1775-1864) & Imaginary Conversation (1824-1829)

- ➢ English poet and writer best remembered for *Imaginary Conversations.*
- ➢ A publication consisting of five volumes.
- ➢ Landor, aged 46, was living with his family in Florence in 1821.
- ➢ He had rooms in the Medici Palace and later rented the Villa Castiglione.

Question 113

Match List I with List II

List I	List II
A. Charles Lamb	I. Imaginary Conversations
B. William Hazlitt	II. Specimens of the English Dramatic Poets who Lived about the Time of Shakespeare
C. Walter Savage Landor	III. Characters of Shakespeare's Plays
D. Thomas Love Peacock	IV. Gryll Grange

Choose the correct answer from the options given below:

1. A-III. B-I, C-IV. D-II
2. A-I, B-II. C-III. D-IV
3. A-II, B-III, C-I. D-IV
4. A-IV, B-I. C-II. D-III

Explanations:
Answer: 3. A-II, B-III, C-I. D-IV

I. "Imaginary Conversations" is a collection of dialogues written by Walter Savage Landor, first published in 1824. The book features fictional conversations between historical and literary figures, exploring various topics and ideas.

II. "Specimens of the English Dramatic Poets who Lived about the Time of Shakespeare" is a work by Charles Lamb, published in 1808. The book contains selected plays and excerpts from plays written by English dramatists who were contemporaries of William Shakespeare, providing insight into the theatrical landscape of that era.

III. "Characters of Shakespeare's Plays" is a book written by William Hazlitt, published in 1817. In this work, Hazlitt offers critical analysis and character sketches of the various characters found in William Shakespeare's plays, delving into their personalities, motivations, and significance within the plays.

IV. "Gryll Grange" is a novel by Thomas Love Peacock, first published in 1861. The book follows the story of Mr. Falconer, who retreats to the countryside estate of Gryll Grange. It satirises various social and intellectual movements of the time, including politics, philosophy, and education, through witty dialogues and humorous situations.

Thomas Carlyle (1795-1881)

- He was an essayist, historian, and philosopher from Scotland.
- A leading writer of the Victorian era.
- There is no doubt that he had a profound impact on the art, literature and philosophy of the 19th century.
- His initial success stemmed from his efforts to disseminate German literature.
- He wrote *Life of Friedrich Schiller* (1825)
- **Past and Present (1843),**
- His first significant work was a novel entitled *Sartor Resartus* (1833–34).
- Carlyle became famous with his *French Revolution* (1837),
- He wrote works like *On Heroes, Hero-Worship, & the Heroic in History (1841).*
- His innovative writing style is known as Carlylese.

- ➢ His style influenced Victorian literature and anticipated the techniques of postmodern literature.
- ➢ **List of Works:**
    - ○ *Wilhelm Meister's Apprenticeship and Travels, Translated from the German of Goethe (1824)*
    - ○ *The Life of Friedrich Schiller, Comprehending an Examination of His Works (1825)*
    - ○ *German Romance: Translations from the German, with Biographical and Critical Notices (1827)*
    - ○ ***Signs of the Times (1829)***
    - ○ ***Sartor Resartus: The Life and Opinions of Herr Teufelsdröckh in Three Books (1831)***
    - ○ ***The French Revolution: A History (1837)***
    - ○ ***Chartism (1840)***
    - ○ ***On Heroes, Hero-Worship, and the Heroic in History (1841)***
    - ○ ***Past and Present (1843)***
    - ○ *Oliver Cromwell's Letters and Speeches: with Elucidations (1845)*
    - ○ ***Occasional Discourse on the Negro Question (1849)***
    - ○ *Latter-Day Pamphlets (1850)*
    - ○ ***The Life of John Sterling (1851)***
    - ○ *History of Friedrich II. of Prussia, Called Frederick the Great (1858)*
    - ○ *Critical and Miscellaneous Essays)*
    - ○ *Marginalia*

Symbols/Clothes:

- ➢ Carlyle rejected all -isms.
- ➢ He believed that man could not fully know the true nature of God.
- ➢ In an 1835 letter, he asked, "Who dares name him? I dare not, and do not".
- ➢ He rejected the charges of pantheism and expressed the empirical basis of his belief.
- ➢ Carlyle saw all things as symbols, or clothes, representing the eternal and infinite.
- ➢ In Sartor, he defines the "Symbol proper" as that in which "there is ever, more or less distinctly and directly, some embodiment and

revelation of the Infinite; the Infinite is made to blend itself with the Finite, to stand visible, and as it were, attainable there."

Question 114

Arrange the following in the chronological order of publication:

    A. Advancement of Learning
    B. The Origin of Species
    C. On Heroes and Hero Worship
    D. The Lives of the Poets

Choose the correct answer from the options given below:

    1. D, A, C, B
    2. D, A, B, C
    3. A D, C, B
    4. A D, B, C

Explanations:
Answer: 3. A D, C, B

"Advancement of Learning" is a work by Francis Bacon, published in 1605. It is considered to be one of Bacon's most important works, and it outlines his ideas about the nature of knowledge and how it should be acquired.

"The Lives of the Poets" is a collection of biographical essays by Samuel Johnson, published in 1779. The essays provide detailed accounts of the lives and works of several important English poets, including John Milton, Alexander Pope, and John Dryden.

"On Heroes and Hero Worship" is a series of lectures by Thomas Carlyle, published in 1841. In the lectures, Carlyle discusses the concept of heroism and examines the lives of several notable figures from history, including Muhammad, Shakespeare, and Napoleon.

"The Origin of Species" is a book by Charles Darwin, published in 1859. It is considered to be one of the most important scientific works ever written, and it outlines Darwin's theory of evolution by natural selection.

Question 115

Given below are two statements :

Statement I: "....he who discovers no God Whatever. how shall he discover Heroes. The Visible Temples of God" is a statement by Thomas Carlyle.

Statement II: "It is not that men are ill-fed. But they have no pleasure in the work by which they make their bread. and therefore look to wealth as the only means of pleasure" is a statement made by John Ruskin.

Considering the above statements. choose the correct answer from the options given below:

1. Both Statement I and Statement II are true
2. Both Statement I and Statement I are false
3. Statement I is true but Statement II is false
4. Statement I is false but Statement II is true

Explanations:
➢ On Heroes, Hero-Worship, and the Heroic in History, by Thomas Carlyle.
➢ John Ruskin - "Unto This Last"

"It is not that men are ill fed, but that they have no pleasure in the work by which they make their bread, and therefore look to wealth as the only means of pleasure. It is not that men are pained by the scorn of the upper classes, but they cannot endure their own; for they feel that the kind of labor to which they are condemned is verily a degrading one, and makes them less than men. Never had the upper classes so much sympathy with the lower, or charity for them, as they have at this day, and yet never were they so much hated by them: for, of old, the separation between the noble and the poor was merely a wall built by law; now it is a veritable difference in level of standing, a precipice between upper and lower grounds in the field of humanity and there is pestilential air at the bottom of it." **THE STONES OF VENICE – BOOK SIX – The Nature of Gothic – paragraph 15.**

Question 116

Which of the following works have been written by Thomas Carlyle?

A. Of Heroes and Hero-Worship
B. The French Revolution
C. Of Human Bondage
D. The Hour and the Man
E. Hudibras

Choose the correct answer from the options given below:

1. A and B
2. A and C
3. A and D
4. A and E

Explanations:
Ans: A and B

"Of Heroes and Hero-Worship" is a series of lectures given by Thomas Carlyle. The lectures explore the idea of the hero in history and society, looking at different types of heroes and how they shape the world around them.

"The French Revolution" is a historical work by Thomas Carlyle that examines the French Revolution from a philosophical and literary perspective. The book presents Carlyle's unique interpretation of the revolution, focusing on the role of individuals and the power of ideas.

Extra Perk:

"Of Human Bondage" is a novel by W. Somerset Maugham. It follows the life of **Philip Carey,** an orphan with a clubfoot, as he navigates his way through life, love, and various philosophical and religious ideas.

"The Hour and the Man" is a historical novel by Harriet Martineau. The book tells the story of **Toussaint L'Ouverture, a slave** who became a leader of the Haitian Revolution and helped Haiti gain independence from France.

"Hudibras" is a satirical poem by Samuel Butler. It tells the story of Hudibras, a Puritan knight, and his squire Ralpho, as they go on various misadventures and satirize the religious and political beliefs of their time.

Question 117

The debate on "the condition of England question' was initiated by

1. William Hazlitt

2. Walter Bagehot
3. Thomas Carlyle
4. Matthew Arnold

Explanations
Answer: 3. Thomas Carlyle

The Condition-of-England question was a debate in the Victorian era over the issue of the English working class during the Industrial Revolution. **Thomas Carlyle first proposed it in his essay *Chartism* (1839).** After assessing Chartism as "the bitter discontent grown fierce and mad, the wrong condition therefore or the wrong disposition, of the Working Classes of England", Carlyle proceeds to ask:

"What means this bitter discontent of the Working Classes? Whence comes it, whither goes it? Above all, at what price, on what terms, will it probably consent to depart from us and die into rest? These are questions."

Question 118

Which of the following works have been authored by Thomas Carlyle

A. Chartism
B. Past and Present
C. The French Revolution
D. Suspiria de Profundis
E. The English Mail Coach

Choose the correct answer from the options given below:

1. A, B and C
2. B, C and D
3. A, B and D
4. C, D and E

Explanations
Answer: 1. A, B and C

List of Thomas Carlyle Works

- ➤ Sartor Resartus: The Life and Opinions of Herr Teufelsdröckh in Three Books (1831)
- ➤ **The French Revolution: A History (1837)**
- ➤ On Heroes, Hero-Worship, and the Heroic in History (1841)
- ➤ Oliver Cromwell's Letters and Speeches: with Elucidations (1845)
- ➤ **Past and Present (1843)**
- ➤ The Life of John Sterling (1851)
- ➤ History of Friedrich II. of Prussia, Called Frederick the Great (1858–1865)
- ➤ Latter-Day Pamphlets (1850)
- ➤ German Romance: Translations from the German, with Biographical and Critical Notices (1827)
- ➤ Wilhelm Meister's Apprenticeship and Travels, Translated from the German of Goethe (1824)
- ➤ The Life of Friedrich Schiller, Comprehending an Examination of His Works (1825)
- ➤ Critical and Miscellaneous Essays
- ➤ In July, he published "On the Sinking of the Vengeur" and in December he published *Chartism*, **a pamphlet in which he addressed the movement of the same name and raised the Condition-of-England question.**

Other Explanations:

The English Mail-Coach is an essay by the English author Thomas De Quincey. A "three-part masterpiece" and "one of his most magnificent works," it first appeared in 1849 in Blackwood's Edinburgh Magazine, in the October (Part I) and December (Parts II and III) issues.

Suspiria de profundis (a Latin phrase meaning "sighs from the depths") is a collection of essays in the form of prose poems by English writer Thomas De Quincey, first published in 1845. An examination of the process of memory as influenced by hallucinogenic drug use, Suspiria has been described as one of the best-known and most distinctive literary works of its era.

Question 119

Which among the following was NOT written by Thomas Carlyle?

1. 'Signs of the Times'
2. Sartor Resartus
3. The Stones of Venice

4. The Life of John Sterling

Explanations:
Answer: 3. The Stones of Venice

"The Stones of Venice" is a comprehensive work on Venetian art and architecture written by the English art historian **John Ruskin.** Originally published in **three volumes from 1851 to 1853**, this treatise delves into a meticulous examination of **Venetian architecture**. Ruskin provides detailed descriptions of numerous structures, including more than eighty churches. Within the book, he explores the architectural styles of Byzantine, Gothic, and Renaissance periods that can be found in Venice, offering insights into their characteristics and significance. Additionally, Ruskin presents a broader historical account of the city of Venice itself, offering readers a comprehensive understanding of its artistic and architectural heritage.

Question 120

Choose the correct order of publication of Thomas Carlyle's works

A. History of the French Revolution
B. Signs of the Time
C. Chartism
D. Occasional Discourse on the Nigger Question
E. Heros and Hero Worship :

Choose the correct answer from the options given below:

1. D,E,B,C,A
2. B,A, C,E,D
3. B,C,D,E,A
4. A,B,C,D,E

Explanations:
Answer: 2. B,A, C,E,D

Thomas Carlyle, a distinguished Scottish historian and essayist born on December 4, 1795, in Ecclefechan, Dumfriesshire, Scotland, passed away on February 5, 1881, in London, England. His seminal contributions to literature include *The French Revolution* (1837), a three-volume work; *On Heroes, Hero-*

Worship, and the Heroic in History (1841); and a six-volume biography titled The History of Friedrich II of Prussia, Called Frederick the Great (1858–65).

- *Wilhelm Meister's Apprenticeship and Travels, Translated from the German of Goethe (1824)*
- *The Life of Friedrich Schiller, Comprehending an Examination of His Works (1825)*
- *German Romance: Translations from the German, with Biographical and Critical Notices (1827)*
- *__Signs of the Times (1829)__*
- *Sartor Resartus: The Life and Opinions of Herr Teufelsdröckh in Three Books (1831)*
- *__The French Revolution: A History (1837)__*
- *__Chartism (1840)__*
- *__On Heroes, Hero-Worship, and the Heroic in History (1841)__*
- *Past and Present (1843)*
- *Oliver Cromwell's Letters and Speeches: with Elucidations (1845)*
- *__Occasional Discourse on the Negro Question (1849)__*
- *Latter-Day Pamphlets (1850)*
- *The Life of John Sterling (1851)*
- *History of Friedrich II. of Prussia, Called Frederick the Great (1858)*
- *Critical and Miscellaneous Essays)*
- *Marginalia*

THOMAS BABINGTON MACAULAY (1800–59)

- **Thomas Babington Macaulay** was an English historian and politician.
- He was known for his **eloquent essays and speeches.**
- **Macaulay's work focused on British history** and governance.
- He helped **reform India's educational system** under British rule.
- He served in Parliament as a **Whig politician.**
- His **writing style was vivid, engaging, and influential.**
- **Macaulay supported the idea of liberal progress** in society.
- He was one of the most **prominent historians of his time.**
- His **"History of England"** remains a classic historical work.
- Macaulay's works reflect his **belief in British imperialism.**
- **Major Works**
  - *Lays of Ancient Rome (1842)*
  - *Critical and Historical Essays (1843)*

- o *The History of England from the Accession of James II (1848–1861)*
- o *Speeches of Lord Macaulay (1853)*
- o *Essays, Critical and Miscellaneous (1860)*
- o *The Miscellaneous Writings and Speeches of Lord Macaulay (1860)*

John Ruskin (1819-1900)

- ➤ English writer, philosopher, art critic, and polymath of the Victorian era.
- ➤ He wrote **essays, treatises, poetry, lectures,** and **fairy tales.**
- ➤ Ruskin gained attention with *Modern Painters* (1843), defending **Turner**.
- ➤ He argued artists' role is **"truth to nature."**
- ➤ From the 1850s, Ruskin supported **Pre-Raphaelites**, inspired by his ideas.
- ➤ His work began addressing **social and political issues**.
- ➤ *Unto This Last* (1860, 1862) marked this **shift**.
- ➤ In 1869, he became the **first Slade Professor** at Oxford.
- ➤ Established the **Ruskin School of Drawing** at Oxford.
- ➤ Published *Fors Clavigera* (1871–1884), letters to **workmen**.
- ➤ Founded the **Guild of St George**, lasting to this day.
- ➤ **Notable Works:**
- ➤ *Modern Painters (1843–1860)*
    - o Written as a defense of the later work of J. M. W. Turner.
    - o **Pathetic Fallacy** Introduced in Volume III, 1856.
    - o It describes the attribution of **human emotions to nature** or inanimate objects.
- ➤ *"Praeterita"*
- ➤ *The Seven Lamps of Architecture (1849)*
    - o The 'lamps' of the title are Ruskin's principles of **architecture**.
- ➤ *The Stones of Venice (1851)*
    - o Three-volume treatise on Venetian art and architecture.
        - ▪ Venetian architecture in detail, describing over eighty churches.
- ➤ *Unto This Last: (1860)*
- ➤ **Sesame and Lilies (1865)**

Question 121

Match List - I with List - II.

List - I (Term / Concept)	List - II (Invented / Coined by)
A. Objectivism	I. John Ruskin
B. Pathetic Fallacy	II. G.M. Hopkins
C. Sprung Rhythm	III. William Carlos Williams
D. Structures of Feeling	IV. Raymond Williams

Choose the correct answer from the options given below :

    (1) A-I, B-II, C-IV, D-III
    (2) A-II, B-III, C-I, D-IV
    (3) A-IV, B-II, C-I, D-I
    (4) A-III, B-I, C-ll, D-IV

Explanations:
Answer: (4) A-III, B-I, C-ll, D-IV

A. Objectivism – III. William Carlos Williams
Introduced in works: Associated with poets like William Carlos Williams, especially in his works such as *Spring and All* (1923).
Explanation: Objectivism in poetry emphasizes clarity, conciseness, and a focus on objects and their inherent qualities.

B. Pathetic Fallacy – I. John Ruskin
Introduced in work: Modern Painters (Volume III, 1856)
Explanation: In *Modern Painters*, Ruskin coined "Pathetic Fallacy" to describe the attribution of human emotions to nature or inanimate objects, often used to critique romanticized descriptions in art and literature.

C. Sprung Rhythm – II. G.M. Hopkins
Introduced in works: Notably in Hopkins's poems such as *Pied Beauty* and *The Windhover* (published posthumously in 1918).
Explanation: Hopkins's *sprung rhythm* is a distinct metrical system that allows varied stressed syllables, aiming to mimic natural speech rhythms.

D. Structures of Feeling – IV. Raymond Williams
Introduced in work: The Long Revolution (1961)

Explanation: Raymond Williams introduced *Structures of Feeling* in *The Long Revolution*, describing the underlying, often unarticulated social and cultural attitudes of a particular time.

Question 122

Arrange the following in the chronological order of their publication:

- A. Past and Present
- B. Leviathan
- C. Unto This Last
- D. The Life of Samuel Johnson

Choose the correct answer from the options given below:

1. (B) (D) (A) (C)
2. (B) (A) (D) (C)
3. (C) (D) (A) (B)
4. (C) (A) (D) (B)

Explanations:

Answer: 1. (B) (D) (A) (C)

- ➢ Leviathan
- ➢ The Life of Samuel Johnson
- ➢ Past and Present
- ➢ Unto This Last

Leviathan by Thomas Hobbes was published in 1651 and is a significant work of political philosophy.

The Life of Samuel Johnson by James Boswell was published in 1791 and is a renowned biography of the prominent English writer and lexicographer.

Past and Present by Thomas Carlyle was published in 1843 and explores social and political issues of the time.

Unto This Last by John Ruskin was published in 1860 and presents his views on political economy and social justice.

Question 123

Some of the following are significant texts of Victorian Criticism. Identify them.

A. Studies in the History of the Renaissance
B. From Rituals to Romance
C. "Hamlet and His Problems"
D. "The Function of Criticism in the Present Time"
E. Modern Painters

Choose the correct answer from the options given below:

1. B, C, and D
2. A, D, and E
3. A, C, and D
4. B, D, and E

Explanations
Answer: 2. A, D, and E

Walter Pater (1839-1894) was a Victorian English essayist, art and literary critic, and fiction writer, regarded as one of the great stylists. His first and most often reprinted book, ***Studies in the History of the Renaissance (1873)***, revised as *The Renaissance: Studies in Art and Poetry (1877)*, in which he outlined his approach to art and advocated an ideal of the intense inner life, was taken by many as a manifesto (whether stimulating or subversive) of Aestheticism.

***Modern Painters* (1843–1860) is a five-volume work by the Victorian art critic, John Ruskin**, begun when he was 24 years old based on material collected in Switzerland in 1842. Ruskin argues that recent painters emerging from the tradition of the picturesque are superior in the art of landscape to the old masters. The book was primarily written as a defence of the later work of J. M. W. Turner. Ruskin used the book to argue that art should devote itself to the accurate documentation of nature.

Arnold is famous for introducing a methodology of literary criticism somewhere between the historicist approach common to many critics at the time and the personal essay; he often moved quickly and easily from literary subjects to political and social issues. His ***Essays in Criticism* (1865, 1888)**, remains a significant influence on critics to this day, and his prefatory essay to that collection, **"The Function of Criticism at the Present Time"**, is one of the most influential essays written on the role of the critic in identifying and elevating literature – even while saying, "The critical power is of lower rank than the creative."

Other Explanation
From Ritual to Romance is a 1920 book written by Jessie Weston. It is an examination of the roots of the King Arthur legends. It seeks to make connections between the early pagan elements and the later Christian influences. The book's main focus is on the Holy Grail tradition and its influence, particularly the Wasteland motif.

Hamlet and His Problems is an essay written by T.S. Eliot in 1919 that offers a critical reading of Hamlet.

Question 124

Which among the following was NOT written by Thomas Carlyle?

1. 'Signs of the Times'
2. Sartor Resartus
3. The Stones of Venice
4. The Life of John Sterling

Explanations:
Answer: 3. The Stones of Venice

"The Stones of Venice" is a comprehensive work on Venetian art and architecture written by the English art historian **John Ruskin.**

Lyotton Strachey (1880-1932) & Eminent Victorians (1918)

- ➤ **Key biographer of Victorian figures, influenced modern biography.**
- ➤ **Known for critical, witty style in historical portraits.**
- ➤ **Best-known work:** *Eminent Victorians* (1918) reshaped biographies.
- ➤ **Member of the Bloomsbury Group, with Virginia Woolf.**
- ➤ **Openly criticized traditional Victorian values and morality.**
- ➤ **Eminent Victorians (1918)**
  - o A collection of short biographical sketches.
  - o **Satirical biographical work** targeting revered Victorian-era

figures.

- o Features **Florence Nightingale, Cardinal Manning, Dr. Arnold, Gordon.**
- o **Challenges traditional Victorian values** with humor and irony.
- o **Uses psychological insight** to reveal flaws and complexities.
- o Influenced **modern biographical writing** with its concise style.

Walter Pater (1839-1894)

- ➤ **Prominent English essayist and art critic** focused on aesthetics.
- ➤ **Key figure in the Aesthetic Movement** in England.
- ➤ **Famous work:** *Studies in the History of the Renaissance* (1873).
- ➤ Advocated "art for art's sake" philosophy in writing.
- ➤ **Influenced writers like Oscar Wilde** and James Joyce.
- ➤ **Good vs. Great Art**: Great art serves humanity, holds universal truth.
- ➤ **Examples of Great Art**: *The Divine Comedy* and *Les Misérables*.
- ➤ **Imaginative Prose**: Essential for capturing complex, modern experiences fully.
- ➤ **Influence on Aesthetic Movement**: Inspired "art for art's sake" philosophy.
- ➤ **Literature's Purpose**: Gains greatness by serving humanity and truth.

Question 125

Which two of the following works does Walter Pater regard as examples of 'great art" in his essay "Style?

A. Iliad
B. The Divine Comedy
C. Les Misérables
D. Faust

Choose the most appropriate answer from the options given below:

1. A and B only
2. A and D only
3. B and C only
4. B and D only

Explanations:
Answer: 3.

Good Art and Great Art according to Walter Pater
At the end of the essay, Pater draws a distinction between good art and great art. The distinction between the two depends not on its form, but on the matter. It is good art when the writer is successful in portraying truthfully his sense of fact. But it is great art when a great subject is treated in a great manner. The great art results only when it 'has the soul of humanity,' when the vision of the artist has nobility, universal truth, and universal validity when it has sound subject matter when it is devoted to the service of humanity. Mere truth to personal vision is not enough; the quality of that vision, its nobility, is also essential. **All art is great in proportion as it is devoted to the service of man and the glory of God. The Divine Comedy, Paradise Lost, Les Miserables, The English Bible are great art.**

Question 126

In the above passage, Walter Horalio Pater's statement, "imaginative prose should be special", implies:

1. abstract language
2. environmental crisis
3. **intellectual complexities**
4. metaphorical functions

Correct Explanations:
In the above passage, Walter Horatio Pater's statement, **"imaginative prose should be special,"** implies intellectual complexities. Pater argues that the chaotic variety and complexity of modern interests make the intellectual issue of the present time incalculable, which suggests that there is a need for a form of literature that can capture the nuanced and complex aspects of modern experience. He suggests that the special art of the modern world is imaginative prose, which is capable of reflecting on the facts of modern experience in a varied and nuanced way, and is not limited by the formal constraints of verse. **Therefore, Pater's statement emphasizes the importance of literature that can grapple with the intellectual complexities of the modern world.**

Algernon Charles Swinburne (1837-1909)

> Born in London, educated at Eton and Oxford.

- ➢ Known for his lyrical and rhythmic poetry style.
- ➢ Explored controversial themes: paganism, sensuality, and rebellion.
- ➢ Influenced by Greek mythology and classical literature.
- ➢ Friends with **Rossetti, part of Pre-Raphaelite circle.**
- ➢ Major works include ***Poems and Ballads (1866).***
- ➢ Opposed Victorian norms; criticized for his radical views.
- ➢ Experimented with meter, rhyme, and poetic forms.
- ➢ Struggled with alcoholism, later reformed by friends.
- ➢ Remembered as a daring, influential Victorian poet.
- ➢ **Notable Works**
  - o **Prose drama**
    - ▪ *La Soeur de la reine (published posthumously 1964)*
  - o **Poetry**
    - ▪ *Atalanta in Calydon (1865)†*
    - ▪ ***Poems and Ballads (1866)***
    - ▪ *Songs Before Sunrise (1871)*
    - ▪ ***Songs of Two Nations' (1875)***
    - ▪ *Erechtheus (1876)†*
    - ▪ *Poems and Ballads, Second Series (1878)*
    - ▪ *Songs of the Springtides (1880)*
    - ▪ *Studies in Song (1880)*
    - ▪ *The Heptalogia, or the Seven against Sense. A Cap with Seven Bells (1880)*
    - ▪ *Tristram of Lyonesse (1882)*
    - ▪ *A Century of Roundels (1883)*
    - ▪ *A Midsummer Holiday and Other Poems (1884)*
    - ▪ *Poems and Ballads, Third Series (1889)*
    - ▪ *Astrophel and Other Poems (1894)*
    - ▪ *The Tale of Balen (1896)*
    - ▪ *A Channel Passage and Other Poems (1904)*
  - o **Criticism**
    - ▪ *William Blake: A Critical Essay (1868, new edition 1906)*
    - ▪ *Under the Microscope (1872)*
    - ▪ *George Chapman: A Critical Essay (1875)*
    - ▪ *Essays and Studies (1875)*
    - ▪ *A Note on Charlotte Brontë (1877)*
    - ▪ ***A Study of Shakespeare (1880)***
    - ▪ *A Study of Victor Hugo (1886)*

- *A Study of Ben Johnson (1889)*
- *Studies in Prose and Poetry (1894)*
- ***The Age of Shakespeare (1908)***
- *Shakespeare (1909)*

Oscar Wilde (1854-1900)

- ➤ **Oscar Wilde** was an **Irish poet and playwright.**
- ➤ Wilde became a **famous London playwright** in the **1890s.**
- ➤ Known for **witty epigrams, plays,** and **The Picture of Dorian Gray.**
- ➤ Faced **criminal conviction** for **homosexual acts,** a **celebrity trial.**
- ➤ Wilde's **parents were intellectuals** from **Dublin.**
- ➤ He was fluent in **French and German** from **a young age.**
- ➤ Wilde studied **Greats** at **Trinity College** and **Oxford.**
- ➤ He followed **aestheticism philosophy** under **Pater** and **Ruskin.**
- ➤ After **university**, he joined **London's cultural and social scene.**
- ➤ Wilde championed **aestheticism** and published **poetry and essays.**
- ➤ He lectured on the **"English Renaissance in Art"** internationally.
- ➤ Known for **wit, style,** and **charisma** in **social circles.**
- ➤ Wilde refined **art supremacy ideas** through **dialogues and essays.**
- ➤ His **only novel,** *The Picture of Dorian Gray*, explored **decadence.**
- ➤ **Turned to drama** for **creative expression** and **social themes.**
- ➤ **Salome** was banned in **England** for **biblical subject matter.**
- ➤ Wrote **four society comedies,** achieving **Victorian success.**
- ➤ **Prosecuted Marquess of Queensberry** in **libel case**; ended poorly.
- ➤ **Libel trial** led to Wilde's **gross indecency conviction.**
- ➤ Wilde served **two years' hard labor, 1895–1897.**
- ➤ **In prison**, he wrote *De Profundis*, a **reflective letter.**
- ➤ On release, Wilde moved to **France** permanently.
- ➤ *The Ballad of Reading Gaol* (1898) recounts **prison life.**
- ➤ Wilde died **in exile** due to **illness,** age **46.**
- ➤ **Legacy endures** for **wit, creativity,** and **philosophy on art.**

Major Works:

- ➤ *Ravenna (1878)*
- ➤ *Poems (1881)*
- ➤ ***The Happy Prince and Other Stories (1888, fairy stories)***
- ➤ *Lord Arthur Savile's Crime and Other Stories (1891, stories)*
- ➤ *A House of Pomegranates (1891, fairy stories)*

- *Intentions (1891, essays and dialogues on aesthetics)*
- ***The Picture of Dorian Gray (first published in Lippincott's Monthly Magazine July 1890, in book form in 1891; novel)***
- *The Soul of Man under Socialism (1891, political essay)*
- ***Lady Windermere's Fan (1892, play)***
- *A Woman of No Importance (1893, play)*
- *The Sphinx (1894, poem)*
- ***An Ideal Husband (performed 1895, published 1898; play)***
- ***The Importance of Being Earnest (performed 1895, published 1899; play)***
- *De Profundis (written 1897, published variously 1905, 1908, 1949, 1962; epistle)*
- *The Ballad of Reading Gaol (1898, poem)*

The Picture of Dorian Gray (1891)

- A philosophical novel.
- First it was published as **Novella** and then as a **Novel**.
- **Dorian Gray**, a handsome young man, meets **artist Basil Hallward**.
- Basil paints a **portrait** that captures **Dorian's beauty**.
- **Lord Henry Wotton** influences Dorian with **hedonistic ideals**.
- Dorian wishes his **portrait would age instead** of him.
- Dorian begins a life of **pleasure without consequences**.
- He falls in love with **actress Sibyl Vane** but **quickly abandons her**.
- Sibyl, heartbroken, **commits suicide** after **Dorian's rejection**.
- Dorian notices the **portrait's expression grows crueler**.
- He hides the **portrait in his attic** to avoid judgment.
- Dorian embraces a **lifestyle of sin and decadence**.
- **Basil confronts Dorian** about his **morality and choices**.
- In anger, **Dorian murders Basil** to protect his secret.
- **Haunted by guilt,** Dorian's life **spirals into paranoia**.
- In a moment of rage, **he stabs the portrait**.
- **Dorian dies**, his body aged; the portrait **restored to youth**.

Lady Windermere's Fan (1892)

- ***Lady Windermere's Fan, A Play About a Good Woman*** is a four-act comedy.
- **Lady Windermere suspects her husband** of infidelity.
- **Lord Windermere befriends Mrs. Erlynne**, a mysterious woman.
- **Lady Windermere confronts her husband** over his actions.

- ➢ **Mrs. Erlynne attends Lady Windermere's birthday ball.**
- ➢ **Lady Windermere considers leaving with Lord Darlington.**
- ➢ **Mrs. Erlynne intervenes to protect Lady Windermere's reputation.**
- ➢ **Lady Windermere realizes Mrs. Erlynne's sacrifice**, saving her honor.

A Woman of No Importance (1893)

- ➢ "*a new and original play of modern life*" in four acts.
- ➢ **The story centers on** Gerald Arbuthnot, an **ambitious young man.**
- ➢ Gerald is offered a **position by Lord Illingworth**, a **wealthy aristocrat.**
- ➢ Gerald's **mother, Mrs. Arbuthnot**, opposes him **working for Illingworth.**
- ➢ **Revelations unfold** that Lord Illingworth is Gerald's **estranged father.**
- ➢ **Mrs. Arbuthnot discloses** Illingworth abandoned her **and young Gerald.**
- ➢ Illingworth tries to **claim his son**, but **Gerald rejects him.**
- ➢ **The play criticizes society's double standards** and **treatment of women.**

An Ideal Husband (1895)

- ➢ A four-act play.
- ➢ **Sir Robert Chiltern** is a respected **politician with a secret.**
- ➢ **Mrs. Cheveley** tries to blackmail **Robert over past corruption.**
- ➢ **Lady Chiltern**, Robert's wife, **believes him to be morally perfect.**
- ➢ **Robert seeks help** from his witty friend, **Lord Goring.**
- ➢ **Lord Goring uncovers Mrs. Cheveley's own deceitful history.**
- ➢ **Lady Chiltern forgives Robert** upon learning the full truth.
- ➢ The play ends with **reconciled relationships and moral redemption.**

The Importance Of Being Earnest (1895)

- ➢ **Algernon Moncrieff** and **Jack Worthing** both lead **double lives.**
- ➢ Jack is known as **"Ernest" in the city** for fun.
- ➢ **Algernon** pretends to visit an ill friend, **Bunbury.**
- ➢ Jack wishes to marry **Gwendolen**, Algernon's cousin.

- ➤ Gwendolen loves **Jack only because he's "Ernest"**.
- ➤ **Lady Bracknell** opposes Jack's proposal due to **his unknown origins**.
- ➤ Meanwhile, **Algernon meets Cecily**, Jack's young ward.
- ➤ Cecily also falls for **"Ernest"**, unaware it's **Algernon**.
- ➤ The **deceptions are revealed**, causing **comic confusion**.
- ➤ **Jack discovers his true identity** and **real name: Ernest**.

The Decay of Lying (1891)

- ➤ It is a **Socratic dialogue** between **Vivian and Cyril**.
- ➤ It promotes Wilde's view of **Romanticism over Realism**.
- ➤ The decay of Lying *"as an art, a science, and a social pleasure"*
- ➤ Vivian defends **Aestheticism and "art for art's sake"**
- ➤ The essay appears in a collection of essays published in 1891 entitled *Intentions*.
- ➤ **Vivian and Cyril** discuss Wilde's ideas in a **Socratic dialogue**.
- ➤ Their conversation is **playful** but leans towards **Romanticism over realism**.
- ➤ Vivian mentions his article, "**The Decay Of Lying: A Protest.**"
- ➤ He believes lying's decline affects **modern literature's quality**.
- ➤ Lying is described as an **art, science, and social pleasure**.
- ➤ Modern literature suffers from **excessive focus on facts**.
- ➤ Emphasis on **social reality** hinders **literary imagination**.
- ➤ In his words, *"if something cannot be done to check, or at least to modify, our monstrous worship of facts, Art will become sterile, and beauty will pass away from the land."*
- ➤ According to Vivian, **life imitates art** more than vice versa.
- ➤ He contends that **nature is no less an imitation of art than life itself.**
- ➤ According to Vivian, art is never representative of any time or place: *"the highest art rejects the burden of the human spirit [...] She develops purely on her own lines. She is not symbolic of any age."*
- ➤ Thus, Vivian argues in favour of **Aestheticism and the concept of "art for art's sake".**
- ➤ Vivian summarizes the doctrines of the "new aesthetics" as follows:
  - o Art never expresses anything but itself.
  - o The essence of all bad art is the return to life and nature and their elevation to ideals.

- o Life imitates Art far more than Art imitates life. Therefore, external nature also imitates art.
- o The purpose of art is to tell beautiful untrue stories.

Questions

Question 127

Which one of the following essays holds that "As a method, realism is a complete failure'?

1. Virginia Woolf, "The Mark on the Wall"
2. Oscar Wilde, "The Decay of Lying"
3. D H Lawrence, "Why the Novel Matters"
4. Mary McCarthy, "My Confession"

Explanations:
Answer: 2. Oscar Wilde, "The Decay of Lying"

In "The Decay of Lying," Oscar Wilde argues that the realist method of art is a failure. He claims that art should not strive to imitate reality but rather create a new and more perfect world. According to Wilde, reality is often dull and mundane, and art should not seek to reproduce it. Rather, art should create an ideal world that is more beautiful and interesting than reality.

Wilde believes that realism is a failure because it is limited by the constraints of reality. Realism can only depict what already exists and cannot create anything new. It is unable to capture the imagination and fails to engage the audience. Wilde believes that art should create a new and better reality that inspires and moves people.

Extra Perk:

Virginia Woolf's "The Mark on the Wall" is a short story that reflects on the nature of perception and the meaning of existence. The narrator begins by describing a mark on the wall, which leads her to contemplate the interconnectedness of life and the passage of time. As she reflects on various thoughts and memories, she realizes the impossibility of truly knowing another person's perspective and the limitations of language in expressing the complexities of human experience.

In "The Decay of Lying," Oscar Wilde argues that art should not aim to imitate life but rather to create a new and more beautiful reality. He criticizes the realist movement in art and literature, which he sees as limited by a narrow focus on the mundane and the everyday. Instead, Wilde champions the art of lying as a means of transcending the limitations of reality and unlocking the imagination.

D. H. Lawrence's essay "Why the Novel Matters" explores the significance of the novel as a literary form. He argues that the novel is uniquely capable of capturing the complexity and depth of human experience, allowing readers to connect with characters on a deep emotional level. Lawrence also emphasizes the importance of individuality in literature, suggesting that the greatest works are those that capture the unique perspective of the author.

Mary McCarthy's "My Confession" is a personal essay in which she reflects on her upbringing in a Catholic family and her eventual rejection of the Church. McCarthy discusses the ways in which her religious upbringing shaped her sense of self and her relationship with the world, but ultimately concludes that she cannot reconcile her beliefs with the tenets of Catholicism. The essay is a frank and insightful exploration of personal identity and the role of religion in shaping it.

Question 128

Arrange the following authors in the chronological order of their birth:

- A. Oscar Wilde
- B. William Langland
- C. Geoffrey Chaucer
- D. John Dryden
- E. Alexander Pope

Choose the correct answer from the options given below:

1. B, C, D, E, A
2. A, B, C, E, D
3. B, C, D, A, E
4. C, B, A, D, E

Explanations:

Answer: 1. B, C, D, E, A

Oscar Wilde (1854- 1900)
> *The Picture of Dorian Gray*
> *The Importance of Being Earnest*

> *Lady Windermere's Fan*
> *An Ideal Husband*

William Langland (1332- 1386)
> *Piers Plowman*

Geoffrey Chaucer (1343- 1400)
> *The Canterbury Tales*
> *Troilus and Criseyde*

John Dryden (1631- 1700)
> *Absalom and Achitophel*
> *Mac Flecknoe*
> *All for Love*
> *The Conquest of Granada*

Alexander Pope (1688-1744)
> *The Rape of the Lock*
> *An Essay on Criticism*
> *An Essay on Man*
> *The Dunciad*

Question 129

Arrange the following in the chronological order of publication :

(A) The Pisan Canw
(B) Ballad of Reading Goal
(C) Mourn not for Adonais
(D) First step up Parnassus
(E) The Complaint of Troilus

Choose the correct answer from the options given below:

1. (E), (D), (E), (C), (A)
2. (C), (A), (E), (D), (E)
3. (B), (C), (A), (E), (D)
4. (E), (D), (C), (B), (A)

Explanations:
Answer: Dropped

The correct chronological order of publication for the given works is as follows:

(D) First Step up Parnassus (1820): This work is a collection of satirical poems by Thomas Love Peacock, published in 1820.

(C) Mourn not for Adonais (1821): This poem is a tribute to the poet John Keats, written by Percy Bysshe Shelley and published in 1821.

(A) The Pisan Cantos (1948): A major work by American poet Ezra Pound, published in 1948, which reflects his experiences and thoughts during his imprisonment in Italy during World War II.

(E) The Complaint of Troilus (1952): A poem by British poet Geoffrey Hill, published in 1952, which reimagines the story of Troilus and Cressida from Greek mythology.

(B) Ballad of Reading Gaol (1898): This poem by Oscar Wilde was written during his imprisonment in Reading Gaol and published in 1898. It reflects on the harsh realities of prison life and the themes of suffering and redemption.

Question 130

Match List I with List II:

List I	List II
(A) O' Henry	(I) The Last Suttee
(B) Rudyard Kipling	(II) Beauty
(C) Oscar Wilde	(II) At Verona
(D) Ralph Waldo Emerson	(IV) Hard to Forget

Choose the correct answer from the options given below:

1. (A)-(I), (B)-(III), (C)-(II), (D)-(IV)
2. (A)-(II), (B)-(IV), (C)-(III), (D)-(I)
3. (A)-(IV), (B)-(I), (C)-(III), (D)-(II)
4. (A)-(III), (B)-(I), (C)-(IV), (D)-(II)
5. **DROP**

Correct Explanation
William Sydney Porter (1862-1910), better known by his pen name O. Henry, was an American writer known primarily for his short stories, though he also wrote poetry and non-fiction. **His works include "The Gift of the Magi", "The Duplicity of Hargraves", and "The Ransom of Red Chief"**, as well as the novel Cabbages and Kings. Porter's stories are known for their naturalist observations, witty narration and surprise endings. Some

Postscripts: "Two Portraits", "A Contribution", "The Old Farm", "Vanity", "The Lullaby Boy", "Chanson de Bohême", **"Hard to Forget"**, "Drop a Tear in This Slot", "Tamales"

Rudyard Kipling (1865–1936) wrote a verse called The Last Suttee in 1889.
"Not many years ago, a King died in one of the Rajpoot States. His wives, disregarding the orders of the English against Suttee, would have broken out of the palace and burned themselves with the corpse had not the gates been barred. But one of them, disguised as the King's favourite dancing girl, passed through the line of guards and reached the pyre. There, her courage failing, she prayed for her cousin, a baron of the King's court, to kill her. This he did, not knowing who she was."

The first version of The Picture of Dorian Gray was published as the lead story in the July 1890 edition of Lippincott's Monthly Magazine, along with five others. The story begins with a man painting a picture of Gray. When Gray, who has a "face like ivory and rose leaves", sees his finished portrait, he breaks down. Distraught that his beauty will fade while the portrait stays beautiful, he inadvertently makes a Faustian bargain in which only the painted image grows old while he stays beautiful and young. For Wilde, the purpose of art would be to guide life as if beauty alone were its object. As Gray's portrait allows him to escape the corporeal ravages of his hedonism, Wilde sought to juxtapose the beauty he saw in art with daily life.

AT VERONA is a poem written by Oscar Wilde. Opening line is given below
How steep the stairs within King's houses are For exile-wearied feet as mine to tread,
And O how salt and bitter is the bread.

Question 131

Given below are two statements :

Statement I: According to W.H. Auden, The Importance of Being Earnest is the purest example in English Literature of a 'Verbal Opera'.
Statement II: Oscar Wilde possessed profound insight into the range of the arts that, in a combined form, make theatre performance possible.

In light of the above statements. Choose the correct answer from the options given below :

1. **Both Statement I and Statement I are true**
2. Both Statement I and Statement II are false
3. Statement I is true but Statement II is false
4. Statement II is false but Statement I is true

Correct Explanations:

The key to decoding the play's meaning lies in its style, which transforms this silliness into a way of life. Wilde's wit floats like a butterfly over the play's absurdities and stings like a bee, exposing the deep triviality of "earnest" social convention. For example, in the play's opening scene, Algernon and his butler Lane glide effortlessly among taboo topics, touching on music and philosophy, science and life, bachelorhood and marriage, and all points. It is one of the most dazzling scenes of comic dialogue ever written in English, a virtuosic pas de deux. **W.H. Auden called The Importance of Being Earnest "the only pure verbal opera in English," and there can be no doubting its crystalline brilliance.**

Question 132

Arrange the following chronologically in accordance with their date of birth:

A. Goethe
B. Oscar Wilde
C. Bertolt Brecht
D. Eugene O'Neill
E. Moliere

Choose the correct answer from the options given below:

1. A, B, D, C, E
2. B, E, A, C, D
3. C, D. A. B. E
4. E, A, B. D, C

Explanations:
Answer: 4. E, A, B. D, C

Molière (1622-1673) - French playwright and actor, known as the greatest writer of French comedy. His works include Tartuffe, L'École des femmes, Le Misanthrope, and Le Bourgeois Gentilhomme.

- ➤ Tartuffe:
- ➤ L'École des femmes
- ➤ Le Misanthrope
- ➤ Le Bourgeois Gentilhomme

Johann Wolfgang von Goethe (1749-1832) - German literary figure considered the greatest of the modern era. He excelled as a poet, playwright, novelist, scientist, critic, and theatre director. His works, including Faust, are central to German literature and the Romantic movement.

- ➤ Faust
- ➤ Wilhelm Meister's Apprenticeship
- ➤ The Sorrows of Young Werther
- ➤ Elective Affinities

Oscar Wilde (1854-1900) - Irish wit, poet, and dramatist associated with the Aesthetic movement. Known for his novel The Picture of Dorian Gray and plays such as Lady Windermere's Fan and The Importance of Being Earnest. He faced legal troubles due to his homosexuality.

- ➤ The Picture of Dorian Gray
- ➤ Lady Windermere's Fan
- ➤ The Importance of Being Earnest
- ➤ An Ideal Husband

Eugene O'Neill (1888-1953) - Foremost American playwright and Nobel Prize winner. His notable works include Long Day's Journey into Night, Beyond the Horizon, and The Iceman Cometh. He is considered one of the greatest dramatists in American history.

- ➤ Long Day's Journey into Night
- ➤ Beyond the Horizon
- ➤ Anna Christie
- ➤ The Iceman Cometh

Bertolt Brecht (1898-1956) - German poet, playwright, and theatrical reformer. Known for his epic theatre style, he departed from conventional theatrical illusion and used drama as a platform for leftist causes. His works include Baal, Drums in the Night, and Die Hauspostille.

> ➤ The Threepenny Opera
> ➤ Mother Courage and Her Children
> ➤ The Caucasian Chalk Circle
> ➤ Life of Galileo

W. B. Yeats: The Bridge Between Victorian Tradition and Modern Innovation

W.B.Yeats (1865-1939)

- ➤ **Yeats**, born in **Dublin (1865-1939)**, had a lawyer-painter father.
- ➤ Educated in **London and Dublin**, summers in **Connaught**.
- ➤ Engaged with **fin de siècle London** and Irish literary revival.
- ➤ Published **first poetry volume in 1887**, early focus on drama.
- ➤ Co-founded **Abbey Theatre** with **Lady Gregory**, chief playwright.
- ➤ **Plays** reflected Irish legends, **mysticism**, and **spiritualism**.
- ➤ Known plays: **The Countess Cathleen, Cathleen ni Houlihan**.
- ➤ After 1910, plays grew **poetical, static, and esoteric**.
- ➤ **Influenced by Japanese Noh**, experimenting with masks, music.
- ➤ Criticized **Nationalist movement's bigotry**, reflected in poetry.
- ➤ **Appointed to Irish Senate** in **1922** for patriotism.
- ➤ Greatest works written **after Nobel Prize win**.
- ➤ **Prize awarded** for drama; remembered for **lyric poetry**.
- ➤ Key volumes: **The Wild Swans at Coole** (1919).
- ➤ **Michael Robartes and the Dancer** published in **1921**.
- ➤ **The Tower** (1928) and **The Winding Stair** (1933) followed.
- ➤ **Last Poems and Plays** (1940) completed his poetic legacy.
- ➤ Themes include **art vs. life**, masks, cyclical life.
- ➤ **Winding stairs** symbolize life's cyclical, winding journey.
- ➤ His work contrasts **beauty and ceremony** with modern life chaos.

Notable Works:

The Wanderings of Oisin and Other Poems (1889)

- ➢ It was published in 1889.
- ➢ Oisin was not a famous poem with modernist critics like TS Eliot.
- ➢ Contents
  - o ***The Wanderings of Oisin***
  - o *The Song of the Happy Shepherd*
  - o *The Sad Shepherd*
  - o *The Cloak, the Boat, and the Shoes*
  - o *Anashuya and Vijaya*
  - o *The Indian upon God*
  - o *The Indian to His Love*
  - o *The Falling of the Leaves*
  - o *Ephemera*
  - o *The Madness of King Goll*
  - o *The Stolen Child*
  - o *To an Isle in the Water*
  - o *Down by the Salley Gardens*
  - o *The Meditation of the Old Fisherman*
  - o *The Ballad of Father O'Hart*
  - o *The Ballad of Moll Magee*
  - o *The Ballad of the Foxhunter*

The Countess Kathleen and Various Legends and Lyrics (1892)

- ➢ The second poetry collection of W. B. Yeats.
- ➢ It includes the play ***The Countess Cathleen.***
  - o **A verse drama.**
  - o **Dedicated to Maud Gonne.**
  - o **Play set in Ireland** during a **famine.**
  - o **Idealistic Countess sells her soul to the devil.**
  - o **Saves tenants from starvation and damnation.**
  - o **Redeemed after death**, ascends to **Heaven** for altruism.
- ➢ Famous Poems in the Collection:
  - o ***"The Lake Isle of Innisfree",***
    - ▪ The style of the Celtic Revival.
    - ▪ The twelve-line poem is divided into three quatrains.
    - ▪ Expresses the speaker's longing for peace and tranquility.

- - "lake water lapping with low sounds by the shore."
    - "purple glow" of heather at noon
  - ***"A Faery Song",***
  - ***"When You are Old",***
    - **Pierre de Ronsard wrote a poem that served to inspire WB Yeats to write his own poem, "When you are Old".**
  - ***"Who Goes with Fergus".***

The Wild Swans at Coole (1917-1919)

- ➢ Represents **Yeats' middle stage**, focusing on **Irish nationalism**.
- ➢ Explores themes of **Irish aesthetic** and national identity.
- ➢ Famous poems in the collection:
  - ***"The Wild Swans at Coole"***
    - Yeats was staying with his friend Lady Gregory.
    - The rhyme scheme in each stanza is ABCBDD.
  - *"The Hawk"*
  - *"Memory"*
  - *"On being asked for a War Poem"*
  - *"In Memory"*
  - *"Upon a Dying Lady"*
  - ***"Ego Dominus Tuus"***
  - *"The Scholars"*

Michael Robartes and the Dancer (1920)

Contents:

- ➢ *Michael Robartes and the Dancer*
- ➢ *Solomon and the Witch*
- ➢ *An Image from a Past Life*
- ➢ *Under Saturn*
- ➢ ***Easter, 1916.***
  - The poem explores **heroism's clash with everyday life**.
  - **Yeats questions the rebels' fanaticism** and their actions' necessity.
  - He admires their **unwavering determination and sacrifice**.
  - **Reluctantly honors their martyrdom**: "A terrible beauty is born."
  - Primarily written in **anapestic trimeter**, creating rhythmic flow.
  - **Iambic lines add emphasis** to key parts of the poem.

- o *Sixteen Dead Men*
- o *The Rose Tree*
- o *On a Political Prisoner*
- o *The Leaders of the Crowd*
- o *Towards Break of Day*
- o *Demon and Beast*
- o **The Second Coming**
    - ▪ The poem uses Christian imagery regarding the Apocalypse and Second Coming.
- ➢ *A Prayer for My Daughter*
    - o It is written to Anne, his daughter with Georgie Hyde Lees.
    - o Yeats married after his last marriage proposal to Maud Gonne was rejected in 1916.
    - o **Poet describes "storm"** as a "howling" force surrounding him.
    - o **Newborn daughter** sleeps "half-hidden" in her cradle.
    - o The **storm symbolizes the Irish War** of Independence.
    - o **Storm overshadows daughter's birth**, giving historical context.
    - o **Setting revealed** as the tower in stanza two.
    - o **Yeats frequently used** the tower as a poem setting.
    - o **Thoor Ballylee** is a Norman tower in Galway.
    - o **Yeats bought the tower in 1917** as his home.
- ➢ *A Meditation in Time of War*
- ➢ *To be Carved on a Stone at Thoor Ballylee.*

- ➢ The Tower (1928)

- ➢ First major collection as Nobel Laureate
- ➢ Recieved the Nobel Prize in 1923.
- ➢ Yeats' most famous poems, including:
- ➢ *"Sailing to Byzantium,"*
    - o **Journey to Byzantium** symbolizes a spiritual quest for eternity.
    - o **Yeats** explores **immortality, art,** and **the human spirit** in harmony.
    - o Poem's **four stanzas in ottava rima** use iambic pentameter.
    - o Speaker leaves a place "no country for old men."
    - o The country is full of **youth, music, and life.**
    - o Speaker sees himself as a "Monument of unageing intellect."
    - o Describes **old age** as a "tattered coat upon a stick."
    - o Seeks wisdom from **"monuments of magnificence"** in Byzantium.

- o **Sages in God's holy fire** are his soul's teachers.
- o Wishes for **freedom from desire** and the "dying animal."
- o Desires to be gathered "into the artifice of eternity."
- o Rejects "bodily form" in favor of an eternal form.
- o Imagines himself as a **singing bird of hammered gold.**
- o Bird sings to keep a "drowsy Emperor awake."
- o Sees himself **singing timelessly** to Byzantium's lords and ladies.

➢ *"Leda and the Swan,"*
- ▪ The poem draws from **Greek myth of Leda** and **Zeus.**
- ▪ **Leda** birthed **Helen** and **Clytemnestra** after Zeus's assault.
- ▪ A sudden blow: the great wings beating still
  - • *Above the staggering girl, her thighs caressed*
  - • *By the dark webs, her nape caught in his bill,*
  - • *He holds her helpless breast upon his breast.*

  - • *How can those terrified vague fingers push*
  - • *The feathered glory from her loosening thighs?*
  - • *And how can body, laid in that white rush,*
  - • *But feel the strange heart beating where it lies?*

  - • *A shudder in the loins engenders there*
  - • *The broken wall, the burning roof and tower*
  - • *And Agamemnon dead.*
    - ▪ *Being so caught up,*
  - • *So mastered by the brute blood of the air,*
  - • *Did she put on his knowledge with his power*
  - • *Before the indifferent beak could let her drop?*

➢ *"Among School Children."*
- o **Yeats visits a school**, observing children with curiosity and reflection.
- o He recalls **his own childhood** and the passage of time.
- o **Ponders aging** and how it changes one's perspective.
- o **Questions the purpose** of life, learning, and wisdom.
- o **Reflects on love and beauty**, remembering Maud Gonne.
- o Imagines **life as a dance**, blending joy and sorrow.
- o **Concludes on unity** of body, soul, and life's journey.

Byzantium (1930)

- **Byzantium's night** brings rest as "images of day recede."
- **Drunken soldiers sleep**, night-walkers' songs fade after cathedral gong.
- The **"starlit" or "moonlit dome"** rejects "mere complexities."
- A **"superhuman" image** floats, "death-in-life and life-in-death."
- **Golden bird** on a golden tree sings with disdain.
- **Bird scorns** "common bird or petal" and "mire or blood."
- At midnight, **flames appear** on Emperor's pavement without burning.
- **"Blood-begotten spirits" die** in "a dance, an agony of trance."
- They leave behind "complexities and furies of life."
- Spirits arrive, riding **dolphins, flooding Emperor's smithies.**
- Marbles on the floor break **furies of complexity.**
- Images upon images form **in a trance-like dance.**
- **Dolphin-torn, gong-tormented sea** reflects life's fury.
- The poem ends on **"that dolphin-torn, gong-tormented sea."**

The Second Coming Line by Line Explanations

"Turning and turning in the widening gyre"
The world spins in chaotic, widening spirals.

"The falcon cannot hear the falconer;"
Control is lost, orders are no longer heard.

"Things fall apart; the centre cannot hold;"
Stability crumbles; central power loses control.

"Mere anarchy is loosed upon the world,"
Complete disorder spreads everywhere in the world.

"The blood-dimmed tide is loosed, and everywhere"
A wave of violence floods all places.

"The ceremony of innocence is drowned;"
Purity and goodness are overpowered and destroyed.

"The best lack all conviction, while the worst"
Good people are passive; evil is determined.

"Are full of passionate intensity."
Wrongdoers are full of fierce determination.

"Surely some revelation is at hand;"
A major change or revelation seems near.

"Surely the Second Coming is at hand."
The Second Coming prophecy feels imminent.

"The Second Coming! Hardly are those words out"
Just saying "Second Coming" brings a vision.

"When a vast image out of Spiritus Mundi"
A vision from the world's collective soul appears.

"Troubles my sight: somewhere in sands of the desert"
I see a troubling vision in desert sands.

"A shape with lion body and the head of a man,"
A creature, part lion, part man, emerges.

"A gaze blank and pitiless as the sun,"
Its eyes are cold and unfeeling, like the sun.

"Is moving its slow thighs, while all about it"
It moves slowly, and desert birds circle.

"Reel shadows of the indignant desert birds."
Birds, disturbed, fly in shadows around it.

"The darkness drops again; but now I know"
Darkness returns, but I sense something new.

"That twenty centuries of stony sleep"
Two thousand years of history lay dormant.

"Were vexed to nightmare by a rocking cradle,"
History awakens to chaos, like a disturbed cradle.

"And what rough beast, its hour come round at last,"
A primal beast's time for emergence has arrived.

"Slouches towards Bethlehem to be born?"
It moves toward Bethlehem, ready for birth.

Line-by-line explanation of "Sailing to Byzantium" by W.B. Yeats:

Stanza 1:

- **"That is no country for old men."**
  - The country doesn't value the old.
- **"The young In one another's arms, birds in the trees"**
  - Young people and birds enjoy life together.
- **"– Those dying generations – at their song,"**
  - Both sing, yet are part of dying generations.
- **"The salmon-falls, the mackerel-crowded seas,"**
  - Nature is vibrant with fish-filled rivers and seas.
- **"Fish, flesh, or fowl, commend all summer long"**
  - All living beings thrive during the summer.
- **"Whatever is begotten, born, and dies."**
  - Everything follows life's cycle of birth and death.
- **"Caught in that sensual music all neglect"**
  - Enchanted by life, people ignore deeper wisdom.
- **"Monuments of unageing intellect."**
  - Ignoring timeless achievements of the human mind.

Stanza 2:

- **"An aged man is but a paltry thing,"**
  - An old man seems weak and insignificant.
- **"A tattered coat upon a stick, unless"**
  - Like a shabby coat on a stick without soul.
- **"Soul clap its hands and sing, and louder sing"**
  - Soul must celebrate and find its own voice.

- **"For every tatter in its mortal dress,"**
  - Singing grows with each flaw of the body.
- **"Nor is there singing school but studying"**
  - True joy comes from studying timeless knowledge.
- **"Monuments of its own magnificence;"**
  - Learning from past achievements of greatness.
- **"And therefore I have sailed the seas and come"**
  - So, I've journeyed here over the seas.
- **"To the holy city of Byzantium."**
  - I have reached the sacred city, Byzantium.

Stanza 3:

- **"O sages standing in God's holy fire"**
  - Wise men dwell in divine, holy light.
- **"As in the gold mosaic of a wall,"**
  - Like a golden mosaic image on a wall.
- **"Come from the holy fire, perne in a gyre,"**
  - Leave the holy fire, spiraling towards me.
- **"And be the singing-masters of my soul."**
  - Become teachers who inspire my soul's song.
- **"Consume my heart away; sick with desire"**
  - Take away my heart, plagued by desire.
- **"And fastened to a dying animal"**
  - Bound to my frail, aging physical body.
- **"It knows not what it is; and gather me"**
  - Confused by itself; gather me into wisdom.
- **"Into the artifice of eternity."**
  - Place me into the immortal realm of art.

Stanza 4:

- **"Once out of nature I shall never take"**
  - Once beyond life, I won't return as human.
- **"My bodily form from any natural thing,"**
  - I won't take any natural form again.

- ➤ **"But such a form as Grecian goldsmiths make"**
  - ○ My new form will be like crafted Greek art.
- ➤ **"Of hammered gold and gold enamelling"**
  - ○ Made of pure, beautiful hammered gold.
- ➤ **"To keep a drowsy Emperor awake;"**
  - ○ Like art designed to inspire, keep alive.
- ➤ **"Or set upon a golden bough to sing"**
  - ○ Or placed on a golden branch to sing.
- ➤ **"To lords and ladies of Byzantium"**
  - ○ Singing for Byzantium's nobles and royals.
- ➤ **"Of what is past, or passing, or to come."**
  - ○ Singing of all things past, present, and future.

Questions

Question 133

Match List I and List II List I

List I (Lines)	List II (Poems)
A. Monuments of unaging intellect"	I. "Leda and the Swan"
B. "in the foul rag-and-bone shop of the heart"	II. "Adam's Curse
C. "So mastered by the brute blood of the air"	III. "Sailing to Byzantium
D. "As weary-hearted as that hollow moon"	IV. "The Circus Animals' Desertion"

Choose the correct answer from the options given below:
1. A – III, – IV, C – II, D – I
2. A – III, B – I, C – IV, D – II
3. A – III, 8 – IV, C – I, D – II
4. A – II, B – I, C – IV, D – III

Explanations:
Answer: 3. A – III, 8 – IV, C – I, D – II

- A. "Monuments of unaging intellect" - "Sailing to Byzantium"
- B. "in the foul rag-and-bone shop of the heart" - "The Circus Animals' Desertion"

C.   "So mastered by the brute blood of the air" - "Leda and the Swan"
D.   "As weary-hearted as that hollow moon" - "Adam's Curse"

Extra Perk:

A. "Monuments of unaging intellect" is a phrase from W.B. Yeats' poem "Sailing to Byzantium". The speaker of the poem is an old man who longs to escape the decay and impermanence of the physical world and achieve immortality through his art. The phrase "monuments of unaging intellect" refers to the timeless works of art and culture that the speaker hopes to create or become a part of in Byzantium.

B. "In the foul rag-and-bone shop of the heart" is a line from W.B. Yeats' poem "The Circus Animals' Desertion". The speaker of the poem is reflecting on his artistic career and feeling disillusioned with the symbols and images that have previously inspired him. The phrase "foul rag-and-bone shop of the heart" refers to the speaker's own creative process, which he sees as a messy and chaotic combination of personal experience, memory, and imagination.

C. "So mastered by the brute blood of the air" is a line from W.B. Yeats' poem "Leda and the Swan". The poem is a retelling of the Greek myth in which the god Zeus takes on the form of a swan and rapes the mortal woman Leda. The line describes the intense physicality and violence of the encounter, with the swan representing the primal, animalistic nature of desire.

D. "As weary-hearted as that hollow moon" is a line from W.B. Yeats' poem "Adam's Curse". The speaker of the poem is reflecting on the difficulty and labor involved in creating true art, particularly in the context of love and relationships. The phrase "weary-hearted" suggests the emotional toll that this labour takes, while the image of the "hollow moon" emphasizes the idea of a difficult, fruitless pursuit.

Question 134

Which of these poets wrote a poem that inspired W B Yeats to write his own poem, "When you are Old"?

1.   Francois Villon
2.   **Pierre de Ronsard**
3.   Edmund Spencer
4.   Heinrich Heine

Correct Explanations:

Pierre de Ronsard wrote a poem that served to inspire WB Yeats to write his own poem, "When you are Old". Though the poem is one of the best-loved of Yeats's works, many people don't realize that it is based on a much earlier sonnet by Pierre de Ronsard, a 16th-century French Renaissance poet.

Question 135

Arrange the following lines of poetry in their chronological sequence:

- A. "An aged man is but a paltry thing."
- B. "The world is too much with us."
- C. "Daddy, I have had to kill you."
- D. "After great pain, a formal feeling comes -"

Choose the correct answer from the options below

1. B, D, A, C
2. D, B, A, C
3. D, B, C, A
4. **B, D, C, A**

Correct Explanations:
"The World Is Too Much with Us" is a sonnet by the English Romantic poet William Wordsworth. In it, Wordsworth criticises the world of the First Industrial Revolution for being absorbed in materialism and distancing itself from nature. Composed circa **1802**, the poem was first published in Poems, in Two Volumes.

The American poet Emily Dickinson wrote "After great pain, a formal feeling comes" around **1862**.

"Sailing to Byzantium" is a poem by William Butler Yeats, first published in the **1928** collection "The Tower. An aged man is but a paltry thing,/A tattered coat upon a stick, unless"

"Daddy" is a poem written by American Confessional poet Sylvia Plath. The poem was written on October 12, **1962**, four months before her death and one month after her separation from Ted Hughes. "Daddy, I have had to kill you. In the waters off beautiful Nauset. I used to pray to recover you."

Read the following poem and answer the questions that follow:

A Prayer for Old Age
God guard me from those thoughts men think
In the mind alone;
He that sings a lasting song
Thinks in a marrow-bone;

From all that makes a wise old man
That can be praised of all;
O, what am I that I should not seem
For the song's sake a fool?

I pray–for fashion's word is out
And prayer comes round again
That I may seem, though I die old,
A foolish, passionate man.

— W.B.Yeats

Question 136

Thoughts true for all time are:

1. born of God's care.
2. for all human hearts.
3. imbued with logic of mind.
4. felt deep inside the self.

Correct Explanations:
The option that best captures the meaning of the phrase "thoughts true for all time" is: felt deep inside the self. Thoughts that are true for all time are those that resonate deeply within the human soul or self, and that are not necessarily determined by external factors such as logic or divine intervention. These are ideas that are universally true and that have the power to transcend time, culture, and individual experience. They may include ideas about love, death, beauty, morality, and the nature of existence, among others. Such thoughts are often felt and experienced at a deeply personal and emotional level, rather than being the product of external factors or logic.

Question 137

In the second stanza, the poet thinks of:
1. **what all makes a wise old man.**
2. what earns all others' praise?
3. what he does not want to appear.
4. what he thinks he is, a fool.

Correct Explanations:
In the second stanza of the poem, the poet reflects on the idea of what makes a "wise old man" and what can be praised by all, but he ultimately concludes that he would rather be seen as a "foolish, passionate man" even if it means being seen as a fool. Therefore, the option that best captures the meaning of the second stanza is: what he does not want to appear. The poet questions what it means to be a wise old man, and suggests that he would rather be true to himself and his creative passions, even if this means going against what is conventionally valued by society. He seems to value creative expression and passion more than wisdom and praise from others.

Question 138

Which one of the following best captures what we infer about the poet?

1. He believes in the efficacy of prayer.
2. He is an old man wise as old are.
3. He is old but happy in not being wise.
4. He is a foolish young man who thinks wisely.

Explanations:
Answer: 3. He is old but happy in not being wise.

The poem reflects the poet's desire to remain passionate and "foolish," rejecting the conventional wisdom and sober thoughts often associated with old age.

Question 139

Arrange the following poems by W. B. Yeats in the chronological order of publication.

A. "The Wild Swans at Coole"
B. "The Second Coming"
C. "Among School Children"
D. "Adam's Curse"

Choose the correct answer from the options given below
1. A, C, D, B
2. **D, A, B, C**
3. C, A, B, D
4. C, A, D, B

Correct Explanations:
"Adam's Curse" is a poem written by William Butler Yeats. In the poem, Yeats describes the difficulty of creating something beautiful. The title alludes to the book of Genesis, evoking the fall of man and the separation of work and pleasure. Yeats originally included the poem in the volume In the Seven Woods, **published in 1903.**

"The Wild Swans at Coole" is a lyric poem by the Irish poet William Butler Yeats. Written between **1916 and early 1917.**

"The Second Coming" is a poem written by Irish poet W. B. Yeats in 1919, first printed in The **Dial in November 1920,** and afterwards included in his 1921 collection of verses Michael Robartes and the Dancer.

William Butler Yeats published "Among School Children" in his famous **1928** collection of poems, The Tower.

Question 140

Which of the following two plays were written by W. B. Yeats?

A. The Land of Heart's Desire
B. Time and the Conways
C. The Silver Tassie
D. The Countess Cathleen
E. The Plough and the Stars

Choose the correct answer from the options given below:

1. C and D only.
2. **A and D only.**
3. A and E only.
4. B and E only.

Explanations:
The Land of Heart's Desire, Time and the Conways, The Silver Tassie, The Countess Cathleen, and The Plough and the Stars are all plays written by Irish playwright and poet William Butler Yeats.

Other Explanations:
The Land of Heart's Desire is a one-act play by Irish playwright William Butler Yeats. The play is a fairy tale set in the Irish countryside, and it explores themes of love, loss, and the supernatural. It was first performed in 1894 at the Avenue Theatre in London and was well received by audiences and critics. The play's success helped establish Yeats as a leading figure in the Irish literary revival.

The Countess Cathleen is a play by Irish playwright William Butler Yeats. The play is based on an Irish folk tale and tells the story of a wealthy woman who sells her soul to the devil in order to save the poor in her community from starvation. The play explores themes of sacrifice, redemption, and the conflict between the material and spiritual worlds. It was first performed in 1899 and was a critical success.

Time and the Conways is a play by British playwright J. B. Priestley. The play tells the story of a wealthy family in Yorkshire, England, and explores the themes of time, fate, and the illusions of youth. It was first performed in 1937 and has been staged many times since. The play is notable for its use of time as a structural device, with the action shifting between 1919 and 1937.

The Silver Tassie is a play by Irish playwright Seán O'Casey. The play is set during World War I and follows the story of Harry Heegan, a footballer who is sent to fight in the war. The play explores themes of loss, disillusionment, and the destructive nature of war. It was first performed in 1928 and was a critical and commercial success. The play is considered one of O'Casey's best works.

The Plough and the Stars is a play by Irish playwright Seán O'Casey. The play is set during the Easter Rising in Dublin in 1916 and follows the lives of several working-class characters as they navigate the tumultuous events of the time. The play explores themes of nationalism, class struggle, and the impact of political upheaval on ordinary people. It was first performed in 1926 and was controversial at the time for its portrayal of Irish nationalism.

Question 141

Choose the correct chronological sequence in which the following texts were published.

- A.   The Tower
- B.   The Hind and the Panther
- C.   The Wild Swans at Coole
- D.   Mac Flecknoe
- E.   The Whitsun Weddings

Choose the correct answer from the options given below:

1.   ABDEC
2.   BCAED
3.   BACDE
4.   **DBCAE**

Explanations:
The correct chronological sequence of publication for the listed texts is as follows:

- ➢   *Mac Flecknoe by John Dryden (1682)*
- ➢   *The Hind and the Panther by John Dryden (1687)*
- ➢   *The Tower by W. B. Yeats (1928)*
- ➢   *The Wild Swans at Coole by W. B. Yeats (1919)*
- ➢   *The Whitsun Weddings by Philip Larkin (1964)*

Question 142

Arrange the correct chronological sequence of the publication of the following texts:

A. *September 1, 1939*

    B. The Collar
    C. Beppo
    D. Paradise Lost
    E. Seeing Things

Choose the correct answer from the options given below:

    1. B, D. C, A. E
    2. B. A, E, C, D
    3. A, E, B. C, D
    4. C, B. A, D, E

Explanations
Answer: 1. B, D. C, A. E

"The Collar" is a poem written by the Welsh poet George Herbert and was published in 1633 as part of his collection of poems titled *The Temple.*

Paradise Lost was **published in 1667** and consisted of ten books comprising over ten thousand lines of verse.

Beppo: A Venetian Story is an extensive poem written by Lord Byron in 1817 while he was in Venice.

"September 1, 1939" is a poem by W. H. Auden, composed shortly after the German invasion of Poland that marked the commencement of World War II. It was initially published in The New Republic on October 18, 1939, and later included in Auden's collection titled Another Time (1940).

Seeing Things is the eighth collection of poetry by Seamus Heaney, the recipient of the 1995 Nobel Prize in Literature.

G.M. Hopkins (1844-1889)

- **Born in 1844**, Hopkins was an English Jesuit poet.
- Known for his innovative style and "sprung rhythm."
- **"The Wreck of the Deutschland"** is a famous work.
- His poetry often explores **nature and spirituality** deeply.

- ➤ He wrote about **inscape and instress** in nature's details.
- ➤ His work was published posthumously, in **1918**.
- ➤ Hopkins struggled with **faith and self-doubt** throughout life.
- ➤ He influenced **20th-century poetry** with his unique style.
- ➤ Poems like **"God's Grandeur"** reflect his religious devotion.
- ➤ **Died in 1889**, leaving a legacy of experimental poetry.

"Pied Beauty"

- ➤ **Pied Beauty** was written in 1877, published in 1918.
- ➤ Poem celebrates **nature's variety**, challenging Platonic ideal of Beauty.
- ➤ It's a **curtal sonnet**: six-line opening, four-line closing.
- ➤ Narrator praises **God for "dappled things"** in nature.
- ➤ **Examples include piebald cattle, trout,** and finches.
- ➤ Describes chestnuts breaking like **coals bursting** in fire.
- ➤ Landscape is **"plotted and pieced"** into fields by farming.
- ➤ Ending emphasizes **God's Beauty as "past change"**.
- ➤ **"Praise him"** contrasts God's immutability with nature's variety.
- ➤ Irony: **God's changelessness** contrasts His creation's diversity.
- ➤ God's **separation and creativity** are emphasized in ending.
- ➤ Poem's **volta** unites opposites: variety and immutability.
- ➤ **Sprung rhythm** captures varied beauty in nature's details.
- ➤ Hopkins uses **alliteration** to emphasize nature's diversity.
- ➤ Aural effects mirror **visual variety** described in poem.
- ➤ **Pied Beauty** reveals Hopkins's skill with form and contrast.

"The Windhover: To Christ our Lord"

- ➤ **"The Windhover"** was written by **Gerard Manley Hopkins** in 1877.
- ➤ Published posthumously in **1918** in *Poems of Gerard Manley Hopkins*.
- ➤ **Hopkins** dedicated the sonnet **"To Christ our Lord."**
- ➤ **"Windhover"** refers to the **kestrel** and its hovering skill.
- ➤ The narrator admires the **bird's grace** and **wind control**.
- ➤ The bird seems to control wind like a **horse**.
- ➤ The kestrel suddenly **dives** and "rebuffed the big wind."
- ➤ The **bird** is interpreted as a **metaphor for Christ**.
- ➤ **Hopkins** considered it "the best thing [he] ever wrote."
- ➤ The poem is widely anthologized and **interpreted diversely**.
- ➤ The poem reveals **Hopkins's spiritual and aesthetic vision**.

Question 143

Match List - I with List - II.

List - I (Term / Concept)	List - II (Invented / Coined by)
A. Objectivism	I. John Ruskin
B. Pathetic Fallacy	II. G.M. Hopkins
C. Sprung Rhythm	III. William Carlos Williams
D. Structures of Feeling	IV. Raymond Williams

Choose the correct answer from the options given below :

(1) A-I, B-II, C-IV, D-III
(2) A-II, B-III, C-I, D-IV
(3) A-IV, B-II, C-I, D-I
(4) A-III, B-I, C-II, D-IV

Explanations:
Answer:
A. Objectivism – III. William Carlos Williams
B. Pathetic Fallacy – I. John Ruskin
C. Sprung Rhythm – II. G.M. Hopkins
D. Structures of Feeling – IV. Raymond Williams

Read the following poem and answer the questions that follow:

No worst, there is none. No worst, there is none.
Pitched past pitch of grief,
More pangs will, schooled at forepangs, wilder wring.
Comforter, where, where is your comforting?
Mary, mother of us, where is your relief?
My cries heave, herds long; huddle in a main, a chief
Woe, wórld sorrow; on an áge old anvil wince and sing—
Then lull, then leave off. Fury had shrieked 'No lingering!
Let me be fell: force I must be brief."'
O the mind, mind has mountains; cliffs of fall
Frightful, sheer, no man fathomed. Hold them cheap
May who ne'er hung there. Nor does long our small

Durance deal with that steep or deep. Here! creep,
Wretch, under a comfort serves in a whirlwind: all
Life death does end and each day dies with sleep.

Gerard Manley Hopkins

Question 144

Which of the following best describes the meaning of the title of the poem, 'No worst, there is none.'?

1. **It is not worst because there is nothing.**
2. Nothing can be so much bad as this.
3. No, it is worst as nothing is there.
4. It is very bad as no one is there.

Correct Explanations:

In the poem's context, the meaning of the title "No worst, there is none" is "Nothing is worse than this." The repeated phrase "No worst, there is none" at the beginning of the poem emphasises the speaker's feeling of utter despair and hopelessness. The following lines describe the speaker's intense grief and the inability of anyone, including the Virgin Mary, to provide comfort or relief. The final lines of the poem suggest that the only comfort lies in the realisation that life and death are inevitable and that each day dies with sleep.

Question 145

Beyond the intensity of known grief, there can be:

1. no grief than being experienced.
2. only a new pain is more painful.
3. only the twisted known pains.
4. **the grief beyond the limits of pain.**

Correct Explanations:

In the context of the poem, the speaker suggests that beyond the intensity of known grief, there can be even greater depths of pain and suffering beyond the limits of what we can bear. The lines "No worst, there is none. / Pitched past pitch of grief, / More pangs will, schooled at forepangs, wilder wring" suggest that the speaker's grief is so intense that it has surpassed any previous experience of pain, and that there are even more intense levels of suffering that can be inflicted upon a person. Therefore, the closest option to being true is "the griefs beyond the limits of pain."

Question 146

Which two of the following are true?

    A.   Not all know the intensity or depth of suffering.
    B.   Death does not put an end to our suffering.
    C.   Suffering is seen as winds that hinder comfort.
    D.   Suffering's intensity or depth is in mind.

Choose the correct answer from the options given below:
1. A and B only
2. C and D only
3. **A and D only**
4. A and C Only

Question 147

Match List I with List II

List I (First Line)	List II (Poet)
A. "Courage!" he said, and pointed toward the land...	I. G.M. Hopkins
B. I am poor brother Lippo, by your leave!	II. Alfred Tennyson
C. I caught this morning morning's minion...	III. D.G. Rossetti
D. Look in my face; my name is Might-have-been..	IV. Matthew Arnold
E. The sea is calm tonight...	V. Robert Browning

Choose the correct answer from the options given below:

1. A-II, B-III, C-I, D-V, E-IV
2. A-IV, B-V, C-I, D-III, E-II
3. A-III, B-IV, C-V, D-I, E-II
4. **A-II, B-V, C-I, D-III, E-IV**

Correct Explanations:
A. "Courage! he said and pointed toward the land" is from **"Ulysses" by Alfred, Lord** Tennyson, not "The Lotos-eaters."

B. "I am poor brother Lippo, by your leave!" - This is the opening line of the dramatic monologue **"Fra Lippo Lippi" by Robert Browning.** The poem is spoken by a Renaissance painter who defends his unconventional lifestyle and artistic methods to a group of monks.

C. "I caught this morning morning's minion..." - This is the opening line of the poem **"The Windhover" by Gerard Manley Hopkins.** The poem describes the speaker's awe and admiration for a falcon in flight and explores the beauty and complexity of the natural world.

D. Look in my face; my name is Might have been" – The Nevermore. Dante Gabriel Rossetti.

E. **"The sea is calm tonight..." - This is the opening line of the poem "Dover Beach" by Matthew Arnold.** The poem reflects on the loss of faith and the decline of Western culture and uses the image of the sea as a metaphor for the changing tides of history.

Robert Bridges (1844-1930) & The Testament of Beauty (1929)

- ➤ Robert Bridges was born in 1844 in England.
- ➤ He studied medicine but later pursued poetry.
- ➤ Served as England's Poet Laureate from 1913 to 1930.
- ➤ Bridges was influenced by classical and romantic poets.
- ➤ His style emphasized clarity and musicality in language.
- ➤ Bridges sought to revive English prosody and rhythm.
- ➤ His poetic works included sonnets, lyrics, and hymns.

The Testament of Beauty

- ➤ The Testament of Beauty was published in 1929.
- ➤ Written in four books, it's a philosophical poem.
- ➤ Explores themes of beauty, truth, and human spirit.
- ➤ Emphasizes harmony between nature, art, and intellect.

> ➤ Uses archaic language to evoke classical influences.
> ➤ Celebrates human creativity and intellectual pursuit.
> ➤ The work reflects Bridges' lifelong poetic ideals.

Question 148

Who among the following were poet Laureates of England?

A. Alfred Austin
B. Robert Bridges
C. Watts-Dunton
D. Oscar Wilde

Choose the correct answer from the options given below :

1. (A) and (C) only
2. (A) and (D) only
3. (B), (C) and (D) only
4. (A), (B) and (C) only
5. **(A) and (B) only**

Correct Explanations

Alfred Austin DL (30 May 1835 – 2 June 1913) was an English poet appointed **Poet Laureate in 1896**, after an interval following the death of Tennyson, when the other candidates had either caused controversy or refused the honour.

Robert Seymour Bridges (23 October 1844 – 21 April 1930) was an English poet who was **Poet Laureate from 1913 to 1930.** A doctor by training, he achieved literary fame only late in life. His poems reflect a deep Christian faith, and he is the author of many well-known hymns. It was through Bridges's efforts that Gerard Manley Hopkins achieved posthumous fame.

This list orders the laureates chronologically, from the first to the most recent.

> ➤ John Dryden (1668–89)
> ➤ Thomas Shadwell (1689–92)
> ➤ Nahum Tate (1692–1715)
> ➤ Nicholas Rowe (1715–18)

- ➢ Laurence Eusden (1718–30)
- ➢ Colley Cibber (1730–57)
- ➢ William Whitehead (1757–85)
- ➢ Thomas Warton (1785–90)
- ➢ Henry James Pye (1790–1813)
- ➢ Robert Southey (1813–43)
- ➢ William Wordsworth (1843–50)
- ➢ Alfred, Lord Tennyson (1850–92)
- ➢ Alfred Austin (1896–1913)
- ➢ Robert Bridges (1913–30)
- ➢ John Masefield (1930–67)
- ➢ Cecil Day-Lewis (1968–72)
- ➢ Sir John Betjeman (1972–84)
- ➢ Ted Hughes (1984–98)
- ➢ Andrew Motion (1999–2009)
- ➢ Carol Ann Duffy (2009–19)
- ➢ Simon Armitage (2019–)

Usage Policy for NerdSchool Notes

Created by: Instructors from NerdSchool
Owned by: NERDSTABLE PVT LTD

The following notes are the intellectual property of **NERDSTABLE PVT LTD** and are made available exclusively to students who have paid for access. By using these notes, you agree to the terms and conditions outlined below:

Policy of Usage:

Personal Use Only: These notes are intended for your **personal study and exam preparation**. You are permitted to **read** and **print** them for your own reference.

No Unauthorized Distribution or Sale: You **may not sell**, **distribute**, or **replicate** these notes in any form, whether digitally or physically. This includes sharing copies with others, regardless of the medium (online platforms, printed materials, etc.).

No Plagiarism: You **may not claim** the contents of these notes as your own. Any form of direct publication or submission under your name, without proper citation, is strictly prohibited.

Non-Transferable Access: Access to these notes is restricted to the individual purchaser. **Sharing your login credentials** or any other means of access to these materials with others is a violation of this policy.

Additional Guidelines:

For Educational Use Only: These notes are designed to help students succeed in their academic exams and should be used responsibly. They are meant to supplement your learning, not to replace the guidance of instructors or textbooks.

No Commercial Use: The content in these notes cannot be used for **commercial purposes**. This includes using the material in any form of paid tutoring or educational courses that you offer without the explicit permission of NERDSTABLE PVT LTD.

Proper Attribution: If you wish to reference any part of these notes in your own academic work, proper **citation** must be made to **NerdSchool and NERDSTABLE PVT LTD**.

Legal Action: Any violation of these terms, including unauthorized distribution or commercial use, may result in **legal action**.